Hilary Putnam

The richness of Hilary Putnam's philosophical oeuvre consists not only in the broad spectrum of problems addressed but also in the transformations and restructuring his positions have undergone over the years. The essays collected in this volume are sensitive to both these dimensions. They discuss Putnam's major philosophical contributions to the theory of meaning, the philosophy of mind, the philosophy of science and mathematics, and moral theory. But, in addition, tracing threads of change and continuity, they analyze the dynamics underlying the unfolding of Putnam's thought. The volume also constitutes a critical introduction to a number of central issues in contemporary philosophy, including quantum logic, realism, functionalism, the 'mind as computer' metaphor, and the fact/value dichotomy.

Yemima Ben-Menahem is a member of the Department of Philosophy at the Hebrew University of Jerusalem.

Contemporary Philosophy in Focus

Contemporary Philosophy in Focus offers a series of introductory volumes to many of the dominant philosophical thinkers of the current age. Each volume consists of newly commissioned essays that cover major contributions of a preeminent philosopher in a systematic and accessible manner. Comparable in scope and rationale to the highly successful series **Cambridge Companions to Philosophy**, the volumes do not presuppose that readers are already intimately familiar with the details of each philosopher's work. They thus combine exposition and critical analysis in a manner that will appeal to students of philosophy and to professionals as well as to students across the humanities and social sciences.

FORTHCOMING VOLUMES:

Paul Churchland edited by Brian Keeley
Ronald Dworkin edited by Arthur Ripstein
Jerry Fodor edited by Tim Crane
Saul Kripke edited by Alan Berger
David Lewis edited by Theodore Sider and Dean Zimmermann
Bernard Williams edited by Alan Thomas

PUBLISHED VOLUMES:

Stanley Cavell edited by Richard Eldridge
Donald Davidson edited by Kirk Ludwig
Daniel Dennett edited by Andrew Brook and Don Ross
Thomas Kuhn edited by Thomas Nickles
Alasdair MacIntyre edited by Mark Murphy
Richard Rorty edited by Charles Guignon and David Hiley
John Searle edited by Barry Smith
Charles Taylor edited by Ruth Abbey

Hilary Putnam

Edited by

YEMIMA BEN-MENAHEM
The Hebrew University of Jerusalem

PUBLISHED BY THE PRESS SYNDICATE OF THE UNIVERSITY OF CAMBRIDGE
The Pitt Building, Trumpington Street, Cambridge, United Kingdom

CAMBRIDGE UNIVERSITY PRESS
The Edinburgh Building, Cambridge CB2 2RU, UK
40 West 20th Street, New York, NY 10011-4211, USA
477 Williamstown Road, Port Melbourne, VIC 3207, Australia
Ruiz de Alarcón 13, 28014 Madrid, Spain
Dock House, The Waterfront, Cape Town 8001, South Africa

http://www.cambridge.org

© Cambridge University Press 2005

First published 2005

Printed in the United States of America

Typefaces Janson Text 10/13 pt. *and* ITC Officina Sans   *System* LaTeX 2_ε [TB]

A catalog record for this book is available from the British Library.

Library of Congress Cataloging in Publication Data
Hilary Putnam / edited by Yemima Ben-Menahem.
    p.   cm. – (Contemporary philosophy in focus)
Includes bibliographical references and index.
ISBN 0-521-81311-5 – ISBN 0-521-01254-6 (pbk.)
1. Putnam, Hilary.   I. Ben-Menahem, Yemima, 1946–   II. Series.
B945.P874H54   2004
191 – dc22

                                                    2004048193

ISBN 0 521 81311 5 hardback
ISBN 0 521 01254 6 paperback

Contents

Contributors

YEMIMA BEN-MENAHEM is a member of the Department of Philosophy at the Hebrew University of Jerusalem. In her publications she has addressed a range of classic problems in the philosophy of science, including explanation, causality, and realism. Her *Conventionalism* is forthcoming from Cambridge University Press.

RICHARD J. BERNSTEIN is Vera List Professor of Philosophy and dean of the graduate faculty at New School University in New York City. He has written widely on political theory, American pragmatism, and critical theory. His books include *Praxis and Action* (1971), *Beyond Objectivism and Relativism: Science, Hermeneutics and Praxis* (1983), *Freud and the Vexed Legacy of Moses* (1998), and *Radical Evil: A Philosophical Interrogation* (2002).

NANCY CARTWRIGHT is a professor of philosophy in the Department of Philosophy, London School of Economics and Political Science, and chair of the London School of Economics Centre for Philosophy of Natural and Social Science. She is also a professor of philosophy at the University of California, San Diego. Among her books are *How the Laws of Physics Lie* (1983), *Nature's Capacities and Their Measurement* (1989), *The Dappled World: A Study of the Boundaries of Science* (1999), and *Measuring Causes: Invariance, Modularity and the Causal Markov Condition* (2000).

ARTHUR FINE is a professor of philosophy and adjunct professor of physics at the University of Washington. He has served as president of the Philosophy of Science Association and of the Central Division of the American Philosophical Association. His works in the philosophy of science focus, in particular, on the foundations of twentieth-century physics and include, among others, *The Shaky Game: Einstein, Realism and the Quantum Theory* (1986; 2d ed. 1996).

JULIET FLOYD is an associate professor of philosophy at Boston University. She has published on Kant, Wittgenstein, and the philosophy of mathematics and coedited *Future Pasts: Perspectives on the Analytic Tradition in Twentieth-Century Philosophy* (2001).

TIM MAUDLIN is a professor of philosophy at Rutgers University. His two main research areas are metaphysics and the philosophy of physics. The author of *Quantum Non-Locality and Relativity* (1994), he has two books forthcoming from Oxford University Press: *Truth and Paradox: Solving the Riddles* and *Metaphysics Within Physics*.

AXEL MUELLER, of the Department of Philosophy at Northwestern University, works in pragmatism, the philosophy of language, and the philosophy of science. His *Referenz und Fallibilismus* (2001) is a study of Putnam's thought.

JOHN STACHEL is a professor emeritus of physics and director of the Center for Einstein Studies at Boston University. Founder of the Collected Papers of Albert Einstein, he has published extensively in the history and philosophy of theoretical physics, especially on the general theory of relativity. His most recent book is *Einstein from 'B' to 'Z'* (2002).

ORON SHAGRIR is a member of the Department of Philosophy and chair of the program in Cognitive Science at the Hebrew University of Jerusalem. His areas of expertise include the philosophy of mind, cognitive science, and the history and philosophy of computing. His recent papers have been published in *Mind, Synthese*, the *Monist, Minds and Machines*, and *Theoretical Computer Science*.

CHARLES TRAVIS is a professor of philosophy at Northwestern University. He works in the philosophy of mind and the philosophy of language, focusing in particular on the interpretation of Wittgenstein's philosophy in these areas. His books include *The Uses of Sense: Wittgenstein's Philosophy of Language* (1989), *Unshadowed Thought* (2000), and *Les Liaisons Ordinaires* (2002).

Acknowledgments

The papers collected here have not been published before. I would like to thank the authors for their responsiveness and patience during the editorial process. I would also like to thank Hilary Putnam, teacher and friend, who over the years has been a source of inspiration and encouragement.

Terence Moore of Cambridge University Press invited me to edit this volume and provided assistance throughout the process. His recent death is a great loss to the philosophical community. The many volumes he brought into the world, however, are a lasting tribute to his vision.

1 Introduction

YEMIMA BEN-MENAHEM

In many ways Hilary Putnam's writings constitute the ideal introduction to his thought. For they are not only lucid and accessible, but also self-reflective, providing numerous signposts to his philosophical motivations, changes of mind and sources of inspiration. Rather than simply 'introducing' Putnam's thought, therefore, the papers collected here are mostly interpretative, seeking, in particular, to trace changes in the broader philosophical environment Putnam's thought was part of – changes that in many cases were precipitated by his novel ideas – and chart the transformation of Putnam's own thinking against the background of these developments. In tracing the evolution of Putnam's thought, they provide a window onto the dynamics of the Anglo-American philosophical arena since Putnam's emergence, in the 1960s, as a leading philosopher. One such transformation is the demise of logical positivism, still dominant in Putnam's formative years, and a growing interest in Wittgenstein and American pragmatism. A related trend is the shift away from the philosophy of science, which loses the primacy it enjoyed in the 1950s and 1960s, and the corresponding repositioning of the philosophy of mind, which takes its place. Most significant, perhaps, is the increasing salience of the ethical perspective in the wake of the growing desire that philosophy play a more direct role in our lives.

Putnam, who has always been politically engaged, never distanced himself from the ethical. Professionally, however, he was educated in analytic philosophy at a time when it tended to relegate ethical and existential issues to the sidelines. As his thought matured, he became increasingly eager to counter this tendency, and his later works bear such ethically oriented titles as *Renewing Philosophy*, *Realism with a Human Face*, *Words and Life*.

Hilary Putnam was born in Chicago in 1926. At the University of Pennsylvania, where he earned his undergraduate degree, Putnam majored, along with Noam Chomsky, in the emerging field of linguistic analysis. His graduate studies were divided between Harvard University, where he studied with Quine, Hao Wang, C. I. Lewis and Morton White, and

1

UCLA, where he wrote his Ph.D. dissertation, under the supervision of Reichenbach, on the concept of probability. Moving to Princeton University in 1953, he made the acquaintance of Carnap and Kreisel, and worked intensively in mathematical logic, proving, with Martin Davis and Julia Robinson, the insolvability of Hilbert's tenth problem.[1] Since 1965, Putnam has been at Harvard, writing on a broad spectrum of philosophical topics; he has also taught and lectured at universities around the world.

Putnam grew up in a home steeped in intellectual and political activity. His father, Samuel Putnam, was a well-known writer and translator, an active communist, and a columnist for *The Daily Worker.* During the Vietnam War, Hilary Putnam, a member of SDS (Students for a Democratic Society), and the Progressive Labor Party, a Maoist group, took an active part in protesting the war and campaigning for social reform. Around 1972, however, he became disillusioned with communism, a turn of events that had considerable impact, it seems, on his subsequent philosophical development.

I. CHANGE AND CONTINUITY

As Putnam's thought is known for its remarkable dynamism and self-critique, I would like to begin with some reflections on methodological issues having to do with intellectual transformations. The identification of change or continuity is of great concern to anyone interested in the history of an idea, a theory, an individual's lifework or a philosophical tradition. Yet a naïve attitude toward the notions of change and continuity in the intellectual sphere is nonetheless not uncommon. This is not the place for a thorough analysis of this complex question; the following remarks are intended only to argue that it calls for deeper reflection than it usually receives. While focusing on Putnam's work, these comments on the problems surrounding the assessment of change and continuity in an individual's oeuvre seem to me to be of more general relevance.

First, we must remember that, like all judgments of difference and similarity, the perception of change is description-dependent. Consider realism. If we choose to frame our description in terms of this rubric, the avowal of realism is a unifying theme running through Putnam's contributions in different areas over the years. If, however, we introduce distinctions between different shades of realism, as Putnam himself does, change will be evident. Furthermore, authors may deliberately or subconsciously use different words to convey similar ideas, or the same words to express different ones. Borges takes the latter possibility to paradoxical extremes in his story "Pierre Menard, Author of the Quixote," where Menard devotes his life to *rewriting* a few chapters of *Don Quixote* – not copying the work or composing a new version, but actually rewriting it. The new text is completely identical to the relevant part of Cervantes's novel, but constitutes, we are told, an entirely different literary work. Even in less dramatic contexts, we must be sensitive to the fact that there is no strict correlation between difference (identity, similarity) in formulation and difference (identity, similarity) in content. For example, having quoted from one of his own earlier papers, Putnam states: "I still agree with those *words*. But I would say them in a rather different spirit now."[2] And this is as true of pronouncements made by the same individual as it is of those made by an author and his colleagues, disciples, critics, sources of inspiration, and so on. An author or interpreter might have any number of reasons (or motives) for seeking to minimize or maximize a difference or similarity by way of a particular formulation: admiration and deference, envy and resentment, the desire to appear original, or, on the contrary, loyal to a tradition, and so on. Apart from their importance in the lives of creative individuals, these considerations are also of immense social, political and cultural significance.

Second, assessment of difference and similarity is value-laden. In most cases we are not interested in change or difference per se, but in *significant* changes and differences, where significance, as well as similar attributes, is not merely found there, but actively *projected* onto the text or problem in question. Consider the following quotation, stripped of names and specific subject matter to emphasize the generic nature of the sentiments expressed:

> How does X's position on L differ from Y's, we must now wonder? Not on any point of substance, it may seem, even though X and Y describe their positions in different philosophical language, and X, even if not always also Y, sees them as opposed.[3]

Here the critic, X, is portrayed as stressing the significance of his disagreement with Y, whereas Y, who is being critiqued, is portrayed as downplaying it. The author of the passage seeks, in turn, to engage the reader in his attempt to find out whether, in fact, there is any significant difference between the two positions. Naturally, no simple answer is forthcoming; it takes the whole paper from which this quotation is taken to reach a conclusion. Works that seek to identify anticipations, points of departure, culminations, partings of the ways, and so on, can hardly be expected to be explicit about all the underlying assumptions involved in such endeavors, but the reader cannot afford to be naïve about the methodological and ethical issues involved.

Third, the individual's self-perception, and the rhetoric used to convey this perception to the reader, affect the reader's interpretation. Putnam's rhetoric is no doubt primarily a rhetoric of change. Expressions such as 'I used to think,' 'I no longer believe,' 'I have come to realize,' and even 'my former self,' recur in his writings, impressing upon the reader the intensely dynamic thought processes that Putnam experiences himself as going through. In comparison, other philosophers, for instance Quine, seem to prefer the language of stability and single-mindedness, yet upon closer scrutiny, their writings reveal realignments that such rhetoric tends to obscure. Though the received image of Putnam's philosophy is Heraclitean – self-critical and ever-changing – the essays in this volume often draw to our attention equally if not more important continuities of content and approach.

From the methodological point of view, the general gestalt we project onto the oeuvre in question is important, for it dictates our working assumptions. Our assessment will determine whether we assume continuity unless we find explicit indications of change, or tend to see earlier positions as no longer upheld if they are not explicitly reaffirmed. Yet we can hardly expect an author to set down each of the changes to older views mandated by newer ones, and still less to reiterate in each work the earlier views and arguments that remain unimpugned by the more recent developments. The interpretation of Wittgenstein's writings is a good example. The common perception of a split, a total break between 'the later Wittgenstein' and the views expressed in the *Tractatus,* engenders readings very different from those which emerge from the more unified picture that has become current in recent years. In Putnam's case, the impression of flux leads many readers to assume that he has retracted his main pre-1976 arguments. The most important example in this context is the externalist conception of meaning developed in "The Meaning of 'Meaning'" (1975b, 12). Although externalism was put forward in 1975 (i.e., prior to the break with metaphysical realism), it also plays a central role in Putnam's later writings, and constitutes the core of *Reason, Truth and History* and *Representation and Reality.* The projection of a dramatic split between an 'earlier' and a 'later' Putnam has led readers to regard the persistent affirmation of the "Meaning of 'Meaning'" approach as a kind of puzzle that Putnam is called upon to resolve. If this is a misconception, as several papers in this volume seek to demonstrate, it should induce us to be more cautious about Putnam's alleged renunciation of other earlier arguments. Indeed, the principal insights of such classic papers as "The Refutation of Conventionalism" (1975b, 9) and "It Ain't Necessarily So" (1975a, 15) continue to inform Putnam's philosophy in later years.

The wiles of terminology may be responsible for some of the confusions surrounding internal realism, a phenomenon familiar from other episodes in the history of ideas. The theory of relativity, for instance, was, much to Einstein's dismay, appropriated by cultural relativists, who applauded its relativistic implications but failed to recognize the crucial role it assigned to invariance across frameworks. In Putnam's case, the term "*internal* realism" has often been associated with images and terminology that turned out to be similarly misleading. First, 'internal' suggests a contrast with 'external,' and thus erroneously implies a contrast between internal realism and the externalist conception of meaning advocated in "The Meaning of 'Meaning.'" As noted, however, the externalist conception of meaning is not merely *retained* in Putnam's later writings, but explicitly employed in arguments defending internal realism against metaphysical realism. Second, the internal–external metaphor is frequently invoked by relativists to convey the difference between truth relative to a framework – truth for an individual or a community – and truth in the objective sense upheld by realists. Putnam's use of the internal–external idiom undoubtedly lent itself to relativist (mis)readings of his position. While he has made a sustained effort to distance himself from relativism, and other terms ("natural realism," "common-sense realism") eventually replaced "internal realism," the confusion wrought by the original terminology has yet to dissipate entirely.

In using the internal–external metaphor, the contrast Putnam wants to highlight is that between the human perspective and a super-perspective purporting to capture reality in itself, unmediated by human language and human concepts. It is the emptiness of the super-perspective that Putnam's internal realism seeks to drive home. Here Putnam is allying himself with the tradition of Kant, the American pragmatists, and (at least) the later Wittgenstein, in urging us to "give up the picture of Nature as having its very own language which it is waiting for us to discover and use" (1994, 302). The relativist, on the other hand, uses the metaphor of the internal-external divide to argue that evaluations of a given proposition's rationality or morality are made from within a particular theory, framework, or culture, and cannot, in general, be weighed against each other. In the context of the philosophy of science, Kuhnian paradigms, allegedly self-contained and incommensurable, reflect this relativistic schema. Where the relativist challenges the notion of objective truth, Putnam stresses its centrality to human life. Giving up the metaphysical super-perspective, he argues, does not compel us to give up the concept of truth cherished by realists, namely, truth independent of what individuals or communities believe and stipulate. And whereas the relativist's use of the internal–external metaphor allows for incommensurable alternatives, neither of which is objectively valid, each making sense on its own 'internal' terms, Putnam's use of the same metaphor, while connoting the vacuousness of the external, upholds truth and objectivity. Once more, we see, similar terminology can serve diverse philosophical agendas.

II. THEMES AND SIGNPOSTS IN PUTNAM'S PHILOSOPHY

Putnam brings to philosophy the analytical tools of the logician, the creative imagination of the theoretical scientist, and the sensitivities of the moral philosopher. He has made substantial contributions to the philosophy of language, the philosophy of mind, and the philosophy of science and mathematics. Indeed, in these areas Putnam's philosophy would be an essential part of any survey of contemporary philosophy. Putnam's oeuvre includes well-known theories and research programs such as functionalism, quantum logic and the causal theory of reference; critical arguments and thought experiments such as the widely discussed Twin Earth argument; and numerous studies of contemporary philosophical positions such as realism, skepticism, relativism and pragmatism. Let me comment briefly on the major issues in Putnam's work that are addressed by the contributors to this volume.

Realism

A persistent theme in Putnam's philosophy is the avowal of realism, a position that creates space for objective truth and objective, albeit fallible, knowledge. An integral part of Putnam's defense of realism is his thoroughgoing critique of nonrealist positions such as instrumentalism and conventionalism, which had been popular with the logical positivists, and relativism, which followed close on the heels of positivism as a result of the impact of Kuhn and Feyerabend. One of Putnam's responses to these nonrealist positions is the argument from success: while realism has a simple explanation for the success of science – it works because it is true – for the nonrealist, the success of science is a miracle. The argument from success, and the inference to the best explanation on which it rests, provoked heated debate but are still the standard defense of realism. Yet the question of why science sometimes *fails*, it has come to be acknowledged, provides a better means of sharpening our intuitions about realism. Putnam's stance on realism started to change as he pondered two related questions. First, is it possible that our best theory of the world, a theory that satisfies every empirical and methodological constraint, is nonetheless false? Inasmuch as realist truth is a radically nonepistemic notion, the realist, it seems, is committed to answering in the affirmative, but in 1976, this answer was beginning to make Putnam uncomfortable. Seeking to avoid such a transcendent notion of truth while maintaining other realist intuitions, he introduced the distinction between metaphysical and internal realism.[4] The second question addresses a different aspect of what it means for a theory to capture truth, namely, its amenability to different interpretations, or, more technically, to different models. How can a theory represent reality objectively if fundamental features of its representation, such as the number of objects it postulates, can vary from one interpretation to another? Model-theoretic considerations thus played a significant role in the transition to internal realism. Putnam now maintains that for the metaphysical realist who believes there must be an objective criterion singling out a uniquely correct reference relation from a range of possibilities, the model-theoretic problem, the problem of the availability of multiple interpretations, is insurmountable. From the perspective of internal realism, however, reference, being an essential component of our conceptual apparatus, is unproblematic; it cannot and need not be anchored in 'objective' reality by yet another layer of theory.

At first glance, the problem of multiple interpretations appears fairly abstract. In his contribution, "Structural Realism and Contextual Individuality," John Stachel shows that, quite to the contrary, the problem looms large in twentieth-century physics. As he explains, one of its dramatic applications is the so-called 'hole argument,' which, for a couple of years, held up development of the General Theory of Relativity. Defending his own *structuralist* version of realism, Stachel examines the relation between the reality of structures and the reality of individuals from the physicist's point of view, but goes on to pursue the implications of his analysis for the relation between the individual and the social dimensions of the human life.

Internal realism, Putnam's position as of 1976, stirred up controversy that has yet to be resolved.[5] Critics typically raise the objection that Putnam's third way between metaphysical realism and nonrealism in fact falls back into one of the two positions he has supposedly rejected. No matter how vigorously Putnam protests attempts to construe internal realism as a type of relativism, there is always a critic from the (philosophical) right, so to speak, who insists on so construing him. And no matter how hard he tries to bring out the differences between himself and the metaphysical realist, there is always a critic from the left who argues that he has not succeeded in distancing himself from that position. Over the years,

Putnam has reworked some aspects of his new position: in the early 1980s he was close to identifying internal realism with verificationism, with long-term warranted assertability replacing the notion of truth; later he rejected this view, as well as attempts to reduce the concept of truth to other concepts or treat it as redundant. Furthermore, under the growing influence of Wittgenstein's work, Putnam makes it exceedingly clear that internal realism is not a philosophical theory that aspires to emulate scientific theories. From this perspective, the argument from success, motivated by the analogy between science and philosophy, seems dated. In "Realism, Beyond Miracles," Arthur Fine and Axel Mueller emphasize the pragmatic dimension of Putnam's realism. Rather than explaining our success in representing reality, they argue, his realism seeks to explain our practices in the realm of inquiry and communication. On their interpretation, this pragmatic motivation serves as a unifying element throughout the dynamic evolution of Putnam's various versions of realism.

Externalism

Generally speaking, the theory of meaning is a central focus of twentieth-century philosophy. Specifically, the controversy over realism has pivoted on such meaning-theoretic considerations as the relation between truth, verification and meaning. The logical positivists' verifiability principle of meaning, for instance, was utilized in arguments against realism, particularly in the philosophy of science. As Putnam recognized, the realist's major challenge is therefore to articulate a realist conception of meaning compatible with a realist view of science as a truth-directed enterprise. The prevailing conceptions of meaning, he argued, either tie meaning too closely to the observable, consigning the theoretical to meaninglessness, or construe meaning as implicitly defined by entire theories, with the result that theoretical change ipso facto constitutes meaning-change. The latter alternative is particularly unsatisfactory if combined with the additional premise that meaning-change is indicative of change of reference, for it then yields an extremely relativistic account of science on which different theories, referring, as they do, to different entities, cannot be rationally compared with one another.

"The Meaning of 'Meaning'" puts forward the sought-after alternative to these nonrealist conceptions of meaning.[6] The central idea here is that "meanings just ain't in the head," that is, the focus of meaning assignment shifts from sensations, ideas and mental states to external reality – the entities spoken of. Moreover, there is a shift from individual to social determination of meaning: to know the meaning of words like 'gold,' speakers are not required to be able to tell gold from similar alloys; it is enough that there are experts in the linguistic community able to do so. Two important consequences follow. On the one hand, speakers can refer to the same entities even if the beliefs, theories, definitions, or images they associate with terms referring to these entities differ radically. This aspect of externalism addresses the threat of relativism. On the other hand, speakers can associate a name or predicate with the same type of mental image yet differ as to its meaning. Putnam's celebrated Twin Earth thought experiment is designed to reinforce the latter intuition. If, on Twin Earth, the substance that looks, feels, and functions like water in fact has a different chemical structure than water does, then despite the identity of the mental images associated with 'water' in the minds of inhabitants of Earth and Twin Earth, we would not (and should not) say there is water on Twin Earth. On Putnam's account, then, it is part of the meaning of words like 'water' that they refer to the stuff we call water in the actual world. Though it is neither analytic nor even irrevisable that the molecular formula of water is H_2O, the meaning of 'water' on Twin Earth, where the chemical structure of the substance called 'water' is different, cannot be identical with the meaning of 'water' on Earth.

To complete the realist account of meaning, Putnam tackled the question of how reference is actually fixed, a question also addressed in Kripke's work on reference and rigid designation. If reference is fixed by theory, it is liable to change with theoretical change. On the Kripke-Putnam alternative, however, reference is fixed by causal relations between speakers and their environment: hence the term 'externalism.'[7] Both Putnam and Kripke present externalism as a critique of, and alternative to, Frege's theory of meaning. Putnam, however, was apprehensive primarily about the nonrealist theories of meaning that had circulated in the 1960s. As Frege's theory of meaning reflects his own avowed realism and champions a robust notion of reference, the question of whether, from the realist point of view, Putnam's externalism has any advantages over Frege's, naturally arises. This is one of the issues considered by Juliet Floyd in her detailed analysis of the historical context of "The Meaning of 'Meaning.'"

As Putnam's philosophy evolved, externalism proved to be central, not only to his philosophy of language, but also to his epistemology and philosophy of mind, and, as noted above, not only to the unqualified realism he had espoused prior to 1976, but also to internal realism. Let me mention two contexts where externalism plays a decisive role. In *Reason, Truth and History*, Putnam presents radical skepticism and metaphysical realism as two expressions of the same untenable outlook. Both these positions, he argues, are premised on the possibility that we are altogether wrong about the totality of our beliefs and knowledge-claims. The skeptic's response to this concern is global doubt; the metaphysical realist's, affirmation of transcendent truth, perhaps beyond the grasp of our human minds. The similarity of these views manifests itself in the willingness of their respective proponents to entertain seriously the possibility that we are no more than brains in a vat. The merit of internal realism, Putnam maintains, is that it need not even consider the brains-in-a-vat hypothesis. Indeed, using his externalist criteria for meaning, Putnam can demonstrate that the very formulation of this hypothesis violates the conditions for meaningful discourse. The insights of "The Meaning of 'Meaning'" thus sustain Putnam's argument against skepticism. The relationship between meaning-theoretic considerations, internal realism and the repudiation of skepticism is further explored in my contribution to this volume, "Putnam on Skepticism" (Chap. 5).

Another context where externalism is invoked is that of Putnam's critique of platonism. In *The Threefold Cord*, Putnam explains the change in his understanding of the idea of a use theory of language. Originating with Wittgenstein, the 'meaning as use' rubric came to be widely disseminated, though variously interpreted. Whereas Putnam initially conceived of use as "described largely in terms of computer programs in the brain," a conception completely alien to Wittgenstein, he later adopted an internal interpretation of use: "On this alternative picture... the use of words in a language game cannot, in most cases, be described without employing the vocabulary of that game or a vocabulary internally related to the vocabulary of that game" (1999, 14). Here internal realism and the externalist conception of meaning combine to create a philosophy of language that is neither naturalistic nor platonistic. On the one hand, meaning is conceptual all the way down, and thus irreducible to the empirical; on the other, concepts are not platonic entities, but evolve through interaction between speakers and their environment. To take one of Putnam's examples, to speak of coffee tables it does not suffice for us merely to have the concept of a coffee table, but we must be in contact with *actual* coffee tables. Yet to be in such contact – for instance, to see an actual coffee table – we need to have the concept of a coffee table and know that it is a coffee table we are looking at. In "The Face of Perception," Charles Travis reflects on the externalist aspects of internal realism, explaining precisely why Putnam's conception of meaning undermines platonism and essentialism.

Philosophy of Mind: Functionalism and Beyond

The 1960s ushered in a series of papers in which Putnam advanced a novel approach to the philosophy of mind, an approach that has come to dominate the philosophy of mind and cognitive science. The new approach, known as functionalism, endeavors to secure the autonomy of mind without positing a nonphysical mind-substance: "The question of the autonomy of our mental life does not hinge on and has nothing to do with that all too popular... question about matter or soul-stuff. We could be made of Swiss cheese and it wouldn't matter" (1975b, 291). What matters, Putnam argued, is functional organization. His guiding analogy for functional organization was the computer, or, more accurately, the Turing machine. Evidently, different machines need not share the same hardware to carry out the same computation. Similarly, Putnam claimed, pain-states, or jealousy-states, can be functionally alike though physically different. In other words, each pain-token has a physico-chemical realization, but no reduction of pain as a general type to a given physico-chemical state is assumed. The computer analogy suggests that mental states are syntactically characterized computational states, the projected research program being to provide the 'software' for their interaction.

In the late 1970s, Putnam began to reconsider this proposal. Here too, the externalist insights of "The Meaning of 'Meaning'" proved to have far-reaching implications, providing a compelling argument against the view that the mind is a solipsistic lockbox of sensations. Thinking of something, a vacation, say, seems like a simple enough example of a mental state, but if, as Putnam now began to think, there are external determinants of meaning, then meanings cannot be identified with internal computational states. Some theorists, notably Fodor and Block, attempted to save the computational account by invoking the distinction between narrow and wide content, a distinction set out by Putnam in "The Meaning of 'Meaning.'" While acknowledging the contribution of physical and cultural environments to meaning in the wide sense, they held onto computationalism with respect to meaning in the narrow sense. Apprehension about intentionality led Putnam to reject this solution. As he argued in *Representation and Reality*, narrow-content computationalism is still an attempt to reduce the intentional to the nonintentional. But since even meaning in the narrow sense calls for interpretation – attribution of beliefs – which in turn calls for charity and reasonableness, intentionality cannot be eliminated. Functionalism had conceived the computational level to be autonomous, that is, irreducible to, even if supervenient on, the physico-chemical level. Putnam's critique of functionalism is equally applicable to the question of the autonomy of the mental vis-à-vis the computational. The story of functionalism is told by Oron Shagrir in "The Rise and Fall of Computational Functionalism."

The Philosophy of Quantum Mechanics

Decades of debate over the interpretation of quantum mechanics have only deepened the sense that, despite its empirical success, quantum theory is replete with conceptual difficulties, impelling Putnam to expend a great deal of philosophical effort on its interpretation. Heisenberg's uncertainty principle imposes a limit on the precision with which the values of certain pairs of physical parameters, such as position and momentum, or different spin components, can be measured simultaneously. On the Copenhagen interpretation, this principle implies that it is meaningless to ascribe simultaneous and determinate values to such pairs of physical parameters, whether or not they are actually being measured. Since, however, when any one magnitude is measured separately, a sharp value is obtained, it appears that it is measurement itself that creates the transition, better known as the collapse, from the indeterminate to the well-defined state. If so, measurement does not reflect a state objectively existing prior to measurement, but rather a state of its own creation. Realists are offended by both the inference from the impossibility of measurement to the meaninglessness of concepts, and the nonclassical understanding of measurement. In "The Logic of Quantum Mechanics" (1975a, 10), Putnam proposed that these difficulties could be overcome by adopting a nondistributive logic first suggested in the context of quantum mechanics by Birkhoff and von Neumann in 1936, and developed by David Finkelstein in the 1960s. In light of the traditional gulf between factual and logical truth, the idea that logic can be revised on the basis of empirical considerations was revolutionary. Putnam saw the situation as analogous to the merging of physics and geometry into an interdependent whole in the framework of general relativity.

Quantum logic raises several questions. First, it is not clear that it is a *logic*, a way of reasoning, rather than a calculus that happens to fit the structure of the Hilbert space of quantum mechanics. Second, the idea that realism can be saved by rejecting classical logic, generally seen as constitutive of realism, seems paradoxical. Putnam's operational definition of the quantum-logical operators, intended to strengthen the analogy with logic, obscures the connection to realism. Third, work on the foundations of quantum mechanics by theorists such as Bell, Gleason, and Kochen and Specker, puts unbearable strain on the realist interpretation of quantum mechanics. Indeed, "Quantum Mechanics and the Observer" (1983, 14), written after Putnam had already moved away from his early realism, is premised on a verificationist understanding of quantum logic. The main thrust of the paper, however, is to argue for yet another interpretation of quantum mechanics – perspectivism – attributed by Putnam to von Neumann. Like quantum logic, perspectivism is a way of avoiding collapse of the wave-function upon measurement. Collapse, on this interpretation, is not a physical process, but an epiphenomenon created by the shift from one perspective to another. Different perspectives, Putnam argued, are empirically equivalent and are all congruent with the predictions of quantum mechanics, hence, they are equally legitimate; but perspectives exclude each other in the sense that statements made from different perspectives cannot be combined to form a quantum state. Realism can be sustained within each perspective, but not across perspectives. Although this seemed an attractive way to avoid metaphysical realism while retaining 'internal' realism, upon realizing that in some cases different perspectives are not empirically equivalent, Putnam became dissatisfied with perspectivism. Even though he no longer subscribes to quantum logic, this provocative research program still garners much attention. In this volume, two chapters are devoted to the philosophy of quantum mechanics: Nancy Cartwright's "Another Philosopher Looks at Quantum Mechanics" addresses the question of the place of Putnam's views on quantum mechanics in his more general philosophy of science; Tim Maudlin undertakes a searching analysis and critique of quantum logic in "The Tale of Quantum Logic."

The Fact/Value Dichotomy and Other Dualities

Putnam is, in general, averse to dualisms. Mind and body, mind and world, fact and value, observation and theory, truth and convention, the analytic and the synthetic, are just some of the dichotomies Putnam has systematically criticized over the years. He has had recourse to various strategies for avoiding such dichotomies. Some dichotomies are simply elaborated on to yield a richer spectrum of possibilities; others are rejected on different grounds. In the case of mind-body dualism, Putnam has argued, as we saw, that generations of philosophers have put excessive emphasis on the ontological question of what the mind is made of rather than on the question of how it functions. He thus rejects the idea that there is an ontological basis for mind-body dualism. Mind and world, he argues, are intertwined in a different way, a way that is perhaps best captured by his dictum, "the mind and the world jointly make up the mind and the world" (1981, xi). Putnam associates the critique of traditional dualisms with the pragmatist tradition, whose champions have indeed questioned such deep-seated dichotomies as that between fact and value. But given the vigor of his protest against what he sees as oversimplified distinctions, it seems that above and beyond his endorsement of the pragmatist orientation, his critique reflects a personal predilection for complexity.

The distinction between the analytic and the synthetic is a good example. The nature of logical and mathematical truth has been an ongoing concern for Putnam, yielding several different positions. Repudiation of the standard alternatives, platonism and conventionalism, has, however, remained a constant. The former, he asserts, is, given the conceptual revolutions in twentieth-century physics, obsolete; the latter, empty: as Lewis Carroll, Wittgenstein and Quine pointed out, conventions cannot ground logic because logic is required for their application. In "It Ain't Necessarily So" (1975a, 15), Putnam proposed replacing necessary truth with the more flexible notion of relative necessity, necessity within a specific conceptual horizon. Necessary truths of this kind, while not to be construed as true in all possible worlds, are not as easily refuted as ordinary synthetic assertions. Later, in "Analyticity and Apriority" (1983, 7), Putnam argued that some logical truths are constitutive of rationality and, as such, cannot be rationally revised, whereas others are defeasible. This view is further elaborated in "Rethinking Mathematical Necessity" (1994, 12), where Putnam presents logical truths as "formal presuppositions of thought" rather than as truths in the ordinary sense. While opposed to the conventionalist account of logic and mathematics, Putnam treasures another insight of conventionalism: the possibility of theories (or descriptions) that appear to be incompatible but are nonetheless equivalent in some specified sense – empirically equivalent, or interpretable in each other's vocabulary. He concurs with the conventionalist's claim that preference for one such alternative over others is a matter of cognitive norm. Conventionalists, however, use the infiltration of norms into the scientific process as an argument against the objectivity of science, whereas Putnam, who rejects the fact/value dichotomy, refuses to identify the normative with the subjective.

The fact/value dichotomy is misguided, in Putnam's view, due to the intractable entanglement of facts and values. Typically, he argues, descriptions of facts are value-laden, and value judgments contain factual elements. When someone is described as cruel, generous, envious or what have you, the description cannot be distilled, so to speak, into a purely factual report and an evaluation. Attempting to do so, by, for instance, unpacking cruelty into taking pleasure in the suffering of others, will not do away with the normative component. Whereas upholders of the dichotomy usually maintain, in addition, that factual judgments, unlike value judgments, are subjective, Putnam casts doubt on this further dichotomy as well. On the one hand, he contends that some value judgments are as objective as human judgments can get, and others more negotiable; on the other, he argues that the establishment of facts, even in the sciences, hinges on negotiable values such as simplicity and elegance. Though critique of the fact/value dichotomy has been a recurrent theme in Putnam's work since 1978, it has only recently become sufficiently central to inspire a comprehensive treatment, *The Collapse of the Fact/Value Dichotomy*, on which Richard J. Bernstein reflects in his contribution to the volume "The Pragmatic Turn: The Entanglement of Fact and Value."

The Collapse of the Fact/Value Dichotomy marks another turning point in Putnam's philosophy. For the first time, he addresses at length questions in social, political and economic theory. The ethical perspective, which has become ever more salient in Putnam's work over the past two decades, has broadened to encompass communities and their political organization. This is the type of philosophical engagement that calls to mind the heritage of American pragmatism, Dewey's in particular.

Whereas Putnam's philosophy of language has come to be increasingly influenced by Wittgenstein, his understanding of his calling as a philosopher seems profoundly different from Wittgenstein's. Wittgenstein's inspiration is manifest in Putnam's internal realism, his insistence that we have no way of shedding our conceptual skin, and his contention that the language-world relation so integral to our conceptual apparatus cannot be naturalized. Dewey's inspiration, on the other hand, is manifest in Putnam's socially oriented moral vision. Remarkably, both these very different leitmotifs are captured by a single metaphor: Putnam's philosophy is (to allude to his own allusion to Dubcek), above all, philosophy with a human face.

Notes

1. The problem was to find an algorithm deciding the solvability of diophantine equations; the proof was completed by Yuri Matiyasevich in 1970.
2. Putnam (1999, 14). Here, what Putnam means is that he now ascribes a different meaning to one of the terms in the earlier quotation, the 'use' of language.
3. Daniel Isaacson, "Carnap, Quine and Logical Truth," in David Bell and Wilhelm Vossenkuhl (eds.), *Science and Subjectivity; The Vienna Circle and Twentieth Century Philosophy* (Berlin: Akademie Verlag Berlin, 1992), 100–130, quotation on 123. X, Y and L stand for Quine, Carnap and logical truth, respectively.
4. "Realism and Reason," Putnam (1978, 123–138).

5. Putnam uses a variety of locutions to refer to this 'third way' – among them, internal realism, pragmatic realism, commonsense realism, natural realism, or just realism (as opposed to Realism).

6. Putnam (1975b, 215–271), but see also the immediately preceding "Explanation and Reference" (1975b, 196–214), which complements "The Meaning of 'Meaning.'" "The Meaning of 'Meaning'" argues that the same image can be associated with different meanings; "Explanation and Reference," that different theories can refer to the same entities.

7. One of the points that became clear with the transition to internal realism is that the notion of causality itself is unpacked differently by metaphysical and internal realists. Thus one can no longer ascribe to Putnam a causal theory of reference, or indeed, a *theory* of reference at all, without further specification.

References

Putnam, Hilary (1975a). *Mathematics, Matter and Method. Philosophical Papers, Volume I*. Cambridge: Cambridge University Press.

(1975b). *Mind, Language and Reality. Philosophical Papers, Volume II*. Cambridge: Cambridge University Press.

(1978). *Meaning and the Moral Sciences*. London: Routledge & Kegan Paul.

(1981). *Reason, Truth and History*. Cambridge: Cambridge University Press.

(1983). *Realism and Reason, Philosophical Papers, Volume III*. Cambridge: Cambridge University Press.

(1988). *Representation and Reality*. Cambridge, MA: MIT Press.

(1990). *Realism with a Human Face*, ed. James Conant. Cambridge, MA: Harvard University Press.

(1992). *Renewing Philosophy*. Cambridge, MA: Harvard University Press (The Gifford Lectures, St. Andrews 1990).

(1994). *Words and Life*, ed. James Conant. Cambridge, MA: Harvard University Press. A collection of essays by Putnam, selected and introduced by the editor.

(1999). *The Threefold Cord: Mind, Body, and World*. New York: Columbia University Press.

(2002). *The Collapse of the Fact/Value Dichotomy*. Cambridge, MA: Harvard University Press.

(2004). *Ethics without Ontology*. Cambridge, MA: Harvard University Press.

2 | Putnam's "The Meaning of 'Meaning'": Externalism in Historical Context

JULIET FLOYD

1. INTRODUCTION

In what sense did Putnam *invent* the doctrine of semantic externalism? His causal treatment of reference, developed in the mid-1960s[1] and most famously defended in "The Meaning of 'Meaning'" (1975; hereafter MoM) was, *inter alia*, a response to the then popular idea that when our beliefs change (as when science progresses), so do the meanings and referents of our terms. Because of the influence of Carnap, Kuhn, and Malcolm, this relativist conception seemed viable at the time, and Putnam's response, accordingly, revolutionary. But surely, one might protest, the founding fathers of early analytic philosophy, Frege and Russell, were not tempted by any such relativism. What prevented *them* from adopting the relativist line of thinking that associated with different theories or criteria different meanings, different referents, even different worlds? Were they *already* semantic externalists? If not, why not?

These questions are anachronistic, but instructively so. They allow us to investigate in what ways Putnam's externalism constitutes a critique of Frege – as Putnam quite explicitly said that it did – and in what ways it constitutes an extension or interpretation of Frege. Similar questions may be asked about Russell and about various stages in his development, for Russell's conception(s) of analysis and doctrine(s) of immediate acquaintance appear on the surface to have lodged logical form (hence, objectivity and meaning) in the mind's immediate contact with extra-mental entities. But in what follows I shall largely focus, as does Putnam, on Frege. For it is Frege, and not Russell, who appears as a primary object of attack in MoM, and it is Frege, not Russell, from whom Putnam has explicitly drawn in the context of his most recent efforts to articulate an anti-Carnapian (that is, anti-conventionalist), anti-Quinean (that is, anti-empiricist) notion of *necessity* relativized to a conceptual scheme.[2] Finally, it is Frege, not Russell, who is nowadays most often regarded as the most important originator of analytic philosophy. By delving into Putnam's own very complex inheritance of

17

Frege, I hope to reach a deeper understanding of his externalism by placing it within the context of a larger question about the nature and origins of analytic philosophy.

2. EXTERNALISM CHARACTERIZED

The core of Putnam's semantic externalism may be variously summarized. Negatively described, it says that the notion of *meaning* is not ambiguous between intension and extension; that individual psychological states do not determine extensions; that an individual in isolation cannot in principle grasp any arbitrary concept whatsoever; that an individual's grasp of his or her concepts does not totally determine the extension of all the individual's terms; that knowledge of meanings is not private property; and – perhaps most radically – that meanings are best not conceived as entity- or object-like at all.[3] Positively described, the position has three central strands. First, our notion of meaning is object- or reality-involving in the sense that, at least in central cases, it is significantly determined by reference rather than vice versa; second, much concept-possession, and much grasp of meaning, is essentially social in character; third, our individuation of meanings, con-cepts, beliefs, and what they are true of are and ought to be settled in *mul-tifarious* ways, by a range of culture- and environment-involving factors, including the purposes and context(s) of a speaker's assertion, her causal links with the objects, the use of stereotypes within a community to gen-erate linguistic obligations, the linguistic division of labor, and, ultimately, judgments as to reasonableness and charity available to speakers in virtue of their "agent-centered" self-conceptions as participants in a variety of practices. Putnam groups these three elements together with his notion of a "meaning-vector" (MoM, p. 269), a suggested template or type of *partial* "normal form description" of the meaning of certain natural kind terms, for example, "water".[4] Putnam has refused, especially in recent writings, to call this a *theory*; indeed, he now explicitly says, against Michael Dummett, that he rejects 'meaning theories' (cf. *Collected Papers Vol. 3*, p. xvii).

The rejection of individualism about concept-possession and the importance of the extension- and reality-involving character of meaning are the two features of externalism most often emphasized in current liter-ature – and were of course also highlighted and exploited by Putnam not only in MoM, but in later works such as *Representation and Reality* (1988) and *The Threefold Cord* (1999). Yet Putnam's commitment to semantic ex-ternalism, it must be emphasized, always reflected and expressed the wider philosophical matrix of his views on *truth, objectivity,* and *value,* and, in particular, his rejection of the fact/value dichotomy, the theme of his latest set of essays (2002).[5] And over time, his various applications of externalism – to undercut external world skepticism (*Reason, Truth and History* [1981]), to refute reductive functionalism about mental states (*Representation and Reality*) and to argue against views positing qualia or internal mental representations as immediate objects of perception (*The Threefold Cord*) – have come to rely more and more explicitly on his pluralism about the notion of truth and on his rejection of the fact/value dichotomy: what I have just characterized as the third element of his externalism. This reflects the increasing importance to Putnam over time of the pragmatists, of Wittgenstein, and of Austin. Moreover, it is also this third element that juxtaposes his version of externalism most interestingly and complexly with Frege's philosophy, and thereby shows what is most original in his version of the doctrine – or so I shall argue. The idea is that Putnam's own "semantic externalism" is an "ism" which is best regarded as an important node in the overall structure of his thought rather than as an isolated doctrine about the nature of meaning or concepts – a way of thinking, rather than an analysis in the classical sense. And this, I shall emphasize, is no accident. For part of Putnam's point in framing semantic externalism was to *reject* the classical notion of *analysis* itself. Since, as he argues in MoM, our uses of the notion of *meaning* neither can nor should be either reduced to a set of necessary and sufficient conditions (p. 271) or assimilated, either to purely conventional, logical stipulations or to theoretically motivated descriptions and/or rules about unobservable entities for explanatory purposes, so much the worse for any philosophy that conceives of analysis as primarily engaged in these sorts of tasks. Conceptual analysis, if such there is to be, must picture itself differently. *That* is the central argument that MoM has with the tradition.

3. STRUCTURE AND AIMS OF "THE MEANING OF 'MEANING'"

From a historical point of view, the most important contributions of MoM were what, in contrast to its predecessors and successors, it did *not* attempt to do. It did not pretend to offer an analysis of the notions of *content, meaning,* or *language* in general. It did not offer a theory of meaning for any especially large class of terms of the language. It offered no real theory of reference either, but at best a few "mild" (as opposed to Rational with a capital *R*) reconstructions of certain elements of the notion of *meaning* in connection with particular examples of predicates. Putnam did frame a few "hypotheses" as to what should be considered central components of the meaning vector, but these were not offered in any deep or foundationalist sense of explanation. MoM did not defend or attack realism, internal or otherwise, though it did provide materials that nicely cohered with a certain *kind* of "internal" realism, and with a certain *kind* of critique of "metaphysical" realism.[6] And it prescinded, in an ecumenical way, from an analysis of the notion of *necessity*, though it exploited the notion in an unsystematized and intuitive way, thereby exposing unexamined assumptions about concept-possession lying behind apparently more rigorous analyses of the modalities, such as those offered by Carnap and the "California" semanticists (MoM, pp. 262ff.). Despite the ways in which they have often been interpreted, then, Putnam's thought-experiments should be construed as being forwarded in a manner most like Wittgensteinian language-games: simplified models of portions of our language use designed to help us reflect on our ways of picturing *meaning*, rather than descriptions whose cogency turns on the existence of ultimately *real* possible worlds.[7]

In general, therefore, Putnam did not insist on his readers adopting any single approach to the notions of *intension, extension,* and *meaning.* What he did do was to show that previous philosophical approaches to these notions, inside and outside of the analytic tradition, had vastly distorted and oversimplified them, and that much work remained to be done in the face of this complexity. This was worth saying, because the dream that one can profitably talk at an overarching level of generality about such notions in terms of a few basic categorial distinctions was (and remains) so very deep-seated, especially within the analytic tradition. Certain starting points were taken for granted as *ideals* for a theory of meaning. Once those are surrendered, there are various alternative approaches one might take, as Putnam has always insisted.

In defense of this interpretation, we note that the overarching dialectical strategy of MoM was to confront philosophers with a starkly rejected *picture* rather than to advance and defend a free standing or universally applicable theory. The main applications of the reconstruction in the article were thus negative, and they applied remarkably broadly, across all kinds of different philosophical positions, ancient and modern, as Putnam explained.[8] Indeed, it is one of Putnam's great contributions to have so accessibly and vividly formulated for his readers *as a picture* certain "myth-eaten" (cf. MoM, p. 216), timeworn, yet utterly natural ways of speaking precisely so as to problematize them. A picture is neither a worked-out theory nor a definition, and for that reason it is all that more powerful. Precisely by confronting the reader with a denial, and asking for assent to it, Putnam kept the discussion from being drawn into those side-thickets philosophers had traditionally shown a hankering to enter; and he thereby vastly widened the class of views to which his criticisms apply. For instance, it doesn't matter to Putnam's arguments that philosophers have differed with one another since at least Plato on what we *mean* by an 'idea' or 'concept'; the tradition, with all its internal dissent, was still largely held captive by certain fundamental starting points about the role of the mind in fixing our take on meaning.

In MoM the picture(s) to be rejected are vividly articulated in terms of two principles, principles that encode a great deal of philosophical history:

1. Knowing the meaning of a term is just a matter of being in a certain psychological state.

2. The meaning of a term (in the sense of "intension") determines its extension (in the sense that sameness of intension entails sameness of extension).

Historically speaking, (1) represents the temptations of empiricism and psychologism, while (2) represents the temptations of rationalism and logicism. Not unlike Kant, Putnam argues that the principles – and, implicitly, the traditions from which they stem – are as they stand jointly incompatible: each ends, if it is viewed as offering the whole truth, by generating hopeless perplexity about our notion of *meaning*. What Putnam demanded – and delivered – is a 'critique' of the principles, that is, adaptations or reformulations of their respective spheres of applicability that allows each a limited and partial role in our characterization of the notion of *meaning*. This is accomplished by designing a newly complex yet intuitively recognizable vocabulary within which to pose and answer questions about the notion of *meaning*. We are thereby shown that a good many of our pretheoretical ways of speaking about and using the notion (e.g., defeasible appeals to the dictionary, deference to those we deem experts, evolving standards applied to concept-individuation) are, on the whole, not only satisfactory but desirable.

Putnam's results were several, and vastly influential within analytic philosophy, which is why this essay is probably the most widely read and cited of any he ever wrote. He rescued the notion of *meaning* from Quinean skeptical onslaught by putting in a fresh and less radically empiricist light Quine's rejection of the analytic/synthetic distinction. He simultaneously rescued it from misuse and abuse at the hands of conventionalists and relativists. He offered several concrete suggestions, along plausible but sometimes contrasting lines, about how the psychological and logical traditions in philosophy might begin to speak to one another across something better than a chasm, and showed that analytic philosophy could, in a constructive and instructive way, overcome its obsession with characterizing meaning in one ideological way rather than another. All that was required was for philosophers to become more nuanced and subtle about their conception of analysis; but this required revisions in the ways they had allowed themselves to talk about the notion of *meaning* for a very long time.

Putnam's famed "Twin Earth" example attacks the notion of *determination* at work in (2) by imagining a context in which we should find it natural to say that though speakers on earth and Twin Earth express the same intension (are in, *ex hypothesi*, identical intensional states) when they use "water", the extension of that term – and hence its meaning – might, by our current lights, differ according to the community's environment. Putnam's claim that he, though a competent speaker of the English words "elm" and "beech", did not know how to distinguish elms from beeches – though he knew them to be distinct species – attacks the idea that the determination of an extension can always be idealized as the activity of an individual speaker: you don't even need to go to Twin Earth to see that a perfectly linguistically competent speaker might (in practice actually *does* and *should*) rely on experts and on frontline, causally immersed observers and ostenders – the social and environmental context – to fix the extension of some terms in her language. There is what Putnam called a *division of linguistic labor.*

Both thought experiments *assume* that natural-kind words like "water" refer to the substance(s) we correctly call by those names in our *current* language, so that there is an admitted kind of ineliminable "indexical" quality to our talk about water, a quality tagged, not only to our time, community, and current state of expert theorizing, but also to our place, to the actual character of our spatio-temporal environment. (Putnam's discussion of 'indexicality' draws an analogy, not an identity, between kinds of words.) Like Kripke, Putnam suggests that the meaning of a natural kind term like "water", typically introduced by ostension, may be taken to be "rigid", that is, assumed to refer to the same substance in all possible situations ("This stuff here"), but in an epistemically defeasible way: "Human intuition", Putnam remarks, "has no privileged access to metaphysical necessity", if such there be (MoM, p. 233). This is a striking and important corollary to externalism. This, MoM argues, is the best way to do intuitive justice to an "agent-centered" point of view on speakers.[9]

Indexicals like "I", "here", and 'now' seem to thwart the idea that *intension* or *meaning* or *concept* determines extension in a fairly intuitive way: such indexicals are usually said to *retain the same meaning* while varying their references from occasion to occasion of use. Thus if the indexical analogy for natural-kind terms is fitting, even if the rigidity idea is wrong, it would still suggest a way to avoid being forced into the kind of meaning- and object-relativism about natural-kind terms associated with Kuhn and Feyerabend. Putnam chose in MoM, however, to push the stronger view that *both* indexicality and rigidity be taken seriously. This allowed him to hold on to a modified ("indexicalized") form of principle (2) by arguing that *because* difference in extension is *ipso facto* a difference in meaning for natural-kind words, meanings must not be conceived either to be concepts or to be (mental) entities (MoM, p. 234).

Moved by the idea that an atheoretical, ahistorical, or transcenden- tal stance on reality (e.g., through "direct", incorrigible, or non–theory- laden observation) makes no sense, conventionalists, instrumentalists and Kuhnians had argued that, since reference is fixed *via* theory, and theory is articulated in language, changes in theory entail changes in meaning. Putnam showed that someone moved by the same underlying idea but prepared both to surrender the analytic/synthetic distinction and to take the social and spatio-temporally situated character of human language use as constitutive of it could avoid this conclusion and retain (or better, re- gain) certain pre-theoretical ways of speaking about meaning. Theory might evolve without meaning-change, and meaning-change might occur without change in theory: it would, it does, and it should, *even ideally*, depend upon our purposes and the context(s) in which we speak. These contexts and pur- poses, Putnam indicates, are not handed down from Mount Sinai once and for all, impersonally and acontextually. They are contingent and various, evolving, and because they are indefinitely open-ended and extendable, also limited and partial. As he writes at the end of MoM (p. 271):

> what have been pointed out in this essay are little more than home truths about the way we use words and how much (or rather, how little) we actually know when we use them. My own reflection on these matters began after I published a paper in which I confidently maintained that the meaning of a word was 'a battery of semantical rules' ["How Not to Talk about Meaning", published in 1965] and then began to wonder how the meaning of the common word 'gold' could be accounted for in this way....
> ... [B]oth learned and lay opinion [have] gone ... astray with respect to a topic which deals, after all, with matters which are in everyone's experience, matters concerning which we all have more data than we know what to do with, matters concerning which we have, if we shed preconceptions, pretty clear intuitions....

MoM is a great work because of Putnam's remarkable ability to write flu- idly, accessibly, and lucidly about notions and problems that had become during his lifetime defamiliarized and overly theorized to the point of ideological surrender. Properly read, the essay is an exercise in recovery – not just recovery from misguided philosophy, but recovery of the activity of philosophy itself as worthwhile. It served as an encouraging reminder that analytic philosophy can venture profitably beyond its origins and apparent conceptual boundaries, partly because it is *not* a tradition constructed around a single insight, doctrine, or method, much less such as could be reductively linked to the notion of *linguistic meaning*.

4. EXTERNALISM AND THE PHILOSOPHY OF PSYCHOLOGY

As Putnam has always seen it, there is something right in the impulse behind (1), the principle of empiricism and psychologism: we need to see what it is about *human beings*, conceived as natural beings situated within their spatio-temporal, causally involved, naturally evolving, epistemically fallible circumstances, that gives us a purchase on the complex, multifarious relationships among our notions of *meaning, objectivity*, and *truth*. What is wrong with (1) is its reductively individualistic, poorly psychologized way of construing this insight. On this Putnam has, so far as I know, never wavered. Yet his way of construing what he takes to be right in principle (2) – the logicizing, rationalist principle – has changed over time, as his own views about psychology have evolved.

Back in 1975, stressing his hope that a positive role could be found for psychology and linguistics in philosophers' talk about meaning and concept-possession, Putnam worked with a distinction (now much discussed by Fodor and others) between *narrow* and *wide* content, between an approach to the analysis of *meaning* that restricts itself to accounting only for individualistic, neurophysiologically discriminable states or properties ("methodological solipsism") and one that aspires to the analysis of a wider class of intersubjectively shareable and discriminable psychological states. In MoM his attack on principle (1) construed it as a thesis about narrow content (pp. 219ff.). This allowed him starkly and vividly to exploit its (individualistically cast) demand for empirical responsibility in criticizing principle (2). Indeed, Putnam argued that principle (2) has traditionally ended in especially murky forms of psychologism and mentalism insofar as it aimed to take speakers of a language into account at all.

Before 1975, Putnam's functionalism about psychological concepts had held him in sway, and it is worth noting that this position, too, aimed at synthesizing the psychological and the logical traditions. His functionalism exploited a (psychologized) version of the logicist principle (2) to reject the individualistic (and neurophysiologically reductionist)[10] construal of principle (1).[11] The central claim of MoM was that not only 'narrow', but also 'wide' content (i.e., the kind we as joint speakers of a language are assumed to be able, in principle, to share and speak about in a public setting) cannot be specified without reference to things external to the speaker's body.[12] The argument as presented applied both widely and narrowly, but the fact is that Putnam had never had much sympathy with Carnap's methodological solipsism, which he always construed as something *more* than a conventionally chosen illustrative basis for an analytic construction, something proposed in the spirit of a kind of positive program for empirical psychology.[13] He complains in MoM that "three centuries of failure of mentalistic psychology" is tremendous evidence against it.[14] Yet it was not until the 1970s, under the influence of John McDowell and Tyler Burge, that Putnam came to reject the coherence of the wide content/narrow content distinction.[15] This squared with his earlier statement that "no important theory of the nature of mind can either be confirmed or ruled out by an examination of the meanings of mental words" (*Collected Papers Vol. 2* [1975], p. xiii), but shifted the insight in a new direction. Spurred on by his use of model-theoretic arguments to attack both global skepticism and global metaphysical realism about truth and reference,[16] in his *Representation and Reality* (1988) he applied semantic externalism to refute functionalism. The core idea here is that the pervasive yet localized relevance of environment, social context, and contextually sensitive standards of good judgment to our notions of *meaning* and *truth* make the Turing machine and the Tarski-style disquotational analysis of truth unsuitable as models of concept possession and reference: they are *both* too individualistic *and* too logicistic.[17] In *The Threefold Cord*, all three elements of semantic externalism are exploited to reject individualistic dogmas in the philosophy of perception (about sense-data, qualia, and "sensory representations") that had, Putnam admits, been invited by his own and Jaegwon Kim's similar forms of functionalism.

Thus, as Putnam now sees it, the unforgettable externalist slogan from MoM, "Cut the pie any way you like, 'meanings' just ain't in the *head*" (p. 227) is a counter-picture that can mislead, however much truth there is in it. For the notions of something's being "in the *head*" and "in the mind" are considerably more problematic than the slogan suggests. Semantic externalism, as Putnam now presents it – despite what the italics in the 1975 slogan might be taken to imply – entails that word- (and sentence-) meanings are best not conceived of as entities of which we could sensibly ask, "Where then *are* they (if not in the *head*)?" The point, then, is that we should stop trying to conceive of them as objects that either do or do not measure up to "truly scientific" scrutiny. This and this alone allows full play to the notion that participation in language and concept mastery are activities, forms of knowing *how* that are not always and everywhere "in principle" reducible to a knowing *that*.[18] What externalism ultimately requires, as Putnam eventually came to emphasize, is a hard-won reassessment of what is meant by the phrases, "entity-like" and "scientific"; a critique of an idea, quite traditional in modern philosophy – to be found, for example, in Kant's explicit rejection of psychology as a proper empirical science – that there is only so much science in a subject as there is mathematics and unified logical articulation of its theory.[19] Reason – and reasonableness – are not, Putnam now emphasizes, formalizeable, idealizeable, or naturalizeable in any such sense.[20]

Putnam's post-1975 applications of semantic externalism – including its use in refuting functionalism – must then be seen ultimately to turn on his pluralistic conception of the variegated, evolving, norm- and purpose-relative quality of our (for Putnam interconnected and inseparable) notions of *concept, meaning, object, language, understanding*, and *truth*. This has allowed him to show how his meaning-vector idea may be used, not only to temper individualism about the mental, but to throw off reductive psychologism generally, even in its nonempiricist, nonindividualist (or neurophysiologically reductionist) forms. In this sense, Putnam's own anti-psychologism has come into its own. In 1975, his anti-logicism and anti-individualism took priority: the notion of *linguistic meaning* had to be wrested away from its conventionalist, positivist burdens. But by the early 1980s, his interest in emphasizing the ubiquity of the normative came to the fore. This allowed him to revisit Frege. Indeed, he now appeals to Frege – or, perhaps more accurately, to a strand of Frege's philosophy adapted by Wittgenstein and to be seen at work in Austin as well – to separate the notion of *sense* – essentially linked to the notions of *understanding, intelligibility*, and *conceptual normativity* – from that of *linguistic meaning*. On Putnam's current view, a sentence's meeting ordinary grammatical standards of sentencehood does not suffice for the expression either of sense or of understanding.[21] This post-Fregean, Wittgensteinian way of drawing the sense/meaning distinction remains true to what was argued against Frege in MoM, but casts it in a new, more complicated light.

5. PUTNAM ON FREGE'S PSEUDO–ANTI-PSYCHOLOGY

The clarity with which Putnam stated his differences with Frege in MoM made it easy for his readers to assume that he had stated in that essay all there was of interest to say on the matter of his attitude toward Frege's notions of *sense, reference, thought,* and *concept.* To begin, however, by supposing that there are two approaches, Fregean and externalist, that exist in Plato's Heaven as primary rivals in the theory of meaning is not only to think anachronistically and far too simplistically about the development of early analytic philosophy; it is to misunderstand the nature and power of the position on *meaning* that Putnam designed and defended.

Frege's name appears explicitly only twice in MoM, each time grouped with that of Carnap; Putnam's explicit remarks are directed at what he treats as Frege's and Carnap's joint form of "anti-psychologism". Implicitly Frege's thought is also at stake in Putnam's critical remarks about Davidson's program of obtaining a meaning theory via a truth theory (MoM, pp. 258ff.): Putnam sees no reason to privilege sentence-analysis over word-meaning, in the style of a truth-conditional analysis of meaning, and this amounts, at least in letter, to a rejection of something like Frege's context principle.[22] Since Frege's own distinctive form of anti-psychologism was explicitly bound up in his advocacy of this principle, we shall have to consider this in some detail.

Putnam's explicit charges against Frege and Carnap in MoM are, first, that their postulation of intensions as abstract entities makes a mystery of the individual mind's contact with concepts, and, second, that Frege's anti-psychologism is weakened by the kind of unpersuasive "straw man" psychologism against which he argued:

> Most traditional philosophers thought of concepts as something *mental.* Thus the doctrine that the meaning of a term (the meaning "in the sense of intension," that is) is a concept carried the implication that meanings are mental entities. Frege and more recently Carnap and his followers, however, rebelled against this "psychologism," as they termed it. Feeling that meanings are *public* property – that the *same* meaning can be "grasped" by more than one person and by persons at different times – they identified concepts (and hence "intensions" or meanings) with abstract entities rather than mental entities. However, "grasping" these abstract entities was still an individual psychological act. None of these philosophers doubted that understanding a word (knowing its intension) was just a matter of being in a certain psychological state (somewhat in the way in which knowing how to factor numbers in one's head is just a matter of being in a certain very complex psychological state). ... (MoM, p. 218)

If our interpretation of the traditional doctrine of intension and extension is fair to Frege and Carnap, then the whole psychologism/Platonism issue appears somewhat a tempest in a teapot, as far as meaning-theory is concerned. (Of course, it is a very important issue as far as general philosophy of mathematics is concerned.) For even if meanings are "Platonic" entities rather than "mental" entities on the Frege-Carnap view, "grasping" those entities is presumably a psychological state (in the narrow sense). Moreover, the psychological state uniquely determines the "Platonic" entity. So whether one takes the "Platonic" entity or the psychological state as the "meaning" would appear to be somewhat a matter of convention. And taking the psychological state to be the meaning would hardly have the consequence that Frege feared, that meanings would cease to be public. For psychological states are "public" in the sense that different people (and even people in different epochs) can be in the *same* psychological state. Indeed, Frege's argument against psychologism is only an argument against identifying concepts with mental particulars, not with mental entities in general. (MoM, p. 222)

"Somewhat a matter of convention" in the second quoted paragraph is an ironic thrust at the irrelevance of Carnap's form of anti-metaphysics. It does Carnap no good, in Putnam's mind, to lean on the analytic/synthetic distinction to try to water down as a matter of "convention" or "meaning-postulate" his talk about intensions as abstract entities. But that is, fundamentally, because *in the dialectical context that Putnam has constructed*, realism versus anti-realism about thoughts and concepts isn't the most important issue on which to focus! To argue that this is a mere "tempest in a teapot" for the notion of *meaning* was a bold and brilliant move on Putnam's part, and absolutely central to his argument in MoM, though it is easily lost sight of, partly because Frege is so often read as an unvarnished 'realist' about thought and meaning, and partly because of what Putnam says in MoM.

Putnam complains that Frege's own arguments for anti-psychologism only work against identifying concepts with "mental particulars", and not with mental entities generally. This is historically just, and by 1975 a fairly well-worn objection, which is one reason Putnam did not waste time justifying or much relying on it. Yet in the context of his treatment of wide and narrow content and his interpolating use of the two principles, Putnam has shifted its significance into a new context, away from ontology and toward the notion of *meaning*. This bears some comparison with the detail of the historical record.

Frege's polemical arguments against psychologism – in, for example, the *Grundlagen der Arithmetik* (1884) and in his widely read essay "Der Gedanke" (1918) – did rely on conceiving *Vorstellungen* as wholly private, fleeting, and image-like, best exemplified by sensations and their qualities and the incommunicable Cartesian "I". Frege seems to have come close to *denying*, as Kant explicitly did, that there could ever be a proper empirical science of psychology. Even in Frege's own day (much less in 1975) such an argument was simply unconvincing. Yet the fundamental difficulty turned on something deeper than Frege's having underestimated the subject matter of empirical psychology or argued poorly. It essentially rested on difficulties internal to logicism's aim to purge logic of psychology.

Heading back in time, we note that Russell and Wittgenstein each rejected Frege's post-1890 distinction between *Sinn* and *Bedeutung* (and with it Frege's conception of thoughts as the senses of sentences), though neither one of them was pleading on behalf of psychology or worrying about Platonism in general. Instead, they worried about Frege's way of talking about the connection between sense and truth in judgment, his way of trying to bring the *expression* of thought in language into his logicized picture.[23] By 1903 Russell accused Frege of having allowed "psychological elements" to intrude into his logical discussions of assertion by having "divorced" assertion from truth (1903, p. 503). By 1913, and again explicitly in the *Tractatus* (cf. its sections 4.064, 4.442, and 5.124), Wittgenstein complained about both Frege's and Russell's respective treatments of truth, sense, and assertion. By 1920, having failed to interest Frege in his own novel way of attempting to logicize the notion of *sense* in the *Tractatus*, Wittgenstein wrote to Frege that he considered Frege's 1918 essay "Der Gedanke" (destined to become one of the most widely read of all Frege's works) to be an "inferior" work, flawed because it attacks Idealism on its weak side.[24] And it is true that Frege's conception of thoughts, though it insists on the independence of thoughts from *Vorstellungen*, fails to tell us *anything* further about what thoughts ultimately are or are made of.

Because of the primacy of logic in framing Frege's notion of *sense*, there are reasons to suppose that this silence is intrinsic to his conception: Frege had no clear stance from which to rule in or rule out any distinctive ontological category for thoughts beyond their being non–cognition-dependent, causally inert, nonspatial, and nontemporal. Thus for all we know, Fregean thoughts are ("mental") Ideas in a Platonic or Absolute Idealist sense![25] At the same time, however, Frege explicitly conceived of understanding a sentence as a matter of an individual speaker's "grasping" the thought it expresses, of judging as a speaker's *act* of acknowledging the thought's truth, and of assertion as an *act* of a speaker manifesting this judgment in language.

So Putnam's primary charge in MoM, that Frege's and Carnap's willingness to conceive thoughts (senses) as abstract objects *necessarily* entangles them in inchoate talk about truth, error, and mental acts of "grasping" and "acknowledging" thoughts has more than a grain of historical and philosophical truth in it, at least in regard to Frege.[26] Yet note that Putnam's objections in MoM do not turn on any *general* anti-realist worries about abstract entities, but instead – just as Russell's and Wittgenstein's had long before – on Frege's particular way of talking about the connection between sense, understanding, and truth with regard to the expression of thought in language. The post-positivist Putnam, however, puts the arguments in a new light by placing a distinctive emphasis upon the notion of *linguistic meaning*, as neither Frege, nor Russell, nor Wittgenstein had.

6. WHAT ABOUT THE CONTEXT PRINCIPLE?

In spite of what we have just conceded about Frege's discussion of thoughts, Putnam's objections to him in MoM seem, on the surface, to be wholly out of order. For Frege was simply not engaged, as Carnap and Putnam were, in the project of offering psychologically responsible accounts of concept-possession. Indeed, the whole purpose of Frege's philosophy was to orient philosophers *away* from looking for such accounts in handling such basic notions as *concept*. Moreover, Frege's anti-psychologism and his context principle were closely linked features of his thought; though interpreters have always differed on how to characterize their ultimate import, it is unquestioned that Frege used each to further the other. Putnam's point about concept-grasp, by focusing on (a certain kind of) word-meaning, seems therefore utterly outside the bounds of the Fregean project. Was not Frege *primarily* concerned with philosophy of mathematics, where, by Putnam's own admission, we do *not* face a mere "tempest in a teapot" about Platonism? And do we not owe to Frege *above all other philosophers* our deepest appreciation of how philosophers are to *avoid* mental-mystery act accounts of meaning by controlling in a scientifically respectable manner the introduction of abstract entities? And is this not precisely to be done by giving primary weight to the use of (something like) the context principle?

The answer for Putnam is No, on all three counts, at least for purposes of analyzing the notion of *linguistic meaning*. *The price of Frege's insistence on the priority of the sentence to the word is an intolerable logicization of concept-possession that the notions of truth and meaning cannot survive.*

Putnam's immediate interest in MoM was in reformulating principle (2) so as to shake off a certain rationally idealized conception of language or theory that had been inherited by Kuhn and Feyerabend from Frege via Carnap. For this it was not enough for him centrally to involve the notions of *object*, *reality*, and *social environment* in our account of concept-possession and of meaning to recover the idea that changes of theory need not entail changes of meaning and reference – something that the pragmatist Peirce, as Putnam points out, also fell into.[27] MoM is also arguing that we need also to alter our view, both of what it is to understand a language and, *a fortiori*, of what form, *ideally*, a theory of meaning and/or concept-possession should take. Putnam's fundamental argument against Frege (and what his successors had tried to take from him) was to reject Frege's ideal of a universally context-encompassing, "first-grade" conceptual scheme (to use Quine's phrase, often quoted by Putnam), a language that would, ideally, provide a canonical way to give a definitive, eternally adequate expression of thought or knowledge. Ideally, for Frege, Carnap, and Quine, such a language would codify in an explicit, rule-governed way the ultimate conceptual bases of our epistemic distinction between the *content* of a belief or judgment and the *process, act,* or *history* of its making. Putnam's arguments in MoM are all intended to reclaim as acceptable *even in our ideal view of a language or theory* the polymorphousness of concept-individuation and contribution, to establish as *fundamental* and *desirable* the contextual and contingently situated complexity involved in our human ways of applying the meaning vector. The contextual complexity of these ways of weighting components of the meaning-vector was what allowed Putnam to soften the notion of *determination* at work in principle (2) to an acceptable one. But it was also intended to outstrip and thereby undercut the way in which Frege's particular form of anti-psychologism and his particular uses of his context-principle were formulated and applied.

MoM did not quarrel with the idea that Frege might be read as a philosopher with a theory of linguistic meaning: after all, post-Fregean theorists of meaning were near the top of the list of Putnam's philosophical targets. Carefully read, however, his remarks do not commit him to such an interpretation; and recently, under the influence of Frege scholarship, he has come explicitly to deny it.[28] And currently Putnam takes himself to have been implicitly relying on (what he later explicitly takes to be) certain deep insights of Frege's, namely, that we ought not to aim at reducing *every* aspect of concept-possession – and especially the notions of *sense* and *understanding* – to our notion of *linguistic meaning* or to any other notions that we dream might one day be wholly formalized or formulated in an ideal scientific language. This, rather than an uncritical metaphysics of thought, is the fundamental mistake about meaning to which principle (2) is tied.

For Putnam knew in 1975 that, when it comes to Frege, one must take the picture of an intension *determining* an extension – enunciated in MoM's principle (2) – quite seriously as a temptation. Anyone wanting to make general scientific sense of the principle's notion of "determines" in such a way as to ensure that there could be no confusion between the act and the content of judgment, no risk of relying at the foundation on any reference to psychological, causal, or spatio-temporally situated features of thinkers, would naturally reach for the mathematician's notion of *function* (recall Kant's dictum that there is only so much science in a subject as there is mathematics). A function "determines" in and of itself, so to speak, an output for every input on which it is defined, and yet the function itself is conceived to be *distinct from* the elements in its domain and range. There can be no doubt that this was the model of "determination" at work in Frege's and Russell's philosophies of logic.[29] The price, Putnam argued in MoM (and ever afterward) is that the notions of *thought* and its linguistic expression became, not just *im*personal, but *a* personal and ahuman, possibly even transmartian: unable *in principle* to be fitted convincingly together with *any* empirical discussion of how the specific capacities, interests, and circumstances of thinkers (whether construed individually or collectively) might affect them, or how our specific linguistic obligations might reflect them.

Now Russell – to his credit from Putnam's point of view – was always able to see this as a central problem, which is to say that he always saw the kernel of truth in the first, psychologizing principle of "MoM", and the need to adjust it to the demands of logicism. However his views evolved – and of course they evolved in many different ways over time – he always aimed at a theory that would put the judger and the proposition, object, and/or fact judged back into the picture in such a way that causal contact could be seen to be made between mind and world, and the philosopher would have *something* to say about the notions of truth, error, and understanding. The persistence with which Russell tried to devise such a view is perhaps one reason why Putnam does not mention him, but only Frege, in MoM.[30]

Frege did enunciate and deploy the Context Principle in his *Grundlagen* as a diagnostic and heuristic device to unmask spurious psychologism about meaning. But this deployment is really just part of an apologia for the primacy and expressive adequacy of his *Begriffsschrift*. Frege holds that the constraints imposed by the Context Principle are and must be utterly general, that is, *purely logical in character*.[31] According to the logicizing picture he develops, for each sense there is just one *Bedeutung*: the senses of sentential occurrences of concept words, of proper names, and of sentences are functions of the senses of their parts that determine the *Bedeutungen* of logically relevant expressions. And he really means *functions* here; this is not intended to be a *vague* notion of determination.[32] Frege appeals *essentially* and *primitively* to this functional model to connect his notion of *thought* with that of *truth*, for he holds that in construing the sense of a name, predicate, or sentence we ought to consider *only* those aspects of an expression that contribute to the purely logical (i.e., purely deductive) role of the relevant sentence.

Frege's post-1890 distinction between *Sinn* and *Bedeutung* was drawn as part of an effort to devise a general way of speaking about that which is preserved when a sentence of ordinary German is translated into *Begriffsschrift*, but it aimed to defend his universalist conception of logic from the encroachments of psychology and empiricism by defending its expressive adequacy as an ideal language for the expression of "pure" thought. It was devised neither as an independent theory of linguistic meaning by means of which to ground logic, nor as an explanation or clarification of the nature of logic.[33]

Frege thus emphatically did *not* take himself to have provided a mere *notation* into which one could transcribe the propositions that mathematicians actually utter, write, and publish in ordinary "mathematical prose", that is, in English or French or German or.... Instead, he took himself to have provided a freestanding "ideal language" or "concept-language" (as we have said, what Quine called a "first grade conceptual scheme") that in some sense *supersedes* ordinary language as a universally applicable science. Moreover, in divising such a scheme he saw himself as providing mathematics with a *foundation* in logic. Ordinary-language (including that of the most expert mathematicians we have or will have in the next hundred years) might be necessary to "lead someone into" the ideal language, but the "elucidations" offered by the logician for this purpose in ordinary language are, so to speak, a ladder that can be thrown away. Frege explicitly argues that ordinary language sentences that we use to explain the ideal notation do not and cannot capture the precise content of the ideal notion.[34]

But this created conceptual tensions that manifested themselves in various ways, some of which we might label Frege's proto-Kuhnian incommensurability problems. These were not problems about conceptual revolutions that would place two theorists, or a layperson and an expert, in different conceptual worlds unable to communicate with one another or refer to the same objects. These were more obscure, more fundamental problems of incommensurability between the standards or criteria we apply to our employment of words in our ordinary uses of language – even at its most currently scientifically sophisticated – and those applied within Frege's idealized picture of a universal, logically articulated theory of reality.[35] On the one hand, Frege insisted that the senses of concept expressions fix definite sharp *Bedeutungen* when they have *Bedeutungen* at all – that concepts with vague boundaries have no *Bedeutungen*, and hence no *genuine* concepts corresponding to them. On the other hand, though he insisted that it is perfectly possible that few *and even perhaps no* speakers of a language, including experts of the current day, may possess a clear or full grasp of the sense of their concept words – by which he meant the kind of ideal grasp of an adequately analyzed sense that would be expressed in its translation into *Begriffsschrift* – he also held that many concepts of our current science have both sense and *Bedeutung*.

The key moral here, relative to Putnam's presentation of externalism in MoM, is that Frege's context principle – and *a fortiori* his discussions of *sense, thought, concept,* and *object* – were, historically speaking, primarily advanced neither to offer a rational reconstruction of the notion of *linguistic meaning*, nor to provide a psychologically realistic theory of cognitive content, nor to provide a general principle or technique for epistemically legitimate postulation of abstract entities. These discussions aimed, rather, at establishing the primacy and universality of (Frege's) logic, expressed in Frege's quantificational (function/argument) analysis of generality.[36] Since for Frege a concept *is* a function, it must yield one and only one output for the inputs on which it is defined: the sharpness of a concept's application – the a priori denial of boundary cases or vagueness – is intrinsic to its concepthood. Since it is defined on all objects, its sphere of application cannot be narrowed down: Frege is offering a univocal analysis of *generality* as a purely logical notion. According to MoM this 'logicization' of our notions of *concept* and *object* is unacceptable.

That this is a primary aim of Putnam's externalism became clearer some years later, when he came to profess, in *Representation and Reality*, that his own version of functionalism had conceded too much to this picture. As he wrote in 1992:

> certain assumptions that were characteristic of positivism remain widespread in analytic philosophy even after the supposed abandonment of positivism. In part this is the case because those assumptions *antedated* positivism; they were, in large measure, implicit in the Fregean revolution. For Frege a "fuzzy" concept was no concept at all; the idea that 'rationality' is not really a proper concept unless it can be reduced to a set of precise rules is simply an application of this picture of what it is to have a real concept. Modern logic was a great and useful discovery; but a certain overestimation of its metaphysical and epistemological significance remains a problem for

contemporary analytical philosophy. In that sense, what I have been trying
to think out . . . is not just what a post-positivist philosophy should look like,
but what a philosophy that refuses to take mathematical logic as its paradigm
of rational thought – a *post-logicist* philosophy – should look like.[37]

Historically speaking, then, it was not only or even primarily the object-
or reality-involving nature of *meaning* and concept-possession that was at
stake in Putnam's articulation of externalism in MoM.[38] Nor was it Putnam's
anti-individualism, central though that is to the essay. If these had been the
only features of Putnam's externalism exploited there, then we might expect
him to have been willing to grant that Frege's notions of *Sinn* and *Bedeutung*
might be taken, *modulo* a few adjustments to the notion of "determination",
to be essentially externalist in nature. Frege did after all conceive of the
sense of a proper name as nothing but the "mode of presentation" of an
object to a speaker.

If one holds – as Frege did not always manage to do – that language,
judgment, and sense are intrinsically public and social, intersubjectively
manifested in our actual uses of words, then it is indeed tempting to construe Frege's conception of sense in externalist terms, as Dummett has
suggested.[39] One might even go on to hold, as David Wiggins has done,
that Putnam's semantic externalism nicely *coheres* with a Fregean-inspired
distinction between sense and reference applied to proper names and to
predicates as their uses are tied to our identificatory and recognitional
capacities: Wiggins specifically suggests identifying the sense of a natural-
kind term with Putnam's idea of a (defeasible) stereotype, since concepts
are, for Frege, as Wiggins argues, extension-*involving*.[40]

Putnam's response is that such an epistemically and practically teth-
ered conception of *sense* shifts Frege's philosophy in a wholly un-Fregean
direction, away from what Putnam thinks it most important to appreciate in Frege's legacy.[41] Being extension-*involving* is not the same as being
extension-*determining*, and Frege's senses are conceived by him to do the
latter: concepts and their "modes of presentation" are for Frege "sharp"
and universally (as well as univocally) applicable, as well as in principle
fathomable (surveyable) by an idealized and formally expressible language
of "pure thought". If one wants to retain Frege's approach to the notion of
concept, one will have to divorce this notion of *sense* altogether from that
of *linguistic meaning*, and thereby surrender, as Frege in the end did, any
hope of a systematic *explanation* of the way in which an intension, in the
sense of a linguistically expressed (or expressible) meaning, "determines"
an extension.

7. PUTNAM ON FREGE, CARNAP, AND QUINE

Carnap thought he had gone beyond Frege in relativizing Frege's picture of *sense*, and even the analytic/synthetic distinction itself, to meaning-
postulates in particular languages, thereby jettisoning Frege's (and, as he
took it, the *Tractatus's*) absolutism with respect to the analysis of thoughts
and concepts. Putnam was always enough of a Carnapian to reject Frege's
ideal of a univocal and universally applicable notion of *object*. Like Carnap,
Putnam saw the need – mathematically and philosophically – for surrendering Frege's idea of a fixed totality of objects over which Fregean "first-order"
quantifiers would univocally range; indeed, though Putnam has so far as I
know never explicitly argued this way, it might be viewed as a kind of corollary to externalism that our notions of *object* and *concept* are both language-
and theory-relative, as well as indefinitely extendible (and malleable) in
the face of future scientific discovery.[42] In contrast to Carnap, however,
Putnam's rejection of Frege in MoM turned on a localized scrutiny of our
ways of talking about word meaning, not a global conventionalism about the
notion of *meaning* itself. By grouping Frege and Carnap together, Putnam
was suggesting that Carnap did not essentially progress beyond Frege on the
most fundamental idealizing assumptions about the expression of thought
in language. Of course Carnap thought he had done so. Nearly everyone in
the analytic tradition thought he or she had. Russell, Carnap, Quine, and
(at least) the later Wittgenstein all defined the core of their philosophies
around a rejection of the Fregean idea that objectivity requires us to regard
various sentences, in the same language or different ones, as reflecting a
determinate content (*Sinn* or *Gedanke*) that can be definitively expressed
in a mathematized, universally applicable theory. They jettisoned Frege's
ideal of an absolute frame of reference for the expression of thought.

Carnap was right, Putnam thinks, to deny that we have – even in ideal,
logical theory – univocal, universally applicable notions of *concept* and *object*
with which to work; this is emphasized, for example, in Putnam's discussions of the bearing of conceptual relativity on realism in *The Many Faces of
Realism*. Carnap's mistake, as Putnam sees it, lay in thinking that this insight
could be defended by tying the conceptual relativity of these notions to the
notions of *meaning, analyticity,* and *truth by convention* as they might be rationally reconstructed in the idealized setting of a formal system. Carnap
retained Frege's rationalistic, logicist ideal, an ideal of understanding and
of the expression of thought in language divorced from particularities of
the local and historically contingent situations of thinkers, even while he
attempted to relativize the application of the notions of *meaning, concept,*

and *object* in an empirically and psychologically responsible scientific way to individual speakers. And it was his failure to make rigorous sense, *by these formalizable standards*, of linguistically relativized notions of *analyticity*, *sense*, and *intension* that left him open to Quine's global attack on the epistemic relevance of these intensional notions (as well as Putnam's less radical empiricist rejection of the analytic/synthetic distinction).[43]

Putnam's MoM rejection of the Context Principle's governing relevance for the notion of *meaning* is thus closely connected to his affinities with, and objections to, Quine on the notion of *meaning*, which is why he discusses Quine's views in two key sections of MoM. Quine – a staunch (at least verbal) advocate of Frege's Context Principle – urged that we retain the Fregean ideal of a universally applicable, logically articulated conceptual scheme or language – retaining thereby univocal notions of *object* and *truth* – while surrendering the effort rigorously to analyze the intensional notions of *concept, intension, proposition, necessity*, and *meaning*, except insofar as these notions find their extensionalized (i.e., naturalized) *Ersätze*. This, Quine felt, would be the best course for devising "an enduring and impersonal formulation of a system of the world" (Quine 1998). Putnam was unwilling to pay the price of Quine's surrender, unwilling to follow him in embracing either an "impersonal", ahuman, cosmic perspective for philosophy or an ideal of language as a unified, total theory of the world without essential "diversity".[44]

In MoM, Putnam was not merely trying to find a middle way between Carnap and Quine without relying on a sharp or generalized distinction between language and the world. He was also recovering a human and agent-centered conception of *meaning*. He did so by jettisoning *both* the Frege-Quine ideal of language as a first-grade conceptual scheme universally applicable to reality on the cosmic scale *and* the conviction (shared by Frege, Carnap, and Quine) that the tools of mathematical logic could be used as an organon to idealize, quite apart from the particular situation of a speaker, that which is central to the expression of cognition or thought in language. Thus, although Putnam concurs with Quine on a localized use of the Skolem-Löwenheim theorem to undercut the idea that a fully regimented theory *could* univocally determine word meaning or essence (Quine's "inscrutability of reference"), he rejects Quine's "ostensive" picture of (first-person) acquiescence in a mother tongue as a "homophonic translation", as a *theoretical* acquiescence for purposes of simplicity of the overall theory. Putnam sees no reason to think that the inscrutability of reference gives us any reason to *deny* as *freestanding* the claim that our words refer to those things (tables, chairs, rabbits) to which we take them, ordinarily, to refer. Thus in rejecting the Quinean ideal of a "first-grade" conceptual scheme (and with it Quine's version of the Context Principle), he rejects Quine's ground for seeing the indeterminacy of translation (at the level of the sentence) as a plausible theoretical hypothesis.[45]

In sum, a key aim of MoM is to show that progress with the notion of *meaning* is to be had only by relieving it of the overly heavy philosophical burdens it had come to carry in connection with the project of analysis – but not simply in connection with the assumption that, ideally, one might set down necessary and sufficient conditions for the application of any and every concept-word (though Putnam does hold that intensions are not something different speakers must share *if* this is the way we construe the notion (cf. Reply to Bilgrami, p. 392). More deeply, Putnam is aiming to alter the kind of picture some philosophers have had of what it is to be and to be master of a language or theory suitable for the expression of knowledge. Putnam's externalism ultimately shows how the notion of *linguistic meaning*, properly construed, may be used to undercut the underlying assumptions about *thought as such* to which post-Fregeans such as Carnap and Quine subscribed, but in such a way that philosophers need not fear falling back either into naïve psychologism or conventionalism in the forms in which these were bequeathed by traditional and logical empiricism.

That this last result had also been an aim of the later Wittgenstein Putnam knew back in 1975. What MoM self-consciously did that was novel, and at the same time perhaps most truly Wittgensteinian, was lucidly to picture and apply this perspective to the contemporary context in a vivid, persuasive way *without* relying on (what was and is frequently taken to be Wittgenstein's) *general*, a priori suspiciousness of theory in philosophy.[46]

Putnam's pragmatic pluralism about truth, his insistence that we have no univocal notion of *object* in the logician's sense that takes account of our notions of *meaning* and *reference*, and his rejection of mathematical logic as a primary model for analyzing the norms governing our concepts all continue to set him against Frege. Yet as Putnam has become more explicit about his externalism's reliance on an underlying appeal to a freestanding, deeper-than-merely-conventional-or-stipulative normativity of many aspects of our practices and our talk about *meaning*, he has come to praise in Frege – much as Wittgenstein did – a thinker who, like Kant, deeply appreciated the ubiquity of the normative (and the normativity of logic), the limitations of empiricism and psychologism, and the centrality to these of our notions of *understanding* and *intelligibility*. Under the sway of his logicism, Frege failed fully to come to grips with these insights. Putnam's suggestion in recent writings is that we ought to adopt what is best in

Frege's anti-psychologism by distinguishing (as Wittgenstein did) between the notions of *sense* and *meaning* in an unFregean, unCarnapian way, so as to cohere with a different kind of pluralism about conceptual normativity than that delivered by Carnap's kind of conventionalism. On Putnam's present version of the sense/meaning distinction, necessities of our present conceptual scheme (including those of logic) evince our present standards of intelligibility and reasonableness, and these notions are, in being constitutive of sense in the here and now, irrevocable in the here and now, though we cannot *say* from a *general* standpoint that they are absolutely, necessarily, or unrevisably true in a descriptively universal way.[47] The important point, relative to Putnam's externalism – and this is a point we can see at work in the background of MoM – is that these standards, though they may count in the allocation of meaning, are neither governing for, nor reducible to, facts about linguistic meaning. This is so *even if* we agree that there are such facts, and *even if* such facts do in certain special cases give us reason to believe in the conceptual relativity of certain truths.[48]

On Putnam's view, the positivists had duped themselves into thinking that they could retain Frege's ideals of rationality and concept-possession while domesticating their metaphysical import through meaning-conventionalism and verificationism. But in so doing they cut themselves off from what Putnam takes to have been one of the deepest insights of Frege's idiosyncratic form of anti-psychologism. For Frege, the norms of logic and mathematics show us something fundamental to our present conceptual scheme, a kind of normativity that, though it is interpersonal, is not to be analyzed in terms of the notions of *necessary* (or *universal, maximally general*) *truth* or *linguistic meaning* – as Frege's own remarks about the need for "elucidations" indirectly suggested. These norms, in being partly constitutive of our ability to make sense of talk about objects, objectivity, and thought, are, in their ubiquity, distinctive norms, governing us differently from the results of any special science – including linguistics, the theory of meaning, psychology, or even ontology. That, for Putnam, is an anti-empiricist insight worth retaining from Frege and the early Wittgenstein. And it is among many lessons that Putnam's 1975 essay teaches us.

8. PUTNAM AND DUMMETT ON FREGE: A CONTRAST

My aim has not been to take sides in the vexed question of how "best" to read Frege. Nor is it my aim to propose an interpretation of Putnam's relation to Dummett, which is a complicated story of its own. It is, however, worth emphasizing that while Putnam has always seen much to admire and agree with in Dummett's philosophy, he has also always differed with him about the form, scope, and character that a theory of meaning ought, ideally, to have (cf. *Collected Papers Vol. 3*, pp. xviff.). And this difference is reflected in how Putnam reads Frege. It also reflects the relatively central influence of Carnap on Putnam, as opposed to Dummett. Perhaps the briefest way of putting this is to say that Putnam differentiates far more sharply than Dummett ever has between the notions of *linguistic meaning* and *understanding*. To appreciate the force of this difference in historical terms, it is illuminating to contrast Putnam's inheritance of Frege with Dummett's.

In his *Origins of Analytical Philosophy* (1993) Dummett sees the origins of analytic philosophy arising with a distinctive treatment of a particular subject matter, what he calls "the philosophy of thought", a branch of philosophy concerned with such questions as What is a thought? What is it to have a thought? What is it for a thought to be about an object? and so on. That subject was pursued, he claims, both by Husserl and by Frege. What distinguished Frege from Husserl is on Dummett's view what distinguished analytic philosophy from all other traditions, and that is a commitment to a kind of fundamental doctrinal "axiom", viz., that a philosophical account of thought can be attained through and only through a philosophical account of language. Frege took the first step, according to Dummett, in sharply separating the philosophy of thought from psychology: in Dummett's vivid phrase, Frege accomplished the decisive step of "extruding thoughts from the mind". That opened up as a generally available subject matter a study of the laws of thought, which for Dummett includes, not merely deductive logic, but a broad theory of meaning, a theory of what a speaker knows when that speaker knows a language.

Dummett does not deny the existence of strongly logicist elements in Frege's philosophy, that it was part and parcel of Frege's view that the contentfulness of language is constituted most fundamentally through our grasp of basic logical laws, laws that express truths in being universally applicable. But he does not take to be fundamental to Frege – as does Putnam – the role of logic in shaping his views of thought, at least after 1890 or so. Once Frege's notion of *Sinn* was in place, Dummett thinks, Frege was to his credit involved in general theory of meaning, and not in a kind of analysis that could be exhaustively carried through in pure logic. Thus, for example, Dummett takes it to be a great advantage of Frege's view that it does not tie the notion of *sense* to that of analyticity, and hence to notions like *logical equivalence*, as did Wittgenstein in the *Tractatus*: we are not, after all, even as mature speakers of a language, logically omniscient, even if we command the meanings of words with which we deductively reason.[49] Mindful of Quine's attack on the analytic/synthetic distinction, Dummett considered Frege to have been right in divorcing the notion of *Sinn* from any conception of the role of synonymy in meaning analysis.

Yet as Dummett construed the development of early analytic philosophy the linguistic turn needed to be made. And it was only fully accomplished *after* Frege. For the price of Frege's anti-psychologism was his postulation of a "third realm", neither mental nor physical, in which thoughts (in a nonpsychological sense) exist independently of our minds. Frege appreciated that the individuation of such *Sinne* was a notoriously difficult matter to untangle, and according to Dummett he left us suggestions and conceptual distinctions (e.g., the Context Principle, the distinctions between sense, coloring, force, reference, and so on) which allow us to state certain principles according to which thoughts may be differentiated and identified. Frege's remarks about a "third realm" had the great virtue, Dummett argues, of making the linguistic turn – the turn to a theory of meaning – virtually inevitable as a reaction. For, as Dummett sees matters, it was the early Wittgenstein – precisely through his reaction to Frege's realism about thought – who completed that turn. The rest is the history of later analytic philosophy.

Now if Dummett's story about the origins of early analytic philosophy were fully satisfactory, then not only would it be unclear how Russell and Moore fit in to the story;[50] it would also turn out that the underlying motivation for what Dummett takes to have been the heart of analytic philosophy, the linguistic turn, would lie in a kind of epistemic verificationism. The trouble Dummett has with Fregean "realism" about thoughts is that they are not publicly sharable; their criteria of individuation are unclear. By focusing on the structure of a theory of meaning for natural language, construed as an essentially social and public phenomenon – the second element of externalism, as I have described it – Dummett believes that we can reconstruct in an epistemically responsible yet nonconventionalist fashion the notion of *meaning*. Yet there is a price: on Dummett's view a *general* metaphysical anti-realism is then required of us, precisely because our concept of what it is to speak a language is to be understood in terms of our grasp of those conditions under which sentences are legitimately assertible as true, and these he understands to be given, ideally, in terms of principles and rules (e.g., the kind of structures articulated in proof theory).[51] Dummett's conception of the expression of thought in language remains, therefore, ultimately quite Fregean in flavor, even if he rejects what he takes to be Frege's ontological excesses: it belongs to the tradition of supposing that we have a handle on the notion of *thought as such* by appealing to the kinds of rules and principles that a theory of meaning can deliver.

Let us contrast Putnam's view of Frege's part in early analytic philosophy as we have so far characterized it. Frege was not, as Putnam reads him, engaged in offering a rational reconstruction of the notion of *linguistic meaning*. Nor was he an unvarnished Realist. Instead, he was involved primarily in imposing upon the traditional logical vocabulary of *concept, intension,* and *extension* a mathematical paradigm rooted in his interpretation of his *Begriffsschrift*. For Frege the *Begriffsschrift* was not just a formalism awaiting interpretation. It was instead *the language* – a freestanding, universally applicable framework for definitively articulating thought as such. The *Begriffsschrift* achieved this status, in Frege's eyes, through its being a logically perspicuous language in which the laws of truth – including those of the most general possible science, logic itself – could be explicitly set forth. As a language, at least ideally, the *Begriffsschrift* would supersede the vagaries of ordinary language, and potentially even the limitations of current scientific concepts as we grasp them, precisely by providing the ultimate expressive means and context within which the contents of knowledge – that is, through their theoretical justification and logical regimentation and articulation – would be expressed.

From this point of view – which, to repeat, I intend here to contrast with Dummett's – Frege (along with Moore and Russell) helped usher in a new and problematic ideal of expression, an ideal of the canonical, maximally explicit or definitive expression of thought (and meaning) in language. This kind of expression would, ideally, allow us to individuate concepts, thoughts, and meanings quite apart from any and every feature of the speaker's spatio-temporal situation, and for all contexts, *just by being explicit and clear enough.* This expressive ideal survived the positivists' turn toward language, verificationism, and anti-metaphysics because it was not fundamentally an idea whose trouble lay in its metaphysical or ontological excesses, but rather in the nature of the demands it placed on acceptable idealizations of human expression. These lay in the background, not only of Moore's strange-sounding efforts to explicate, by means of wholly impersonal true assertions, the notions of *judgment, concept,* and *certainty,* but also of Frege's and Russell's powerful formalizations of certain fundamental (and quite traditional) logical and mathematical notions. The demands led the earliest analytic philosophers to fear the psychologizing elements of traditional empiricism far more than the unbridled excesses of Platonism, and to resist, at least for a time, offering anything but inchoate remarks about *linguistic meaning, understanding, error,* and *truth.*

On this telling, the development of analytic philosophy has not been centrally defined and driven forward either by any "axiom" about the manifestability of thought's expression in language or by an epistemologically motivated preference for verificationism and anti-metaphysics. It has instead been primarily engaged in a quarrel over the coherence, scope, and status of an underlying ideal for the expression of thought in language – inherited from Frege, Moore, and Russell – that seemed inevitable if the pitfalls of historicism, psychologism, and idealism were to be avoided. Putnam's contributions, including especially his semantic externalism, have centrally revolved around taking the complexity of our powers of expression seriously as a basis for avoiding these pitfalls without miscasting or oversimplifying the misconceptions rooted in the original ideal.

Notes

This essay was written with generous sabbatical support from The American Philosophical Society. I should like to thank Ruth Anna Putnam – with whom I first discussed "The Meaning of 'Meaning'" some twenty-one years ago – for her teaching and encouragement, as well as Robert Briscoe, Thomas Ricketts, Gary Ebbs, Sanford Shieh, and Charles Travis for writings and conversations about Putnam and Frege that have stimulated and instructed me for many years. Thanks are due to Yemima Ben-Menahem for posing the questions with which this essay begins. A version was read to the Boston Colloquium for the Philosophy of Science, and I profited from my audience's comments. And last but certainly not least, I am grateful for being able to call Hilary Putnam my longstanding, ever generous teacher and friend.

1. See "Is Semantics Possible?", delivered in 1967 as a lecture, published in 1970, reprinted in Putnam's *Philosophical Papers Vol. 2*.
2. Cf. especially "Rethinking Mathematical Necessity" (a lecture of 1990) in *Words and Life*, ed. J. Conant (Cambridge, MA: Harvard University Press, 1994), pp. 245–265, and part one, lecture three of *The Threefold Cord* (1999, delivered 1994), "The Face of Cognition".
3. For the last statement, compare *Representation and Reality*, p. xiii; "Introduction to *The Twin Earth Chronicles*", p. xix.
4. Putnam writes (MoM, p. 269):
   Thus the normal form description for "water" might be, in part:

SYNTACTIC MARKERS	SEMANTIC MARKERS	STEREOTYPE	EXTENSION
mass noun, concrete;	*natural kind; liquid*	*colorless; transparent; tasteless; thirst-quenching; etc.*	H_2O *(give or take impurities)*

5. This has been emphasized by Ebbs in his readings of Putnam (cf. Ebbs 1992 and 1997). The ubiquity of the normative, as a theme, was foreshadowed in many works of Putnam, including MoM, but an especially important series of texts to consider in this vein are: "It Ain't Necessarily So" (1962), republished in *Philosophical Papers Vol. 1: Reason, Truth and History*; parts 2 and 3 of *Realism with a Human Face* (essay written between 1976 and 1999); and *Renewing Philosophy*, chap. 5.

6. Putnam, "Reply to Ebbs", in Hill, ed. (1992), p. 349.

7. Of course, the tone in which Putnam described "Twin Earth" in MoM did not highlight this. What he says (p. 230) is that the notion of a *possible world* may be taken as a 'primitive one', as one (and here he cites Kripke's logical work on the modalities) that "makes sense and is scientifically important even if it needs to be made more precise". This reflects not only the fact that he had not yet fully broken with the image of philosophical theories as scientific in explanatory form and subject matter (as he began to do in the 1976 "Realism and Reason" and "Reference and Understanding"), but also part of his ecumenical dialectical strategy: in general, Putnam is *scharfsinnig* enough as a logician *never* to bring in *more* than he needs to in an argumentative context, a feature of his thought that readers must constantly bear in mind. Besides, he wished to ward off the then-all-too prevalent Wittgensteinian tone of a *general, a priori* hostility to theory. What, however, he later wrote about Wittgensteinian 'pictures' and Wittgenstein's own investigations of our notions of *necessity* and *meaning* is perfectly consistent with the arguments offered in MoM, and one can even find similar-sounding remarks in essays of the early 1960s (e.g., "Review of *The Concept of a Person*" [1965], *Philosophical Papers Vol. 2*), as Putnam points out in his "Reply to Ebbs" (1992).

8. MoM, pp. 216ff.; compare Putnam's introduction to Sessin and Goldberg, eds., 1996, pp. xvff.

9. MoM, pp. 229ff.; the idea of an "agent-centered" view comes to the fore in *The Many Faces of Realism*.

10. In the introduction to his *Philosophical Papers Vol. 2*, p. xiii, Putnam admits that he was originally led to functionalism by a desire to *defend* materialism, but by 1975 he has come to see functionalism as supporting a refutation of reductionism. Compare, for a brief discussion of Putnam's post-functionalist, externalist arguments against reductionism about mental states, his *Threefold Cord*, and his introduction to Sessin and Goldberg 1996.

11. See, for example, Putnam's "On the Nature of Mental States" (1967). An account of the evolution of Putnam's functionalist phase, 1960–1975, and the reasons lying behind its evolution and dissolution, may be found in the article "Putnam, Hilary", in Guttenplan, ed., 1994, pp. 507–513. Relevant functionalist essays may be found in *Philosophical Papers Vol. 2*. Functionalism's rejection is explored in several essays in *Words and Life*.

12. Cf. Putnam's "Reply to Bilgrami", in Hill, ed., 1992, p. 359.

13. On the topic of how to read Carnap's methodological solipsism in the *Aufbau*, see the debate between Putnam and Ricketts in Hill, ed., 1992, and compare *The Collapse of the Fact/Value Dichotomy*, pp. 23–24, n. 38, and Putnam 1998.

14. MoM, p. 221: "Only if we assume that psychological states in the narrow sense have a significant degree of causal closure . . . is there any point in making the assumption of methodological solipsism. But three centuries of failure of mentalistic psychology is tremendous evidence against this procedure."

15. See the papers in Sessin and Goldberg, chap. 7–17, Putnam's introduction to this volume, and his "Reply to McDowell", in Hill 1992.

16. See, e.g., "Realism and Reason", *Meaning and the Moral Sciences*, Part 4; *Reason, Truth and History*, chap. 2. Putnam continues to explore model-theoretical considerations to this day, always to attack the idea that we can coherently conceive of truth and/or reality as if they are or could be expressed in a global language or theory, fixed once and for all for all contexts. Compare his *Many Faces of Realism* (the 1985 Carus Lectures), his "Model Theory and the Factuality of Semantics" (from 1989, reprinted in his *Words and Life*, chap. 18), and his recent discussions of nonstandard models of arithmetic and Wittgenstein's remarks on the Gödel incompleteness theorems (Floyd and Putnam, 2000).

17. This does not mean, of course, that Putnam insists that there is nothing whatsoever in cognitive science; his arguments are limitative, constituting a kind of philosophical critique of the general, motivating pictures certain theorists have had. On this, see "Computational Psychology and Interpretation Theory" (first published 1983), "Model Theory and the Factuality of Semantics", "Reflexive Reflexions" (from 1985, reprinted in *Realism with a Human Face*), and his 1987b.

18. Cf. "Reply to Bilgrami", in Hill, ed. 1992, Putnam's introduction to Sessin and Goldberg, eds., 1996; and *Reason, Truth and History*.

19. This argument is given by Kant in his *Metaphysical Foundations of Natural Science*, 1786, pp. 469–472.

20. See, for an especially important essay, "Why Reason Can't Be Naturalized", chap. 13, of *Philosophical Papers Vol. 3*.

21. See "Rethinking Mathematical Necessity" and *The Threefold Cord*; in some ways "It Ain't Necessarily So" (1962; reprinted in *Philosophical Papers Vol. 1*) already broached this kind of view.

22. Putnam's rejection of truth-conditional semantics may be seen in his "Reference and Understanding" (delivered 1977), part 3 of *Meaning and the Moral Sciences*.

23. There is a growing and opinionated literature on Russell's and Wittgenstein's respective attitudes toward Frege's doctrine of thoughts as senses, and indeed, Russell's and Wittgenstein's attitudes toward each other. The primary sources crucially include Russell (1903); Wittgenstein (1921, 1979, 1989); and Frege's own writings – cf. especially the correspondence with Russell (Frege 1980, pp. 149ff.) and with Wittgenstein (Frege 1989), as well as Wittgenstein's correspondence with Russell (cf. Wittgenstein 1995, Russell 1913). A useful survey of the issues may be gleaned from sampling Anscombe (1971); Dummett (1981a, 1991, esp. pp. 237–248); Hylton (1990, 1995, 1997); Ricketts (1996b, 2001); the 2002 papers by Ricketts, Diamond, and Proops (in Reck 2002); and those by Goldfarb and Ricketts in Floyd and Shieh, eds. (2001). The early Wittgenstein's attitude toward Frege on thoughts, as it connects to the fact/value dichotomy and Wittgenstein's early attitude toward solipsism are discussed in Floyd (1998), with an interesting reply by Putnam (1998).

24. Frege (1989), cf. letter of 3 April 1920. We have only Frege's side of the correspondence, but Geach (1977, pp. vii–viii) substantiates by anecdote what is implied about Wittgenstein's objections by Frege's responses to Wittgenstein's letter. The phrase "an inferior work" is thus due to Geach, reporting a later conversation with Wittgenstein about the exchange between him and Frege.

25. Frege responded to Wittgenstein in 1920 by saying that it was not part of his aim to argue against Idealism at all. On the vexed question of whether Frege's doctrine of thoughts as senses can or cannot constitute a kind of foundation for his views of knowledge, see Burge (1991, 1992, 1998); Diamond (1991), chaps. 2–5; Ricketts (1985, 1986a, 1986b, 1996a); and Weiner (1986, 1997a, 1997b).

26. Whether or not Putnam's charges are fair to Carnap is another disputed question. See note 13 above.

27. *Philosophical Papers Vol. 2*, p. ix.

28. The most important Frege scholars for Putnam in this respect include Tyler Burge and especially Cora Diamond, Burton Dreben, Warren Goldfarb, Thomas Ricketts, and Joan Weiner; compare his "Reply to Ebbs", in Hill, ed., 1992.

29. One index of this is that each found himself explicitly approving of Dedekind's theorem 66 in his 1888, an argument that George Boolos (Putnam's student, to whom *The Threefold Cord* is dedicated) calls "one of the strangest pieces of argumentation in the history of logic" (1988, chap. 13). Dedekind takes the phrase "the thought of" to refer to a 1–1 function, and purports to establish what is now, after Frege, seen to require a special axiom: the existence of infinite sets. See Frege's "Logic" (1897), in his 1979, esp. p. 136n (where Frege explicitly says that Dedekind "uses the word ['thought'] as I do"), and Russell (1903), pp. 357–358. Russell's eventual dissatisfaction with Dedekind's "Platonic" assumptions were expressed much later, in his 1919, pp. 139ff. So far as I know, Putnam has never commented on this argument in print; for a discussion of its assumptions and history, see Webb (1980), who remarks that "twentieth-century logic, excepting intuitionism, has reacted to the inherent difficulties of Dedekind's argument by gradually replacing considerations of thought by those of language and symbolism" (p. 61). The MoM, historically speaking, concerns itself with how the notion of *meaning* figured in that replacement.

30. Of course Russell never did manage to make room for the force of what I have called the second and third elements of Putnam's externalism: the essentially social nature of much concept-possession and the variegated, contextually sensitive ways in which we establish criteria for understanding. Perhaps this is because Russell remained forever tempted by the appeal to incorrigibly self-evident (and private) knowledge of perceptions, facts, and universals, to the fact/value dichotomy, and to an anti-Jamesian, anti-pluralistic conception of truth and knowledge. There is a large literature on the relation of Putnam's externalism to Russellian theories of "direct reference" that we cannot survey here. It should be noted, however, that historically speaking Russell did not come to think of language and the notion of *meaning* in particular as of primary interest – and certainly not as causally construed – until 1918, when, still under

the influence of the young Wittgenstein, he read James and the behaviorist Watson in prison (on this see Dreben 1996, and compare Hylton 1990 and Ricketts 2001 on details of Russell's development).

31. In Aristotelian fashion, Frege opens the *Grundlagen* with an account of his predecessors' errors, pressing upon them a question up to that point in time treated, Frege feels, with far too little seriousness, viz., "What is the number one?" When mathematicians and traditional philosophers bothered to ask this question, Frege says, they largely tended to make the mistake of focusing on the *word*, without sufficiently attending to its logical role within sentences as a whole. This led them into two kinds of temptation. Some cast about for an entity – usually a mental idea or representation – corresponding to the word "one". But this amounted, Frege charges, to selecting a something, "anything we please", to *call* the number one. Others, noting the generality of the number words' applications, became formalists, insisting that there *are* no entities to which the number words correspond, but that instead the objectivity of arithmetic inheres in the ways in which we operate with uninterpreted algebraic letters in mathematics, allowing the letters arbitrary reinterpretation according to our extramathematical needs. This counterreaction to objectionable mentalism suffers, Frege points out, from the same word-myopia as that which it tries to overcome: the formalist focuses on the variable in splendid isolation, quite apart from an understanding of how, in instantiation, generality and particularity are to be understood as relating to one another logically.

32. Whether, of course, it *is* vague is another question; one that moved Wittgenstein to his purely truth-functional *(operational)* conception of *sense* in the *Tractatus*. Compare Dummett's discussion of Frege in his 1981a and 1981b.

33. For three differing readings of Frege along these lines, see references to Burge, Ricketts, and Weiner in the References.

34. For example, for the case of what Frege takes to be his primitive or undefinable notions (e.g., *function, concept*) see Frege's "On Concept and Object" (1892), pp. 204ff. (in Frege 1984, pp. 193–194); "On the Foundations of Geometry" (1906), pp. 301ff. (in Frege 1984, pp. 300–302); and "Logic in Mathematics" (1914, unpublished), in Frege 1979, pp. 207, 214, 235; compare Frege (1893) appendix 2, n. 1 (p. 240). For *truth* as undefinable, see "Der Gedanke" (1918), pp. 59ff. (in Frege 1984, pp. 351ff.).

35. Burge (1991) gives a very useful survey of passages that bring out this tension.

36. Cf. Ricketts 1986b.

37. "Reply to Miller", pp. 369–370.

38. Note Putnam's emphasis, in his (2001) and in Part II of *Words and Life* that Reichenbach was, for example, *both* a "realist" *and* a "verificationist": one moral of Reichenbach is that "realism" about entities is not enough to overcome the traditional positivist dogmas about *meaning*.

39. For an early paper, see Dummett's "The Social Character of Meaning" (from 1974), reprinted as chapter 23 of his 1978.

40. Wiggins 1994, p. 210. Compare his 2002.

41. Cf. his "Reply to Wiggins", in Clark and Hale, eds., 1994.

42. This idea of open-endedness may also be derived both from Putnam's conceptual relativity arguments and from the model-theoretic considerations that he has often invoked; compare his "Reply to Dreben", in Hill, ed., 1992.

43. On Putnam as Girondiste and Quine as Jacobin radical, see Dreben 1992 in Hill, ed. Compare Wiggins's remarks on Quine with his 1994.

44. Cf. Part VII, *Words and Life*, on "the diversity of the sciences".

45. Compare *Philosophical Papers Vol. 3*, chap. 13, and "Reply to Dreben", in Hill, ed., 1992: these all flesh out moves against Quine that are made in MoM, pp. 257ff.

46. It is doubtful that Putnam ever believed that this idea was completely true to Wittgenstein, but he certainly knew that there were among his readers some who would subscribe to it.

47. There is a connection here with Putnam's fascination with the possibility of alternative logics – say, for quantum theory – and the relation of such possibilities to the notion of *meaning*. Putnam's tolerance of revision under the pressure of physics – or even just an interest in human expressive complexity (as in the case of set theory, which may or may not ever achieve empirical applications), forms a distinctive way of avoiding Frege's sharp dilemma (posed most polemically in his *Grundgesetze*) between a formalist conception of logic as an empty structure awaiting arbitrary interpretation and a conception of logic as contentful through universal applicability conceived as descriptive adequacy. In "Rethinking Mathematical Necessity" (p. 262, n. 12), Putnam rejects paraconsistent logics on the ground that such logic is, at least at present, a *mere* formal system. Presumably Putnam means by this that it does not shape in a fundamental way (more than classical logic does) our ways of thinking about intelligibility and sense (in *Putnam*'s sense of these notions). Similar considerations allow Putnam to avoid caving in wholly to Quine's empiricistic "indispensability" arguments about the ultimate rationale for postulating abstract entities such as sets, as this essay also makes clear.

48. See especially "Rethinking Mathematical Necessity", chapter 12 of *Words and Life*.

49. Wittgenstein's aim, however, was to depsychologize, i.e., extensionalize and logicize, Frege's notion. At least arguably, the *Tractatus*'s conception of "belonging to language" is not to be understood, pace the Vienna Positivists, as something to be analyzed via a notion of *linguistic meaning*, especially one construed in terms of epistemic procedures conceived as rules of verification.

50. This is emphasized by Peter Hylton in his review of Dummett (Hylton 1995).

51. For Putnam's explicit criticisms of Dummett's vision on this score, see *The Threefold Cord: Mind, Body and World* (New York: Columbia University Press, 1999), especially pp. 43ff., which draw on Diamond (1991, chap. 9).

References

Anscombe, G. E. M. (1971). *An Introduction to Wittgenstein's Tractatus*, 2nd ed. (1st ed. 1959). Philadelphia, PA: University of Pennsylvania Press.

Barrett, R., and Gibson, R., eds. (1990). *Perspectives on Quine.* Oxford: Basil Blackwell.

Bell, D., and Cooper, N., eds. (1991). *The Analytic Tradition: Meaning, Thought and Knowledge.* Oxford: Basil Blackwell.

Boolos, G. (1998). *Logic, Logic and Logic.* Cambridge, MA: Harvard University Press.

Burge, T. (1991). "Frege on Sense and Linguistic Meaning", in Bell and Cooper, eds.

(1992). "Frege on Knowing the Third Realm". *Mind* 101, 404:633–650; reprinted in Tait, ed.

(1998). "Frege on Knowing the Foundation". *Mind* 107, 426:305–347.

Clark, P., and Hale, R. H., eds. (1994). *Reading Putnam.* Oxford: Blackwells.

Dedekind, J. W. R. (1888). *Was Sind und Was Soll die Zahlen?* English translation in Ewald, ed., 1996.

Diamond, C. (1991). *The Realistic Spirit: Wittgenstein, Philosophy and the Mind.* Cambridge, MA: MIT Press.

(2002). "Truth before Tarski: After Sluga, after Ricketts, after Geach, after Goldfarb, Hylton, Floyd, and Van Heijenoort," in Reck, ed., 2002, pp. 252–283.

Dreben, B. (1992). "Putnam, Quine – and the Facts", in Hill, ed., pp. 293–316.

(1996). "Quine and Wittgenstein: The Odd Couple", in *Wittgenstein and Quine*, ed. R. Arrington and H. Glock. London and New York: Routledge, 1996, pp. 39–61.

Dummett, M. (1978). *Truth and Other Enigmas.* Cambridge, MA: Harvard University Press.

(1981a). *Frege: Philosophy of Language*, 2nd ed. Cambridge, MA: Harvard University Press.

(1981b). *The Interpretation of Frege's Philosophy.* Cambridge, MA: Harvard University Press.

(1991). *Frege and Other Philosophers.* Oxford: Clarendon Press.

(1993). *Origins of Analytical Philosophy.* Cambridge, MA: Harvard University Press.

Ebbs, G. (1992). "Realism and Rational Inquiry", in Hill, ed., pp. 1–34.

(1997). *Rule-Following and Realism.* Cambridge, MA: Harvard University Press.

Ewald, W., ed. (1996). *From Kant to Hilbert : A Source Book in the Foundations of Mathematics.* New York: Oxford University Press.

Floyd, J. (1998). "The Uncaptive Eye: Solipsism in Wittgenstein's *Tractatus*", in L. S. Rouner, ed., pp. 79–108.

Floyd, J., and Putnam, H. (2000). "A Note on Wittgenstein's 'Notorious Paragraph' about the Gödel Theorem". *Journal of Philosophy* 45, 11:624–632.

Floyd, J., and Shieh, S., eds. (2001). *Future Pasts: Perspectives on the Analytic Tradition in Twentieth Century Philosophy.* New York: Oxford University Press.

Frege, G. (1893). *Grundgesetze der Arithmetik, Bd I.* Jena: H. Pole; reprinted with Bd. II by Georg Olms Verlagsbuchandlung, Hildesheim, 1966. Partially translated into English (through §52) by M. Furth, as *The Basic Laws of Arithmetic.* Berkeley: University of California Press, 1964.

(1979). *Posthumous Writings.* ed. H. Hermes et al., trans. P. Long and R. White. Oxford: Basil Blackwell.

(1980). *Philosophical and Mathematical Correspondence.* Ed. G. Gabriel et al. Chicago: University of Chicago Press.

(1984). *Collected Papers on Mathematics, Logic, and Philosophy.* Ed. B. McGuinness, trans., M. Black et al. New York: Blackwell.

(1989). "Briefe an Ludwig Wittgenstein aus den Jahren 1914–1920". Ed. A. Janik, in McGuinness and Haller. English translation by J. Floyd and B. Dreben (forthcoming) in J. Hintikka and E. De Pelligrin, eds., *Festschrift in Honor of Professor Georg Henrik von Wright.*

Geach, P. T., ed. (1977). Frege, *Logical Investigations,* trans. P. T. Geach and R. H. Stoothoff. New Haven, CT: Yale University Press.

Goldfarb, W. (2001). "Frege's Conception of Logic", in J. Floyd and S. Shieh, eds., pp. 25–42.

Guttenplan, S., ed. (1994). *The Oxford Companion to the Philosophy of Mind.* New York: Oxford University Press.

Hill, C., ed. (1992). *The Philosophy of Hilary Putnam, Philosophical Topics,* vol. 20, no. 1. Fayetteville: University of Arkansas Press.

Hylton, P. (1990). *Russell, Idealism, and the Emergence of Analytic Philosophy.* New York: Oxford University Press.

(1995). "Review of M. Dummett, *Origins of Analytical Philosophy.*" *Journal of Philosophy* 92:556–563.

(1997). "Functions, Operations and Sense in Wittgenstein's *Tractatus*", in Tait, ed., 1997, pp. 91–106.

Johnson, D. M., and Erneling, C. E., eds. (1987). *The Future of the Cognitive Revolution.* New York: Oxford University Press.

Kant, I. (1786). *Metaphysische Anfangsgründe der Naturwissenschaft,* vol. IV: *Kants Gesammelte Schriften,* ed. Royal German Academy of Sciences. Berlin: Walter deGruyter & Co., 1900–. English translation: *Metaphysical Foundations of Natural Science,* trans. J. W. Ellington. Indianapolis, IN: Bobbs-Merrill, 1970.

Proops, I. (1997). "The Early Wittgenstein on Logical Assertion". *Philosophical Topics* 25, no. 2 (fall 1997): 121–144.

(2002). "The *Tractatus* on Inference and Entailment", in Reck, ed., pp. 283–307.

Putnam, H. (1975). *Mind, Language and Reality: Philosophical Papers Vol. 2.* Cambridge: Cambridge University Press.

(1976). *Mathematics, Matter and Method: Philosophical Papers Vol. 1,* 2nd ed. (1st. ed. 1975). Cambridge: Cambridge University Press.

(1978). *Meaning and the Moral Sciences.* Boston: Routledge and Kegan Paul.

(1981). *Reason, Truth and History.* Cambridge: Cambridge University Press.

(1983). *Realism and Reason: Philosophical Papers Vol. 3.* Cambridge: Cambridge University Press.

(1987a). *The Many Faces of Realism.* La Salle, IL: Open Court Publishing.

(1987b). "Functionalism: Cognitive Science or Science Fiction?" in Johnson and Erneling, eds., pp. 32–44.

(1988). *Representation and Reality*. Cambridge, MA: MIT Press.

(1990). *Realism with a Human Face*. Ed. J. Conant. Cambridge, MA: Harvard University Press.

(1992). *Renewing Philosophy*. Cambridge, MA: Harvard University Press.

(1994). *Words and Life*. Ed. J. Conant. Cambridge, MA: Harvard University Press.

(1998). "Reply to Juliet Floyd's 'The Uncaptive Eye: Solipsism in Wittgenstein's *Tractatus*'", in L. S. Rouner, ed., pp. 109–114.

(1999). *The Threefold Cord: Mind, Body, and World*. New York: Columbia University Press.

(2001). "Hans Reichenbach: Realist and Verificationist", in Floyd and Shieh, eds., pp. 277–290.

(2002). *The Collapse of the Fact/Value Dichotomy and Other Essays*. Cambridge, MA: Harvard University Press.

Quine, W. V. (1998). "Reply to Hintikka", in L. Hahn and P. Schilpp, eds., *The Philosophy of W. V. Quine*, LaSalle, IL: Open Court Publishing, pp. 227–228.

Reck, E. H., ed. (2002). *From Frege to Wittgenstein: Perspectives on Early Analytic Philosophy*. New York: Oxford University Press.

Ricketts, T. (1985). "Frege, the *Tractatus*, and the Logocentric Predicament". *Noûs* 19:3–14.

(1986a). "Objectivity and Objecthood: Frege's Metaphysics of Judgment", in L. Haaparanta and J. Hintikka, eds., *Frege Synthesized*. Dordrecht: D. Reidel, pp. 65–96.

(1986b). "Generality, Meaning, and Sense in Frege". *Pacific Philosophical Quarterly* 67:172–195.

(1996a). "Logic and Truth in Frege". *The Aristotelian Society Supplementary Vol. 70*, pp. 121–140.

(1996b). "Pictures, Logic, and the Limits of Sense in Wittgenstein's *Tractatus*", in H. Sluga and D. Stern, eds., 1996, pp. 55–99.

(2001). "Truth and Propositional Unity in Early Russell", in Floyd and Shieh, eds., pp. 101–122.

(2002). "Wittgenstein against Frege and Russell", in Reck, ed., pp. 227–252.

Rouner, L. (1998). *Loneliness*. Boston Studies in the Philosophy of Religion. Notre Dame, IN: University of Notre Dame Press.

Russell, B. (1903). *Principles of Mathematics*. Cambridge: Cambridge University Press.

(1913). *Theory of Knowledge: The 1913 Manuscript*. Ed. E. R. Eames. Published 1984, 1992. New York: Routledge.

(1919). *Introduction to Mathematical Philosophy*. New York: Simon and Schuster.

Sessin, A., and Goldberg, S., eds. (1996). *The Twin Earth Chronicles: Twenty Years of Hilary Putnam's "The Meaning of 'Meaning'"*. Armonk, NY: M. E. Sharpe.

Sluga, H., and Stern, D. G., eds. (1996). *The Cambridge Companion to Wittgenstein*. Cambridge: Cambridge University Press.

Tait, W. W., ed. (1997). *Early Analytic Philosophy*. La Salle, IL: Open Court Publishers.

Webb, J. (1980). *Mechanism, Mentalism, and Metamathematics: An Essay on Finitism.* Dordrecht: D. Reidel.

Weiner, J. (1986). *Frege in Perspective.* Ithaca, NY: Cornell University Press.

(1997a). "Frege and the Linguistic Turn". *Philosophical Topics.* 25, 2:265–287.

(1997b). "Has Frege a Philosophy of Language?" in Tait, ed., 1997.

Wiggins, D. (1994). "Putnam's Doctrine of Natural Kind Words and Frege's Doctrines of Sense, Reference, and Extension: Can They Cohere?" in Clark and Hale, eds., pp. 201–215.

(2001). *Sameness and Substance Renewed.* Cambridge: Cambridge University Press.

Wittgenstein, L. (1921). "Logische-Philosophische Abhandlung", final chapter in, Ostwald's *Annalen der Naturphilosophie.* English translation: *Tractatus Logico-Philosophicus* by C. K. Ogden. New York: Routledge and Kegan Paul, 1922. A critical edition in German containing the *Prototractatus* is Wittgenstein 1989.

(1979). *Notebooks 1914–1916.* Ed. G. H. von Wright and G. E. M. Anscombe, trans. G. E. M. Anscombe. Oxford: Blackwell.

(1989). *Logische-philosophische Abhandlung-Tractatus Logico-Philosophicus, Kritische Edition.* Ed. F. McGuinness and J. Schulte. Frankfurt: Suhrkamp Verlag.

(1995). *Cambridge Letters.* Ed. B. McGuinnes and G. H. von Right. Oxford: Blackwell.

3 The Face of Perception

CHARLES TRAVIS

Near the end of his Dewey lectures, Hilary Putnam remarked:

> Part of what I have been trying to show in these lectures is that what we recognize as the face of meaning is, in a number of fundamentally important cases, also the face of our natural cognitive relations to the world – the face of perceiving, of imagining, of expecting, of remembering, and so on – even though it is also the case that as language extends those natural cognitive relations to the world, it also transforms them.[1]

The aim of this essay is to say what it is for perceiving to have a face, and how it matters that it does. At its core, I will show, is a bit of vintage Putnam – an idea that has run consistently through the centre of all his philosophy, from at least 1960 to the present. It is one of the most important ideas in twentieth-century philosophy.

One main theme in the Dewey lectures is endorsement of what might be called *naïve realism*. That is, roughly, just the view that perception is awareness of one's surroundings; so that the objects of perception are, at least typically, what does in fact surround us – notably, objects, such as pigs and Marmite, and facts of things being ways they are, such as that pig's staring at one through the railings of its sty. One main theme of this essay will be that the idea of a face of perception is essential if naïve realism, so conceived, is to be tenable. In fact, perception must have a face, in the way Putnam intends, if there is to be such a thing as perception at all.

Putnam's idea about faces can be rendered as an idea about the special nature of a conceptual capacity, or of those that we enjoy. A second theme of this essay concerns the idea so rendered. It might be put this way: if we think about conceptual capacities in the way Putnam shows we must, we will see that, while conceptual capacities are required to see such things as the face of perception, and while they may be required for some conceptual achievements, they are not inevitably involved either in perceptual achievements or in thought. I will indicate what it means to say that, and why one should.

1. THE FACE OF MEANING

Putnam speaks of a face of meaning. The image is new. It comes from Cora Diamond.[2] But the idea, radical as it is, is just the main burden of such classic works as "The Analytic and the Synthetic" and "It Ain't Necessarily So".[3] For Putnam it was originally a way of accommodating what physics had made inescapable. The resultant view of meaning shares much with Wittgenstein's. Each view is a form of the anti-platonism that is one of the main themes of philosophy in the second half of the twentieth century.

What physics, if nothing else, had made untenable is a certain traditional view of concepts. That view is contained in a short answer to a simple question. Suppose we ask what the world has to do with what fits a given concept. For many concepts the agreed answer would be, "Quite a lot". Take, for example, the concept of a pig. Uncontroversially, there could have been more or fewer pigs, or different ones from those there are. What would have fit that concept in such a case is not what does. But suppose we ask what the world has to do with *when* something would fit a given concept, with what something's being what it is a concept of might be. The short traditional answer is, "Nothing". The idea is: *when* something would fit a given concept – what it would take for something to do so – is something intrinsic to that concept, part of its being the concept it is. So that what would be something's fitting a given concept is what it is depends on nothing (other than the concept's being the one it is). So the facts as to when something would fit it are what they are no matter how the world might be. That is a form of platonism; a form that Putnam, early on, saw would not do.

What it takes to fit a given concept is not all that is intrinsic to it on this view. A concept is also identified as the one it is by its being of what it is. The concept of being a pig is identified by the fact that it is of *being a pig*. That is part of the problem with the traditional view. For, though one might at first not notice it, there are now multiple things to be presumed as to what a concept is – what it takes to fit the concept of a concept. As things stand (in our present circumstances), those presumptions rest on equal footing when it comes to identifying what it is we are speaking of in speaking of a concept. And, to adumbrate, what Putnam has shown most convincingly is that, in philosophy as well as in sublunary affairs, the phenomena may always show multiple presumptions to conflict: one can hold onto one only if one gives up another. In which case, it just may be the Platonism that has to go.[4]

In any case, in the tradition to which Putnam belongs, it was probably Hans Reichenbach who showed that the traditional picture will not do.

Reichenbach's point was that, at least in many cases, a concept cannot partition the world into that which fits it and that which does not at all unless its
application is governed by at least some principles which, if they do govern
application, had better be true, but which cannot be necessarily so. One
might, for example, consider the concept of a length, such as that of being
six feet long.[5] There is then the principle that objects do not change length
merely by changing spatial position. Deny that principle as things stand (or
stood not so long ago), and it becomes undetermined what a measurement
would be, so, too, what being six feet long might be. But the principle is not
necessarily true. It is not as if space could not have had – or turn out to have –
a geometry that makes it false. If the principle is true, then it determines
in part when something would count as six feet long. If it is not, then it
does not do that: whatever, if anything, it would be for something to be six
feet long would not be fixed in that way. That makes the traditional story
untenable.

Putnam's response to Reichenbach's point turns on an idea about how
something is identified as the concept such-and-such (and how what a concept is a concept of is identified as what it is). To adumbrate again, that idea
is the idea of a face of meaning. A contrast will help to bring it out. Someone else who took Reichenbach's point, but responded differently, is Paul
Feyerabend. On Feyerabend's view (as of 1958, at least), for any *putative*
concept there is a set of principles (a 'theory') that represent what is to be
presumed as to how the supposed concept works (what would, with right,
be presumed in our position), and that are what one might call *conditionally
analytic*: if the concept is genuine – if there is really such a thing as what it
is a concept of – then those principles are true. Contraposing, if they are
not true, then the concept is bogus. And they are not (all) necessarily true.
As it may be, part of the relevant theory for the concept of being a pig may
be that pigs are mammals. Then either pigs are mammals or there is no
such thing as being a pig. If the supposition that pigs are mammals, and
the other things to be supposed as to what it is for something to be a pig,
are not all true of anything, then it is not (just) that there are no pigs, but
rather that there is no such thing as being one.

Putnam differs from Feyerabend at a crucial point. Suppose there is
some putative way for things to be (and a putative concept of something's
being that way). Suppose that, in the position in which we find ourselves,
there are certain things one would most reasonably presume as to what way
for things to be that is – as to when something would, and when something
would not, be that way; how the world partitions. For the sake of argument
we may suppose that these presumptions amount to a theory that could be
made explicit. Now suppose the world turns out to be such that that theory

could not be (entirely) true of anything. There is, perhaps, no relevant physical quantity that remains constant under change of spatial position. Or those things we would have supposed to be pigs all 'suckle' their young on a silicon compound; they are not mammals. Then *perhaps* we dealt in bogus concepts. Perhaps there is no such thing as being a pig, or being six feet long. But perhaps some of what was to be presumed – some of the relevant theory – is just false of that very way for things to be of which, in our condition of ignorance, we were presuming it. Perhaps there is such a thing as something's being a pig, and those beasts whose haunches we so lovingly preserve *are* pigs. We were just mistaken in supposing that pigs are mammals. Perhaps the length of an object is what it measures as outside of a certain anomalous region of space. The point here would hold for *any* theory that might fix how the world would partition into that which is F and that which is not: that theory is not necessarily so of *being F.*

So where given things are to be presumed as to what being F would be, and they cannot all be true of any way for a thing to be, perhaps that shows that there is really no such thing as being F; or perhaps there is such a thing, and it merely shows that some of those presumptions are false of that. What decides which alternative is so in a given instance, and, where it is the second alternative, what decides which presumption is (or presumptions are) false – and what, instead, really does fix the way the world partitions? A crucial part of Putnam's answer is that there is no formula for deciding such things. (If there were, it would just constitute another presumption that *might* have to be given up.) We must give up the idea that there is such a thing as being F if, without presumptions we cannot retain, what we were speaking of would be unrecognizable as being F. We must not give up that idea if there remains a way for things to be for us to speak of which, given its role in our thought and action, is recognizably being F, which we explicably supposed to operate in such-and-such ways that it does not (and that nothing can).

Such things, as Putnam has shown, are often recognizable. But they are not (in general) calculable. There are no statable principles from which one can, in general, deduce correctly when the one thing, when the other, has occurred. Rather, we must rely on the fact that we can sometimes see such things, and on the actual operations of our abilities by which we do so. That is the idea of a face of meaning. In given circumstances, with a given perspective on the world, people spoke of some putative way for things to be. They spoke of it, say, as being F. In given other circumstances, from a different perspective on the world, people speak of a (putative) way for things to be of which certain other things are to be presumed. In each case the putative notion plays a certain role in the thought and action of those who so speak. Sometimes we can see the face of the one notion in the other way of speaking (and thinking) of things. If the first practice is one thing speaking of being F might be, then so, visibly, is the second. If the second practice is coherent – if the world makes no problems for its way of doing things – then that is what being F really is (and shows how that way for things to be in fact partitions things). There are two different forms of speaking of being F where such things are thus visible (and there are no principles that decide where they would be). The facts as to where there are, where not, such forms show what, if anything, it really is for something to be F.

2. RECOGNIZING AND CONCEIVING

We have now seen what the notion face of meaning comes to. But the image may mislead. For it may put us in mind of literal facial recognition – a phenomenon a psychologist might aim to understand. And we may then misunderstand what the psychologist's aims would be. Most of us can recognize some faces: we see them to confront us just when they do – abstracting, roughly, from peripheral sources of error. A psychologist might seek an account of that. We have compelling ideas as to what success would be. The psychologist's main concern will be to identify that to which we are sensitive in particular cases: visible features – perhaps highly abstract ones – to which we respond, when they are detected, by taking a presented face (or figure) to be a given one – so-and-so's face. If he succeeds, he will be able to say just what otherwise-specified inputs will result in our seeing the presence of a given face. He will be able to state the conditions for our so responding. Since what is at stake is an *ability* to *recognize* – that is, an ability to get things right, to take a given face to be present roughly just when it is – the psychologist may also be reasonably seen as identifying, in other terms, conditions under which a given face would be present (at least on one notion of a face).

Suppose this project could be carried out for faces of meaning. The psychologist would identify in a given deployment of a notion – the notion of being six feet long, say, as applied from a given perspective on the world – features, perhaps highly abstract ones, which made that notion recognizable as the one deployed in a different way of thinking of the world, carried out from a different perspective on it. He would thus identify, in other terms, conditions for some notion, used in some way, being recognizable by us as such-and-such a notion. Since, on the idea described above, for it to be being a pig, or being six feet long, that is, being spoken of on a given way of speaking of the world just is, for that to be visible (from a suitable perspective on the world), the psychologist will also, ipso facto, have identified conditions for its *being* such-and-such that is spoken of on some given way of speaking of things. If he has succeeded at that, it would seem, then he has made the world's role in determining what, if anything, it would be for something to fit a given concept calculable. Our ability to see faces of meaning would be, in principle, eliminable. That would do away with Putnam's idea.

We have no principled reason to believe that a psychologist who sought an account of facial recognition could not succeed in his ambitions. Nor is there a principled reason to think he could not succeed for any other recognition ability he chose to study. But to think that this threatens Putnam's point is to misunderstand a psychologist's ambitions. It will help to be clearer on what it is he aims to describe. To begin with, he aims to describe something we do, or can do, when we know, or can tell, or can recognize, such-and-such – a pig, say, or a tango, or heliotrope – when we see or hear one, or encounter one in such-and-such a way. What he aims to describe is a particular way of doing what we thus can do; a way on which, in some sense, we rely. If we call what he describes a recognition capacity, we can think of such a capacity as characterized by the following four features.

First, it should be determinate just what results the capacity would achieve (if working flawlessly). There should be some one set of results that are just those which (without interference) it would achieve. It should be determinate just when – for what (registered) inputs – its exercise would result in identifying, or seeing, something as the relevant thing (a pig, Jones, heliotrope); just when, according to the way it works, something is so to be identified.

Second, there should be a specifiable way that the capacity works: statable principles by which those environmental factors to which it is sensitive are transformed into the capacity's outputs. There should, that is, be a describable, identifiable function from relevant inputs to the capacity's deliverances. So it must be possible to specify the arguments of such a function – just what it is to which the capacity is sensitive.

Third, a capacity to recognize F, or Fs, is – so far as a psychologist is interested in such things – under no obligation to be sensitive to features that are *essential* to being an F. It need only be sensitive to features that in fact distinguish Fs (or an F) from other things. Pia may be recognizable by her face. A capacity to recognize her may exploit that fact. But plastic surgery may give her a new face. For all that she would still be Pia.

Fourth, and relatedly, a given recognition capacity, fixed by its results, and by its way of achieving them, may only work in hospitable environments. Since, by definition, a capacity gets things right, it may only be a *capacity* in hospitable environments. That capacity to recognize Pia by her face ceases to be a capacity to recognize her after the plastic surgery. A capacity to recognize pigs by their shape may cease to be if its environs are inundated with perfectly porcine-shaped antipodean marsupials.

So far as we know, any recognition capacity we have, at least with respect to perceptually encountered denizens of our sublunary world, is, in fact, hostage to the hospitality of our environments. Our ways of telling sheep from goats are always liable to cease to be effective if the environment goes wrong. We have nothing to rely on when it comes to telling a pig when we see it, or Pia when we see her, that is not liable to cease to be reliable if our environment changes. If a psychologist claimed to solve the problem of how people tell sheep from goats, he would not be refuted merely by showing that there are *conceivable* circumstances in which (genuine) sheep would share with goats all the features which, according to him, lead us to distinguish between them. This shows that, in solving the problem he addresses, the psychologist does not (or need not) identify what it is for something to be a goat, or when, in general, something would so count.

Suppose we think of a conceptual capacity, for the concept of being F, as a capacity to tell what would count as something's being F, or when something would so count. Our conceptual capacities would then be defined by what we are able, or equipped, to see in such regards. They are just our capacities to see that. It is such capacities that we exercise in seeing faces of meaning. We see that what people are speaking of, in speaking from such-and-such a perspective, in such-and-such a way is, say, being a goat: something's being what they thus speak of just would be its being a goat. Our confidence that the psychologist could succeed at his chosen task – explaining how we distinguish sheep from goats or tell a goat on sight – is not in itself reason to think that our conceptual capacities, as just conceived, will submit to the same treatment. Our confidence is that the psychologist can describe capacities with the first two of the above features. But, given the limits of his ambitions, we have no reason to think that capacities with those features could enable us to see all that we in fact can see with the conceptual capacities we have.

No recognition capacity is a way of seeing when its own limits have been exceeded. A given capacity to tell pigs at sight lacks the means for deciding when *that* way of telling pigs at sight is no longer a way of telling pigs at sight. Our conceptual capacities allow us to see such things – how something could still be a pig while lacking the features on which a given such recognition capacity relies, or fail to be a pig while having those features. They thus also allow us to see, given sufficient access to the way things are, when some such thing is a possibility. A conceptual capacity could reduce to a recognition capacity – that is, it could have the first two of the above features of such a capacity – only where there are no such possibilities, or none that might be visible to us; only where there is no such thing as something's being an F by the capacity's way of deciding things, but for all that, not an F, or vice versa (or at least no such thing so far as we are equipped to see). Putnam's thesis, in response to Reichenbach, clothed as it now is in the image of a face of meaning, can now be put this way: our conceptual capacities, at least in sublunary matters, do not so reduce. They do not have those first two marks of a recognition capacity in the present sense.

3. ARTICULATIONS

Perception, where, if ever, it occurs, is awareness of one's surroundings. Such awareness normally includes awareness of the presence of particular features in one's surroundings – of that pig before one, or the presence of a pig there, or of the pig's pawing the ground, or of the fact that pig droppings are strewn about. How does what one perceives of one's surroundings at a given moment articulate into the particular features one then perceives? Just what features is one then perceptually aware of? Here are three theses about that.

1. What a perceiver perceives – what he is perceptually aware of – depends on but two factors: how he is at the time (just how sensitive he is, or his sense organs are, to what is around him; what it is then like for him); and how his surroundings are. Since there is room for no other factor to play a role in answering this question, there is a unique way that his awareness of his surroundings articulates into awareness of particular features of it; a unique right answer to the question of which features he perceives.

2. Here is how the world makes its contribution to fixing an articulation. It (the way things are) articulates in a unique way into particular ways things are. The question of what the perceiver is perceptually aware of is then simply a question of which of these ways he has noticed, which he has missed, or to which he is not properly sensitive.

3. Any particular way things are, so any way the perceiver is aware of how things are, articulates in a unique way into objects and/or ways for an object to be, and is structured in a unique way in terms of what objects are which of these ways. (The articulation of a statement in terms of the particular things its parts speak of is a model for this.)

I am about to suggest that all three of these theses are false. I will concentrate first on the third.

Frege held (at least sometimes) that a thought articulates only relative to an analysis.[6] If we were to accept that, and hold that a thought is identified by the way things are according to it, we might well reject the third thesis. But another, currently more popular, idea speaks in favor of it. One may see that idea (or a form of it) as inspired by a thought of Strawson's: that facts are mere doppelgängers for statements.[7]

Strawson's idea has two components. It may begin from the good idea that there is no more to identifying a thought than identifying the way things are according to it: the thought just is that things are *that* way. If one were to think that thoughts and ways for things to be were fully and determinately countable, one might say that thoughts and ways for things to be are isomorphic. The second component is more questionable. It is the idea that thoughts and statements are isomorphic. The words used in making a statement are structured: they have recognizable constituents syntactically related in recognizable ways. This imposes a structure on the things those constituents speak of. The idea is that a thought is (or has) that same sort of structure of things to be spoken of; and that thoughts are to be counted by such structures: each thought is structured in some one definite way. That is just to ignore Frege's careful distinction between *Gedanken* and *Aussagen*.[8]

But this Strawsonian idea, to say the least, diverges from our usual ways of dealing with such matters. Consider the following descriptions of the way things are. There is a pig in the sty. That thing in the sty is a pig. That pig is in the sty. The sty contains some ambulatory pork. Porcineness is so distributed as not to leave that sty utterly bereft of it. These descriptions, fixed by the words that give them, are not structured all in one way. If we thought they had logical forms, we could not suppose they all had the same form. Nor do they even all mean the same. They are not all logically equivalent. (It is not a logical truth that all pigs are ambulatory – there may be quadraplegic pigs – nor that all ambulatory pork is [part of] a [current] pig. There are, for example, conceivable transplants.) But suppose we had to describe a given situation. Style aside, which of these would do the job? Say there is some particular way we want to say things to be. Which of them would say things to be that way? Often, for many purposes, we would count any of these as but different ways (some stylistically better advised than others) of saying the same thing to be so. If there is a given way we want to say things to be – a given situation we want to say to obtain – we could find no basis for saying that only some, as opposed to others, say that situation to obtain. That that is a pig in the sty, and that there is ambulatory pork there both equally capture what it is we think, and the point we wish to make.

So far I speak of intuitions. Perception gives us some extra reason to take them seriously. For if these nonequivalent descriptions ipso facto, from the mere fact of their nonequivalence, describe different ways for things to be, then for any pair it should be possible for someone to see things to be the one way but not the other. Suppose, now, that Sid is staring at the (pig-blessed) sty. Which of these descriptions identifies a way he sees things to be, and which does not? Just what is supposed to decide that question? What should Sid be doing, or how should he be, to see things to be the one way that he need not be doing to see them to be the other? If he does see them to be some one of these ways, what else, or different, should he be doing to see them to be another? How could he, say, merely be seeing there to be a pig in the sty while missing the fact that that pig is in the (or a) sty? In many such cases, for many purposes, we have no idea how to answer such questions. Where Sid sees things to be the way that fits some one of these descriptions, we have no idea what *else* he should be doing to see them to be the way that fits some other.

But there is something that makes it difficult to take these intuitions seriously. To take the most glaring case, there is, as noted, no logical equivalence between the sty containing a pig and its containing ambulatory pork. Conceivably, pork could be transplanted into sheep. Conceivably, some future pigs will have to make do with their wings, their atrophied legs having become useless for walking. Where it is possible for there to be pigs in the pen but no ambulatory pork there, or vice versa, that is just to say that things might be the one way but not the other; something we could not so much as say unless there were two different ways for things to be. And the nature of the possibility makes clear what one should notice to see things to be both ways: that the pig is ambulatory, say, or that it (still) contains pork, or that the pork in the pen is currently part of a viable pig, or whatever the possibility demands. Again, someone may fail to know where pork comes from. Perhaps he thinks it swims up river to spawn in the spring. So he may see a pig to be in the sty without realizing that there is, ipso facto, ambulatory pork there.

In some situations, then, it is imperative to distinguish two different ways for things to be, one of which would be a pig's being in the sty, the other of which would be ambulatory pork being there. That drives us to the Strawsonian idea only if we accept this principle: *what would sometimes be so must always be so*. But we need not buy that. The alternative idea would be that what count, and what do not, as two ways of speaking of some one way for things to be depends on the occasion for the counting: on how one then *ought* to think of ways for things to be, given the distinctions the world, and our purposes, make it necessary to draw; and sometimes just on how we *are* thinking of ways for things to be in the discourse in which this particular decision about how to speak is to play a part. Sometimes, given our world, and ourselves, there is just no way for there to be a pig without ambulatory pork, or vice versa; nothing else ambulatory pork might be but a pig, and vice versa; and no way that someone might see there to be a pig but miss the fact of ambulatory pork, or vice versa. In such situations we may correctly see one way for things to be, specifiable in either way. But that we may sometimes do that does not mean that we always may.

Simple predicates, such as 'has red hair', provide a model for this way of looking at the matter. What that predicate speaks of is having red hair. But different understandings are possible as to what having red hair would be. There are different (sometimes) legitimate ways of thinking of the matter. If a genetic brunette dyes his hair, say, candy-apple red, then there is an understanding of having red hair on which that is how he has made himself, and another on which he still does not have it. If we said someone to have red hair, we might say what would be true of him in such a situation, or we might say what would be false. For we might speak of his having it on either of these understandings of that. An occasion may make it pointful to speak in one way or another of having red hair. It may even be that, on a given occasion, there is one thing or another which is what one *would* then say in so speaking; something that would then count as having red hair. Abstracting from occasions, there is a truth to be told in describing our sample man as having red hair. There is also a falsehood thus to be told. There is also a truth to be told in saying him not to have red hair; one to be told in saying him to have brown hair; one to be told in saying him not to have brown hair, and so on. Of course, not all these truths are to be told at once. There is never truth to be told in saying him to have, and not to have, red hair; and perhaps none to be told in saying him both to have red hair and to have brown hair. For one tells a given one of these truths only in speaking of having red (brown) hair on the appropriate understanding of having that. And where one speaks on some one understanding of this, one does not speak on any other.[9]

Now the idea is that ways for things to be are occasion-sensitive in just the way the phenomenon of having red hair is. There are various legitimate ways of thinking of what ways there are for things to be, or what ways things in fact are, and are not. One may think of how things are in such a way as to discern one way for things to be, identifiable in a variety of ways, as illustrated above. One may also legitimately think of things in such a way as to discern one or another way for things to be, identifiable in some of those ways, but not in others. There are indefinitely many different ways of doing this. (Of course, for any of these ways of thinking, there are occasions for thinking in that way. And there are occasions on which there are ways one *ought* to think of ways for things to be. The world might create the need for us to do so [the ubiquity of pork transplants]; so might our purposes or needs on an occasion.) It is sometimes correct to take there to be just one way for things to be that one may describe equally by speaking of pigs or by speaking of ambulatory pork. But, again, what is sometimes so need not always be.

Our intuitions, and the limits of what we can thus see, do, then, provide a cogent case for rejecting the Strawsonian idea, which is to reject the third assumption on the list with which I began. And, though the point merits fuller treatment, we have caught a glimpse of why one should reject it. Particular circumstances, in fixing, inter alia, ways it is possible for things to be, may allow us a grip on what it is one might miss in 'merely' seeing that there was a pig in the sty, but failing to see that there was ambulatory pork there, or that *that* pig was in a sty. But it takes particular circumstances to make it determinate what that might be. If we were to adopt the Strawsonian idea and distinguish ways for things to be accordingly, we should be at a loss (in principle) to say what would qualify one as seeing, or noticing, or knowing, that things were such-and-such a way. (I do not deny that some philosophers have tried to say this.)

I have attacked the third thesis. If it goes, then so do the other two. The third thesis was that any given way for things to be articulates in some unique way. That is false, since there are many structurally (and logically) distinct ways of saying things to be a given way. What allows this to be so is that it is an occasion-sensitive matter which ways of saying how things are, are ways of saying things to be the same way, which means that it must be an occasion-sensitive matter how the world articulates into ways for things to be. For we must sometimes discern two ways for things to be where, at other times, there counts as only one. So the second thesis is false. It follows immediately that the first is as well. That is, there is no one way that is, occasion-independently, *the* true way in which someone's awareness of his surroundings articulates into particular ways he is aware of how things are. He is, of course, aware of some of the ways there are to be aware of. But what these are is an occasion-sensitive matter. (There is a further question as to when, for a given way, he would count as aware that things are that way.)

We have arrived at a view of articulation that is just what Putnam still retains of 'internal realism'. In the Dewey lectures Putnam continues to reject

> the traditional realist assumptions of (1) a fixed totality of all objects; (2) a fixed totality of all properties; (3) a sharp line between properties we 'discover' in the world and properties we 'project' onto the world; (4) a fixed relation of 'correspondence' in terms of which truth is supposed to be defined.[10]

There is much more in point (1) than has been approached here. But we have now filled in the form such a rejection may take. We have also seen how that rejection is consistent with the naïve realism Putnam now espouses. It remains to show how naïve realism positively requires it.

The present position is that articulation is an occasion-sensitive affair: how the way things are articulates into particular ways things are depends on the occasion for distinguishing such ways; how a perceiver's awareness, at a moment, of how things are around him articulates into awareness of particular features of how things are depends on the occasion for holding him to be aware of one thing or another. We have seen some reason for holding this position. There are now two points left to make. The first is that articulation must take that shape if there is to be such a thing as perception at all, and if naïve realism is to be correct. For it is a triviality, which naïve realism insists on, that perception, where, and if ever, it occurs, *is* awareness of how things are around one: to see a pig to be before one is to be aware that that is how things are. But such awareness could only be an occasion-sensitive affair. The second point is that we could not see perception to have such a shape unless our conceptual capacities, directed at that phenomenon, fit Putnam's conception of such a capacity: the capacity to see the face of a perceptual achievement.

Taking up the first point, why must articulation in perceptual achievement be an occasion-sensitive affair?[11] The answer is that perception is, in the nature of the case, a source of a certain sort and quality of information about one's surroundings. And it can only be an occasion-sensitive matter when we are in possession of information of that quality. To see features of how things are is to have (what might be) reasons to think things. What one sees is that the pig is loose; reason to remove the baby from the porch. Now a proper reason, one might think, is what is liable to be better or worse, conclusive or no reason at all, depending on circumstances. As one might also say, its goodness depends on the cogency of an inference from it to what it is a reason for. The presence of fresh pig droppings in the

yard is, in some circumstances, good reason to think there are pigs about;
but perhaps not when the loaded stock transporter is lumbering down the
drive toward the abattoir. Suppose one wanted to reject these restrictions
on what a reason is. Then we might extend the notion to include what I
will call degenerate reasons. A degenerate reason for thinking P cannot be
better or worse, and how good it is does not depend on circumstance. Nor
does it depend on the cogency of any inference from it to something else.
For a degenerate reason for thinking P is not thus distinct from P itself.
That there is a pig on the porch is a degenerate reason for thinking so. In
this terminology, the point is that perception of a feature of how things are
always supplies degenerate reason for taking something to be so as to how
things are. If you see there to be a pig in the sty, then what you see – that
there is a pig in the sty – is a degenerate reason for thinking there is a pig
in the sty. Such is the quality of information that perception, in the nature
of the case, supplies.

A degenerate reason leaves no further room for knowledge to be an
occasion-sensitive affair. Suppose Pia noticed the fresh pig droppings. Does
she know that there are pigs about? One might think (though I do not rec-
ommend this view) that that depends, in part, on how good a reason the
droppings are for taking there to be pigs. How good they are *might* be an
occasion-sensitive matter. Or one might think that the answer depends on
Pia's ability to appreciate the cogency of some substantial inference from
what she noted to ambient pigs; and what her credentials are in that matter
might be an occasion-sensitive affair. But with degenerate reasons there
is no such place where occasion-sensitivity might arise. If Pia's reason for
taking there to be pigs is what she saw – namely, that there are pigs about –
then she cannot do any less than know that there are pigs. So we need to
note that knowledge is an occasion-sensitive affair. Pia is weekending at Sid's
country retreat. On an early morning stroll she passes some outbuildings
and suddenly confronts a pig in the sty. She is surprised, and a bit pleased,
that Sid actually practices husbandry. She returns and tells Zoë, "There's a
pig in the sty out back". "Nonsense", says Zoë. "No", Pia replies, "I know
there is. I saw it for myself". Pia speaks truly. In another place, at a slightly
later time, Max is talking with Des. Des has just read an (as it happens false)
article in a weekly of some repute. According to the article, gentleman farm-
ers in Sid's district have been substituting a sort of chic, and terribly porcine,
antipodean marsupial for pigs in their livestock collections. An amateur
could not tell by looking that these marsupials are not pigs. Now suppose
Max says, "Well, at any rate, Sid still keeps pigs. Pia knows he does. She saw
for herself that there are pigs in his sty". Max would thus speak falsely.

What Pia knows is an occasion-sensitive matter. In the context of some discussions, on some occasions for viewing her, she counts as knowing that there was a pig in Sid's sty. In the context of others, she does or would not. Where she does count as knowing this, she also counts as having seen there to be a pig in the sty. That is *how* she knows. But where she does not count as knowing this, she cannot count as having seen there to be a pig there. In fact, in the case at hand, and in the context of that discussion, she does not count as in a position to be able to see whether or not there is a pig in the sty, at least in Sid's district. Sometimes she cannot so count. But, for all that, sometimes she does. (We would not know a cat when we saw one if we were invaded by sufficiently feline Martians. We would lack the ability to see such things. But, for all that, we do know a cat when we see one.) The occasion-sensitivity of knowledge, if nothing else, requires occasion-sensitivity in the articulation of a perceiver's perceiving how things are into his perceiving of particular ways things are. That is one reason why Putnam's view of articulation is mandatory.

There is now the second question: the importance of Putnam's view of our conceptual capacities. The face of perception is the faces of perceptual achievements: seeing the cat to be curled up on the rug, hearing that the phone is ringing, or that the wind is rattling the tiles on the roof, and so on. The idea is that, say, the face of seeing there to be a pig in the sty is part of the view of Pia's perceptual awareness that one gets from certain perspectives on the world, absent from the view available from others. Has Pia seen a pig in the sty? Is she up to seeing such things (in her current situation)? Can, or could, she see whether that is how things are? To answer this we must first grasp when she would fail to see whether that is how things are; what mistakes she would, or might, make if there were occasion for them. She might, for example, miss discrete enough marsupial pouches. We must then assess whether her capacities are fit for dealing with the situations she actually confronts. Ought they to count as adequate? Or does epistemic mishap lie that way? Is there any point in depreciating her capacity, conditions being what they are? Or would it be pointless and stupid to do so, forcing us to discount too many of our capacities as, equally, not really ones to recognize how things are in this or that respect? It is a more than plausible idea that the right assessments in such matters are not calculable from some set of fixed principles plus antecedently specified factors in situations on which such statuses depend. What one needs is openness to all, whatever that might be, that makes a given assessment pointful, and a good one, or pointless and stupid. For that one needs human sense and sensibility.

There is a more general point here. Thinking occasion-sensitively, so detecting occasion-sensitive phenomena, always invokes irreducible conceptual capacities in the present Putnamian sense. The problem to which Putnam's view was first directed has this form. From a given perspective on the world, there were things to be presumed as to how a given phenomenon, being F, sorts the world into its instances and other things. That fixes what the right way of sorting instances would be, provided the world permits itself to be sorted in that way, and the result is recognizably what we had in view in thinking of (things) being F. But suppose that condition is not met. How, then, if at all, does the world sort into instances of being F? Putnam's answer is that we must be able to see what militates in favor of one or another answer to that question, and then to adopt the answer that, all considered, is the best one. Seeing such things, he argues, exhibits an irreducible conceptual capacity. (Seeing such things cannot, he argues, be merely seeing what is calculable from some principles that are part of what being F was to be taken to be. For such principles, if there were any, would just be a further part of that scheme for sorting instances which has proven not to work. What to do with them would just be another part of what we would have to be able to see.)

Occasion-sensitivity simply raises a slightly different species of the same form of problem. From our perspective on the world, there are things to be presumed as to how the world should sort into instances of being F. Red things are not green. Red things are typically visibly so (one can tell by looking). Red things are stably so, barring physico-chemical changes, and so on. (It may, of course, be an occasion-sensitive matter just what is to be presumed.) There need be no doubt that these presumptions are correct as to what it would be for something to be F. The trouble is that, in some cases that concern us, they simply do not decide how the world sorts. One might sort in various ways while preserving all of them. For example, it is not fixed precisely when, or where, one should look to see whether an item of a certain sort is red. The problem is then to see whether, on a given occasion for sorting relevant items, there are any additional constraints on sorting – additional aspects of how this is to be done – which it would be right to take as part of the right way of doing the sorting under the conditions in which it is to be done. How should this sorting be done, given that such-and-such would be the right way if, in fact, it effected a sorting of the cases we want? The point about occasion-sensitivity is that sometimes such questions have recognizably correct answers. But those answers cannot follow simply from some true principles about what it is for something to be F. For by hypothesis we are dealing with cases that are not decided just by what it is for something to be F. Whatever principles do govern being F are thus ones that do not decide what it is we want to know. There is no point in trying to calculate an answer from them; rather, we must be able to see the right thing to say given that an answer is not thus calculable. Seeing such answers thus invokes a conceptual capacity with respect to being F that does not reduce to such principles, one that fits Putnam's conception of what a conceptual capacity is.

The idea, then, is that we invoke irreducible conceptual capacities in seeing the shape perceptual (and epistemic) achievements take. That is not to say that we invoke, or inevitably invoke, such capacities in achieving them. There is an idea abroad that our perceptual achievements rest on such capacities. I will next examine one thing that might, in some sense, make this so.

4. OBJECTIVITY

Here is one way our cognitive relations to the world rest on irreducible conceptual capacities: such capacities make us proof against one source of inevitable loss of objectivity in the picture we may gain of how things are. But it is possible grossly to overestimate the loss with which we would thus be threatened. Thompson Clarke, in "The Legacy of Scepticism",[12] identifies that threatened loss. But he both overestimates the threat and misconstrues its source.

Clarke begins from an example:

> Pilots are being taught to identify enemy aircraft. Ten kinds of enemy aircraft, A, B, . . . J, are characterized in terms of their capabilities and mutually distinguishing features. The pilots are instructed to identify *any* enemy aircraft by running through a provided checklist of features. It is recognized that this may result in misidentifications: there are types of enemy aircraft, antiquated, rarely used, intentionally not covered by the checklist, which specifies features sufficient for distinguishing the ten types one from another but none from X, Y, Z, the antiquated types which the pilots are instructed to ignore. This procedure is adopted for certain overriding practical advantages.[13]

Clarke takes the pilots to model two things: first, the skeptic's view of us; and, second, the actual human condition unless we satisfy a certain condition. If we do not, then, with respect to whether the water has boiled yet, or the grass is turning brown, or foot and mouth disease has spread to Cumbria, or any other matter that might concern us, we are cut off from seeing how, objectively, things really are. It is this second idea that concerns us here.

To see how, objectively, things *really* are in any particular respect, Clarke thinks, we would need (with respect to that) to 'escape the plain'. Escaping the plain would be attaining a position in which, in asking 'A?' or saying 'A',

> what *we* ask, or affirm, is what the words with their meaning do *per se*.[14]

For that each concept we employ in the asking, or the saying,

> must be divorceable intact from our practices, from whatever constitutes the essential character of the plain, from elemental parts of our human nature.[15]

Then, but only then, we can be

> purely ascertaining observers who, usually by means of our senses, ascertain, when possible, whether items fulfill the conditions legislated by the concepts.[16]

Suppose that, in some given area, we cannot escape the plain. Then, Clarke says, we suffer just that loss of objectivity modeled by the pilots. For, he says, confined to the plain,

> we should be intellectually frustrated just because prohibited access to the *objective*. We could ask "What type is this aircraft?", but we wouldn't thereby be managing to inquire what the objective fact really was, to raise an issue to be settled solely by the concepts and the item. . . . The limiting eyeglasses of the restricted would prevent us from seeing, even trying to see, things and ourselves as they and we really are.[17]

Clarke calls it a 'visible fact'

> that the objectivity attainable within the plain is only skin-deep, *relative*. We want to know not how things are *inside* the world, but how things are, absolutely. And the world itself is one of these things.[18]

Wherever we think in terms of occasion-sensitive phenomena we do not escape the plain. For what we state or ask in speaking, say, of someone having red hair, is not fixed by the concepts our words express (say, the concept of having red hair), but depends also on the understanding on which we speak of what those concepts are concepts of. In fact, the phenomena we think and speak of are occasion-sensitive. Things would be otherwise only where we spoke of a way for things to be that did not admit of understandings: no matter how things were, there were no two views of what it would be for a thing (or things) to be that way, both compatible with all that is so as to what the way in question is. I (with Wittgenstein and Putnam) do not think it in our power to think of such 'uninterpretable' ways for things to be. We just cannot have in mind something *that* fully determinate. We cannot have something in mind in a way so as to, as Wittgenstein puts it, stop up all the cracks where a doubt (two ways of thinking of that which we have in mind) might creep in.[19] In the end, Clarke agrees that we cannot escape the plain. So it is agreed on all sides that if this entails loss of access to how things objectively are, then we suffer that loss.

Since occasion-sensitivity is at least one form of implainment, it would be odd if the mere fact of implainment entailed any loss of objectivity. For occasion-sensitivity is, in the first instance, the dependence of *what* is said or asked on the occasion of the saying or asking. Normally, if we are told that a car is blue, we do not scrape the paint off to see whether that is right. We do not because what we would discover if we did so does not bear on whether the car is as it was thus said to be. But whether that is so depends on the occasion of the saying. For there *are* understandings of a car's being blue on which scraping paint is highly relevant. And it is possible, on some occasions, to speak on such an understanding in calling a car blue. Nothing in this, so far, suggests that we cannot see whether things *really, objectively* are as they were said to be on a given occasion in calling the car blue. Grasping the understanding on which it was said to be that, we keep our pound coins in our pockets and just look. What we see *is* how the car really is in that respect.

What worries Clarke, in terms that are not his, is really the occasion-sensitivity of proof. Pia, walking past the sty, gains what sometimes counts as proof that there is a pig there; for she sometimes counts as having seen for herself. But she is not in a position that would always count as having such proof, independent of the occasion for the counting. That grunting from behind the barn proves that there are pigs about. But it would not always do that regardless of the occasion on which proof is called for. Nor would the proof it does supply, such as it is, always count as gapless. Our occasion-sensitive notion of proof allows things sometimes to count as proof that would not always do so. Clarke's worry is, *au fond*, that we cannot allow such occasion-sensitive proof to count as *real* proof, while retaining the idea that when we have proof, we are really seeing how things objectively are. Let us see why one might think that.

How do the pilots model the loss of objectivity we are supposed to suffer? To find out what type a plane is, the pilots follow the instructions in the manual. Those instructions describe the workings of a particular recognition capacity in the present sense. So insofar as the pilots confine themselves to the manual, they confine themselves to one specific recognition capacity. Every recognition capacity has its limits: it works only in hospitable environments. And I think that, for the pilots to model anything interesting, we must take very seriously the idea that they are confined to this one recognition capacity. When they have exercised it (correctly), they have exhausted their means for finding out how things are with respect to the type of a plane, say, flying by. We must suppose the pilots to lack relevant conceptual capacities – the capacity to see when the limits of their single recognition capacity has been reached. This means that while they may know that there is such a thing as a plane being an A so far as the manual gives a way of telling, but not an A, or vice versa, they lack any grasp of what it would be for that to be so. They must lack any adequate grasp of what situations would so count. For if they had such a grasp, they could, in principle, carry their investigations further. Suppose they knew that to be type A was, inter alia, to have such-and-such provenance. Then they would know what might show that a plane which was type A by the manual's way of telling was not really an A. They might, for boring peripheral reasons, be blocked from ever gaining the information that would in fact show this. But that, I take it, is not Clarke's point. It is only if we suppose the pilots to lack relevant conceptual capacities that their reliance on the manual leaves them with residual questions that they could not, in principle, investigate. It is the existence of such questions that makes for Clarke's envisioned sort of loss of objectivity.

What makes it difficult to view the pilots in this way is that to suppose them to lack such conceptual capacities is to suppose them not to be normal human beings. But as soon as we see that, we also see that they do not model our condition. We have a grasp of what it might be for our recognition capacities to have reached their limit. We tell pigs by their physiognomy. But we do understand what it might be for there to be a pig without that physiognomy, or vice versa. Where the world provides ways for that to happen, we can, as a rule, recognize them as such. We can recognize reason, where there is such, to think that things might be some given such way. We can then, often enough, see how investigating that possibility might go. Of course, we might happen never to be so placed as to gain the information needed to carry out such an investigation successfully. And of course our imagination, insight, savoir-faire, and patience sometimes fail us. Perhaps one can make skepticism out of merely that. But that is not the predicament the pilots are meant to model. We are not in that predicament. Just that makes it difficult to see just what the pilots model.

Clarke's depreciation, or neglect, of conceptual capacities makes it difficult for him to see how an occasion-sensitive notion of proof can fail to carry with it loss of true objectivity. That same neglect of conceptual capacities makes it difficult not to mishear a certain genre of philosophical point, most often associated with so-called 'ordinary language' philosophers. A case very much to the present point is Austin's remark "Enough is enough; it doesn't mean everything."[20] Austin's idea is this: knowing that P requires having proof;[21] but that proof need not contain, for every conceivable way for P to fail to be so, a proper subproof that things are not that way. My proof that it is a finch before me – what I see, say – need not contain as subproof a proof that what is before me is not stuffed.

If one conflates conceptual with recognition capacities, one will inevitably hear this point as meaning that convention, or custom, or the meanings of words, or usage, or their proper use, determines something equivalent to a manual from which follow results like this: in such-and-such situation, there is such-and-such that you must have checked on, and such-and-such that you need not have, in order to know that (or whether) what is before you is a finch. Somehow, our ordinary concept, or conception, of knowledge, or of finches, or so on, works like a set of principles from which one may derive the specifics of what would, and what would not, count as having proof of such-and-such when. One need not check for stuffing, say, unless such-and-such is so. In present terms, knowledge, or knowledge that P, is governed by a specifiable recognition capacity: one knows that P just when that is what the output of the (properly working) capacity would be; thus just when those specifiable factors to which it is sensitive are present.

Any such conception of knowledge is objectionable. The objection can be put as follows. The concept of knowledge is fairly tightly tied to fixed elimination policies. If you know you have turned the gas off, no further checks are called for. If you *know* that Sid keeps pigs, then (discretion and *delicatesse* aside) you may flatly say so. Whereas if you do *not* know, then, for many purposes at least, if you are to speak correctly, you must really hedge what you say. Roughly speaking, knowledge licenses action; failure to know calls for reservation. Given that, if our concept of knowledge were governed by a recognition capacity, as described above, then that concept would fix a particular, inflexible introduction policy: when someone has done such-and-such checks, then the concept fits. The problem then arises whether such a concept is harmonious. It follows from what knowledge is, the idea would be, that I know there is a finch before me even if I have not checked for stuffing. But perhaps I should check for stuffing before I start strewing seed? Is it really prudent to act according to such a policy – on such grounds? If the question can be raised in that form then, it seems, it is always up for discussion, and not to be settled by even a conceptual decree. If that really is our concept of knowledge, then perhaps our concept of knowledge is just ill-advised. That, I take it, is another take on the problem Clarke uses the pilots to model.

But this cannot be the right way of reading Austin. For one thing, it is central to Austin's epistemology that one cannot derive epistemic statuses from meaning, or from 'the concepts involved'.[22] On his view, meaning does not determine such things as what is evidence for what, what is proof of what, what requires proof, or when someone knows such-and-such. Rather, just as it is meaning plus circumstance that fixes the truth condition for a statement, and not meaning alone that does so, so it is the content of a statement plus circumstance that determines what would be evidence for what was said, when someone might be said to know it, and so on. Here Austin shows himself to share Putnam's grasp of what a conceptual capacity must be. If the question is whether P, we generally have good reason for wanting certain kinds of proof before we will count that question as settled, so for demanding that someone have certain sorts of proof before he counts as knowing that P, or whether P. We may, of course, think we have good reason where there is none. Where that is so, there is something that shows it so; it is thus recognizably so if we avail ourselves properly of our conceptual capacities. Conversely, for any way for P to fail to be so – a feathered bomb, say, masquerading as a finch – there may be good reason for checking whether things are that way before taking it to be settled whether P. But then our conceptual capacities allow such good reason to be recognizably such, where, in fact, there is such reason. What we must ask for by way of proof that P, before we allow ourselves, or others, to know that P, is no less than what our circumstances require.

To see, then, on a given occasion, whether someone then counts as knowing that P, we must, by exercising our conceptual capacities, see what proof there is good reason to want, what proof there is no good reason to insist on; just how might one actually be wrong, in this situation, as to whether P. Against this background, Austin's point is simply that there is never good reason for demanding everything that there might ever be good reason to demand by way of proof. In fact, the very idea of demanding that patently makes no sense. To see what introduction policy the concept of knowledge requires in a given case, then, we must exercise our conceptual capacities. We could not get by with some fixed recognition capacity. Is there good reason why P cannot, or should not, count as settled without such-and-such investigation? Then carrying out that investigation is part of settling whether P, so part of what the relevant introduction policy demands. When epistemic status is so viewed, questions of harmony are no longer ones of the legitimacy of some concept of knowledge, or of whether invoking it cuts us off from true objectivity. They are rather questions as to what introduction policy our concept of knowledge in fact requires, in given situations, and, perhaps, for given purposes. For the introduction policies it requires are just those that in fact harmonize with those fixed elimination policies we want to be part of that concept. Those questions, of course, are ones whose answers only suitable conceptual capacities allow us to see. But as soon as the problem takes that form, the mere fact of the occasion-sensitivity of proof is no longer, as such, a barrier to true objectivity.

The pilots do not model us. But how different from us are they? Just how thorough, or pervasive, is their loss of objectivity? Clarke's idea seems to be this. Consider the proposition G (of a given plane): *This plane is an A going by the manual but it is not an A.* The pilots cannot investigate, much less establish, whether G is true. They can investigate, and perhaps establish, whether the plane is an A going by the manual. Suppose that in doing so they were establishing whether the plane was an A. Then they would have established both that it was an A going by the manual, and that it was an A. Which settles G. So they would have established whether G. But, by hypothesis, they cannot do that. So, in establishing whether a plane is an A going by the manual, they cannot (ever) be establishing whether the plane is an A. So they can never really know whether a plane is an A.

But is this the right way of viewing their predicament? By hypothesis, the pilots lack a grasp of how it could be that a plane was an A according to the manual but not an A. They could not recognize cases of that being so as such. So, for any such way for things to be, they could not construct a proof that things were that way (if they were). Nor could they construct a proof that things were not that way. (If they can ever have, or construct, what count as proofs that such-and-such plane is an A, these could not form part of what would count as the last-mentioned sort of proof.) More pertinently, no proof that things were not some such way (a way such that the plane was an A going by the manual, but not an A) could be a subproof in any proof available to them (if there are any) that the plane is an A.

Suppose it really might be that the plane in question is an A going by the manual but not an A. The world really affords such a possibility. The pilots cannot prove that that possiblity does not obtain. (They cannot even recognize it for what it is.) So they cannot prove, nor have proof, so nor know, that that plane is an A. But suppose there is no chance that the plane, if an A going by the manual, could fail to be an A. That is just not a way that things might be. The manual was meant to give instructions for telling whether a plane is an A. What it describes, in these hypothesized circumstances, is, in fact, a way of telling whether a plane is an A. Why, then, deny that, in these circumstances, those instructions are just what they purport to be, so that in following them in these conditions the pilots really are finding out whether the plane is an A? Their proof that the plane is an A would contain no subproof that the manual had not misled. But then, there is no way for it to have misled. Why, then, should such a subproof be required? Pia's way of establishing that there are pigs in Sid's sty would not work if there were certain sorts of marsupials, and if such marsupials were about. It would be folly to deny, on that ground alone, that she is really able to establish whether there are pigs in Sid's sty. So far, the pilots are in just Pia's position. The occasion-sensitivity of proof is precisely what allows us to avoid such folly without loss of objectivity. For, given such a notion, where there might be such marsupials, where the plane might be merely an A going by the manual, Pia would not be establishing whether there were pigs, at least not by those methods – though she might resort to others. And, similarly, the pilots would not be establishing whether the plane was an A, though, unfortunately in their case, they have no other methods to resort to.

The pilots cannot always tell whether a plane is an A. Sometimes the manual is not enough. But sometimes it is; then there is very good reason to say that what they are establishing is whether the plane is an A. Where that is what they are doing, they establish no less than how things really are in that respect. They have less potential grip on the world than we do; but their loss is limited. We remain, then, in this position. Conceptual capacities are needed for seeing the shapes of our cognitive relations to the world. They are sometimes needed for standing in such relations. But so far we have seen no reason to suppose that they are inevitably needed for this – that there can be no perceptual achievements, or knowledge of how things are, without them. The next section is a last attempt to find such reason.

5. PERCEPTUAL ACHIEVEMENTS

The face of perception is visible only to those with suitable conceptual capacities. Are perceptual achievements, notably, seeing the world to be thus and so, available only to those with such capacities? I will assume that cats and dogs and such lack conceptual capacities. They may have their batteries of recognition skills, and these may, perhaps, change over time; but not through the sort of reflection on what is going on that our conceptual capacities permit us. Now, a cat watches a bird alighting on a bush, and then keeps track of it perching there. Has the cat seen the bird to alight there? Does it see that the bird is continuing to perch?

If the cat's recognition capacities had reached their limit, or where, for certain purposes, those capacities leave the cat out of its depth, the cat would, of course, be at sea. If there are Martians about, or mechanized finches, indistinguishable to a cat from finches, that might impugn the cat's claim to have seen a *bird* to have alighted. If someone is seriously (but wrongly) concerned that many so-called 'finches' today are really mechanized, we cannot assuage his fears by pointing to the cat's perceptual achievements. For those purposes, such is beyond what the cat counts as having attained. But, as we have seen, it does not follow from what it *would* be right to say in such strange and counterfactual situations that the cat does not know a bird when it sees one, and cannot see a bird to have alighted, as things stand (that is, where there is no possibility of such strange things).

There is, though, another line of thought. It begins from the idea that seeing things to be thus and so is, inter alia, awareness that they are that way; and that awareness that things are thus and so entails *taking* them to be that way. Perhaps there are counterexamples to these principles. But, for present purposes, they may stand unchallenged. It then continues with the idea that one cannot count as taking things to be thus and so without appreciating sufficiently what it means for things to be that way. To make a very long story very short, the idea would be that it is through one's appreciation of the way one takes things to be that we see how it is one takes things to be; and that that connection is anything but accidental. I take this last idea to be correct. At any rate, it will remain unchallenged.

The idea that cats and dogs are incapable of genuine perceptual achievements of the present sort depends on putting a certain spin on what are, so far, unobjectionable ideas. On this spin, the idea that one cannot take it that P without seeing sufficiently what P means becomes: one cannot grasp, or think, the thought that P without grasping sufficiently its place in a system of thoughts. Now how must we think of P as having a place in such a system? ("What system?" one might ask.) On the line of thought I am now setting out, we get our grip on the system, and the place, through the idea that a thought is essentially structured.[23] It is a particular organization of elements drawn from some stock of elements. (And, at least for a given thinker of the thought, at a time, there is a given stock of elements from which these are drawn.) As it may be, the thought is about Sid, and to the effect that he is getting fat. It thus is, essentially, of the form Fa. (I bracket the possibility of analyzing *getting fat*.) That *that* is the form the thought has is part of what identifies it as the thought it is; and, on the line I am now setting out, part of what one must grasp to think *it*. Now, as Wittgenstein once noted (just before becoming later), it makes sense to ascribe such a form to a thought (Wittgenstein spoke of a *Satz*, or proposition) only if its elements also figure in other combinations; that is, only if the thought is part of a system that also includes such thoughts as Fb, Fc, and so on, and Ga, Ha, and so on. An element, to *be* an element, must have a systematic role. (Wittgenstein notes that one cannot say a priori just how big such a system must be.) So we can see the structure of a thought as reflecting its place in a system of thoughts, or at least as identifying the sort of system to which it must belong, and the sort of place in that system which it must have. One might also see the structure of the thought as that in virtue of which it occupies the place it does in the sort of system it does – as what *makes* it have the inferential role, so meaning (in the system) that it does.

Now let us return to the cat. The present spin has put the cat in the following position. In order to see the bird to have alighted, the cat must grasp a certain thought. That thought has a certain structure. It is of the form *Fa*, where the element in it that takes the *F* place is something that makes it about having alighted – the concept of having alighted – and the element that takes the *a* place is a certain concept, or idea, or anyway a representation, of that bird. Grasping that much about the thought is essential for seeing why it has the meaning, or implications, that it does. For it has that meaning in virtue of, inter alia, its place in a system of thoughts. And it is that structure that gives it that place. But to grasp that structure is to grasp from what concepts the thought is composed, so to grasp, or have, those concepts – inter alia, the concept of having alighted. By hypothesis, the cat has no concepts. So it cannot grasp such structures. So it cannot see what the bird's having alighted means. So it cannot take the bird to have alighted. So it cannot *see* it to have done so. That sort of perceptual achievement is closed off from cats.

There is, though, something very wrong with this spin on an innocuous idea. In fact, there are many things wrong with it. But one will do for our present purpose. The sort of structure to which the spin appeals is, essentially, *representational* structure. The element *a* in a thought *Fa* has a systematic role in the way a range of items represent things. It makes a systematic contribution to their *truth conditions*, that is, to the conditions on which things will be as represented. Whereas meaning, or meaning of the sort the cat needs to appreciate, is in the world. What the cat needs to appreciate sufficiently is what it means *for the bird to have alighted.* To avoid confusion, I will call this sort of meaning factive meaning. Some ways the world is mean that it is also, or was also, other ways. That the world is, or was, those other ways follows from, or on, its being those ways. (And some ways the world might be *would* mean, if it were those ways, that it was also further ways.) The wind's howling as it is outside my window as I write this means that the power will soon be out. (And if the power does not go out, then it did not, after all, mean that: if A means B in the present sense of 'mean', then A and B.) And if it is the meaning of the world's being a way it is that one needs to appreciate, then, as we saw in considering articulations, there is no one way that is, intrinsically, the – or even a – way that a given way things are articulates: no one articulation of that way one must appreciate to grasp that that is how things are.

The point, then, is that to see things to be thus and so one must appreciate sufficiently the factive meaning of what one thus sees. That is what the cat must do to see the bird to have alighted. To do that, the cat need make no detour through systems of representations as described above. Representations are not what it needs to deal with. The cat, we may suppose, is sensitive to the bird's presence in the way cats are. That presence occupies its attention. It treats what is present as the presence of comestibles, of what is apt to flee if caution is not exercised, as the presence of something with certain size and heft and possibilities for motion, and so on. It treats the bird on the branch just as it would be fit for a cat to treat comestibles, and so on. The cat's manifest sensitivity to the presence of the bird on the branch is nothing short of appreciation (of a feline sort) of what it means for there to be a bird there; of what further features of the world follow on from the presence of that one. One might quibble as to whether the cat's appreciation of the meaning of that feature of the world is *sufficient* for it to count as taking things to be that way. By our ordinary standards it is. And once we are rid of the idea that such appreciation must proceed via a detour through representations, we have no reason to discount those standards – to think that we ordinarily speak metaphorically, or anthropomorphically, or extend to cats courtesies they really do not deserve.

Suppose a pig rounds the corner of the barn and starts to approach Pia as she is taking her morning walk. How could she fail to see there to be a pig approaching? Perhaps her attention is elsewhere, or she is in a daze. Perhaps she does not know a pig when she sees one or regularly confuses pigs with sheep. Perhaps there has been an invasion of a certain sort of antipodean marsupial. More generally, perhaps, for one or another specific reasons, for all she can see, there might not be a pig approaching. But where there is no such specific failing to point to – nothing that she missed which, if missed, leaves it open that there might not be a pig approaching, it would be correct description to say that she sees a pig approaching. Similarly, when the bird landed on the branch, the cat's attention may have been elsewhere. If it is an eccentric enough cat, it may regularly fail to distinguish birds from random detached feathers. If there are mechanized finches about, the cat may be in insufficient touch with how things are. It may be, for one or another specific reason, that for all the cat sees, or can see – for all it has taken in – no bird may have landed on the branch. But the cat's sensitivity to the way things are may rule out any such specific failing. What the cat can see may leave no other way things might be than that a bird had alighted on the branch. In such a case, lack of conceptual capacities on the cat's part is no reason to deny that the cat has seen a bird to have alighted. Only a tenuous and convoluted philosophical picture of what cognitive relations to the world *must* be, resting on a misplaced emphasis on cognitive relations to *representations* of the world, suggests that we not take our ordinary ways of describing cats in these regards at face value. We need not need that suggestion. That leaves us where we started: we need cognitive capacities to recognize perceptual achievements where they occur, or their absence where it occurs. But the perceptual achievements themselves do not inevitably – though they may sometimes – require conceptual capacities.

6. FACES

In the preceding I hope to have shown some of what the idea of a face of perception comes to, and how it derives from a prior core idea of a face of meaning, with its attendant conception of a conceptual capacity. That core idea is one that Putnam has developed and defended over more than four decades. As developed it makes meaning neither a myth (as with Quine) nor a source of a special sort of truth, insulated absolutely from the world's influence and accessible to pure armchair reflection. Nor, correlatively, is meaning, as on a platonist conception, something that decides, univocally, all decided questions as to what counts as what (as a case of knowing that P, say); at least, it certainly does not do so independently of what, on particular occasions, proper and irreducible conceptual capacities bring into view. One feature of a face of perception, emphasized in the preceding, reminds us of a feature of faces of meaning that must be kept in view. It takes proper conceptual capacities to see the shapes that meaning takes – what form, say, talk of water or of length would take in given conditions for conducting it.

This does not mean that it always takes conceptual capacities to think about water, or about length. A dog may see, and so be aware, if it is so, that there is no water in its dish.[24]

Notes

I would like to thank the Arts and Humanities Research Board of the United Kingdom for their very generous support of this research. Many people have helped me shape this work. Most notably, I have benefited greatly from discussions with Mark Kaplan, Joan Weiner, Michael Martin, Mark Sainsbury, Jennifer Hornsby, António Zilhão, and João Branquinho.

1. These lectures are reprinted in Hilary Putnam, *The Threefold Cord: Mind, Body and World* (New York: Columbia University Press, 1999). The quote is on p. 69 there.

2. Diamond introduces this image in her "The Face of Necessity", in *The Realistic Spirit* (Cambridge, MA: MIT Press, 1991).

3. The first is published in his *Philosophical Papers*, vol. 2; the second, in his *Philosophical Papers*, vol. 1 (both Cambridge: Cambridge University Press, 1975).

4. For further discussion of this idea, see my "Order Out of Messes", *Mind* 104 (January 1995): 133–144.

5. According to Putnam, Reichenbach gave this example in lectures at UCLA.

6. See his "Ueber Begriff und Gegenstand", *Vierteljahrsschrift für wissenschaftliche Philosophie* 16 (1892): 192–205.

7. See P. F. Strawson, "Truth", collected in *Logico-linguistic Papers* (London: Methuen and Company Ltd., 1971), pp. 190–213, especially pp. 196–197.

8. Gareth Evans, following Strawson, insists emphatically on doing just this. See his *The Varieties of Reference* (New York: Oxford University Press, 1982), especially chapter 4, and most especially section 4.3.

9. For further discussion of this general phenomenon, see my "Pragmatics", in *A Companion to the Philosophy of Language*, ed. Bob Hale and Crispin Wright (Oxford: Basil Blackwell, 1997), pp. 87–107.

10. Ibid, p. 183 (n. 41). As for correspondence, I take Putnam to be endorsing Wittgenstein's view that there are many ways in which words that speak of *given* things may (purport to) correspond or be true to reality, so that saying that truth consists in 'correspondence to reality' does not yet tell us how things should be in order for a given description of the world (as being such that such and such) to be true. Cf. *Wittgenstein's Lectures on the Foundations of Mathematics: Cambridge 1939*, ed. Cora Diamond (Chicago: University of Chicago Press, 1975), especially lecture 7.

11. To repeat, perceptual achievements come in at least two forms: awareness of objects and awareness of things being particular ways they are. The occasion-sensitivity of achievements of the first sort has been discussed cogently by Thompson Clarke (see his "Seeing Surfaces and Seeing Physical Objects", in

Philosophy in America, ed. Max Black [Ithaca, NY: Cornell University Press, 1965], pp. 98–114). The present discussion is indebted to Clarke in several ways. Our present concern, though, is with the second sort of perceptual achievement.

12. *The Journal of Philosophy* 69 (1972): 754–769.

13. Ibid, p. 759.

14. Ibid, p. 760.

15. Ibid, p. 761.

16. Ibid.

17. Ibid, pp. 761–762.

18. Ibid, p. 762.

19. Cf. *Philosophical Investigations*, §84.

20. J. L. Austin, "Other Minds", *Philosophical Papers*, 3rd ed. (New York: Oxford University Press, 1961), p. 84.

21. Having proof is not quite the same as being able to give proof. Pia enters the room just as Zoë, glove-clad, shoots Sid, carefully places the smoking gun in Pia's hands, and phones the police. Pia has proof – the evidence of her eyes – that Zoë did it; she knows. But, quite likely, she cannot prove it – to the police, or to anyone else.

22. Austin's ideas on this are spelled out in *Sense and Sensibilia* (Oxford: Clarendon Press, 1962), lecture 10.

23. Again, Gareth Evans is the current reference point for this idea. See note 8 above.

24. The view I ascribe here to Thompson Clarke, while wrong as charged, is also, I now think, wrongly ascribed. He expresses it to reject it.

4 Realism, Beyond Miracles

AXEL MUELLER AND ARTHUR FINE

Two things about Hilary Putnam have not changed throughout his career: some (including Putnam himself) have regarded him as a "realist" and some have seen him as a philosopher who changed his positions (certainly with respect to realism) almost continually. Apparently, what realism meant to him in the 1960s, in the late seventies and eighties, and in the nineties, respectively, are quite different things. Putnam indicates this by changing prefixes: scientific, metaphysical, internal, pragmatic, commonsense, but always *realism*. Encouraged by Putnam's own attempts to distinguish his views from one time to another, his work is often regarded as split between an early period of "metaphysical realism" (his characterization) and a later and still continuing period of "internal realism". Late Putnam is understood to be a view that insists on the primacy of our practices, while the early period is taken to be a view from outside these, a "God's Eye view". As Putnam himself stresses (1992b), this way of dividing his work obscures continuities, the most important of which is a continuing attempt to understand what is involved in judging practices of inquiry, like science, as being objectively correct. Thus Putnam's early and his current work appear to have more in common than the division between "early" and "late" suggests. In fact, Putnam's earlier writings owe much of their critical force to his adopting the pragmatic perspective of an open-minded participant in practices of empirical inquiry, a stance not explicitly articulated in these writings but rather taken simply as a matter of course.[1] Thus insofar as Putnam's early writings defend a form of representational realism, they can be regarded as attempts to articulate a realist position at work *inside* our ordinary practices of making empirical judgments. For this reason, we begin our review of Putnam's realisms by extracting from the early writings a core of principles that carries over into his current work but underwent significantly different interpretations over time. The most consequential of these reinterpretations was Putnam's attempt to mold this core into "scientific realism", a development that called for leaving the pragmatic perspective of the earlier work in favor of a picture of a unique external reality that underlies all the claims we are entitled to regard as objective. Putnam's current position can then be seen, in his own words, as the attempt "to recover our ordinary notion of representation (and of a world of things to be represented)" (1994a, p. 300) without committing the "philosophical error of supposing that the term *reality* must refer to a single superthing" (1999, p. 9).

In the following, we proceed in these steps. First, we present Putnam's position from the late fifties to, say, the early seventies (secs. I–III). In these writings, Putnam excavates a realist core that participants in fallible practices of inquiry take for granted when they make and exchange factual claims. He does this by opposing a pragmatic perspective on public practices of inquiry to the antirealist reductions of empiricism. This core can be characterized by four basic assumptions (or presuppositions), which we lay out in the next section. Three of them connect reference, truth and objectivity, and we shall refer to them as the *referential principles*. The fourth concerns a publicly shared context for empirical inquiry, and we shall call this the *environmental principle*.

The second step we shall take is to discuss some of Putnam's reasons first to adopt and then to reject scientific realism (secs. IV–VI). The appearance of "scientific realism" in Putnam's pragmatic outlook marks the beginning of an extended period of reflection on realism. In spite of the fundamental role in inquiry of the presuppositions just mentioned, any attempt to take them for granted faces a challenge from the fact, emphasized by Putnam, that we can always go wrong. Indeed, over time we have seen well-entrenched theoretical claims come to be regarded as false and terms once explanatorily fruitful lose their reference. Thus the question arises of whether the core presuppositions are merely illusions, and whether theoretical claims we make are, as vulgar instrumentalism suggests, merely tools for organizing experience. Are empirical descriptions really capable of objective truth or falsity? In reaction to this challenge, Putnam experimented with a defense of these core commitments by re-presenting them as a substantive view alternatively called "scientific realism" or "metaphysical realism". According to it, the correspondence of our true claims and referential terms with a unique mind-independent reality explains the success and the communicability of scientific claims. Thus, the referential principles are embedded in a picture of objective knowledge that tries to account for the objectivity (as opposed to the acceptance) of our empirical beliefs, and the environmental principle is substituted for by the picture of a mind-independent reality. We shall see, as Putnam came to realize, that such a defense fails badly; that it neither lends support to realism nor excludes anti-realism; in particular, instrumentalism.

Putnam's reaction to the failure is not to give up the referential principles, but to revert to the participant's perspective and to deepen his reflection
on their use in evaluating empirical claims. In the course of this reflection he
gradually dismantles the metaphysical realist picture of a mind-independent
reality and recovers the environmental principle as its pragmatic counterpart. The final step in our presentation (sec. VII) will be to characterize
some of the key features of Putnam's current work. This work undermines
the realist picture without giving up the view that the correctness of empirical statements has an objective basis. The key element here is Putnam's
insistence on the fact that, from the participant's perspective, there is no
access to any reality but by describing it in a certain way – that is, by using
certain conceptual systems. The idea of an absolutely mind-independent,
totally unconceptualized reality, since indescribable, is also not usable for
any purposes. The upshot is that our notion of a statement's objective correctness does not entail commitment to any theory-neutral domain, but
only commitment to the public revisibility of our claims. Moreover, Putnam
suggests that from ordinary language to high-level science there exist many
different conceptual systems that are perfectly capable of describing a given
situation in ways that can be and often are objectively correct. If we recognize that no particular system is forced upon us, this leads to pluralism.
Pluralism is the basis of his "common-sense realism", which urges that as
long as none of these systems accommodates the possibility that, in a given
case, a statement and its contrary could be equally correct, all of these ways
of describing our environment are on a par as far as objectivity is concerned.
For any of these descriptions, to take them as empirical amounts to applying the referential principles. According to Putnam's current view, the use
of referential semantics does not depend on relations of "correspondence",
for instance, between our sentences and the facts themselves. It simply relies on disquotation. That allows us to subject each other's assertions to the
usual inferential practices guiding our evaluation of empirical claims. By
means of disquotation, each way of making correct empirical statements
is in effect a way of organizing the situation into objects and properties.
Putnam concludes that taking all the various systems that are applicable
in a context as capable of issuing empirical statements is at the same time
taking the entities, properties and relations denoted in any system to be as
real as the ones in the others.

This constitutes his doctrine of "conceptual relativity", the view that in
some cases there is more than one way to represent the same situation, none
of which stands out as the best, because each is fully interpretable in terms of
one another (even though, if simply joined, their existential commitments

yield contradictions). Putnam uses cases of conceptual relativity to drive home the lesson that no "superthing", like the realist's picture of a mind-independent reality, is needed to ground objective judgments. Putnam's considered position thus finds a way to reconcile the core principles underlying his earliest views with a mature, reflective stance toward our practice of empirical inquiry.[2]

I. BACKGROUND: GENERAL REVISIBILITY AND THE CONTEXTUAL APRIORI

According to his own testimony at the time, and to recent self-evaluations, Putnam's earlier writings were not avowedly realist.[3] Rather, he was attempting what he called a "*mild* rational reconstruction" (1992b, p. 349) of epistemic and interpretative practices. Those reconstructions sought to correct distortions of earlier "reconstructions" in the empiricist, anti-realist tradition. Putnam begins from the perspective of the practices and, in consequence, turns out to be what we shall call "anti-antirealist" on all relevant counts.

Putnam's rejection of empiricism is built on a pragmatic, fallibilist view of inquiry. This involves a presumption of *general revisibility*, and it is expressed by Putnam in the following way: "any principle in our knowledge can be revised for theoretical reasons" (1962a, p. 48). This idea is hedged by two caveats (which also help to distinguish him from Quine on this score): "unless it is *really* an analytic principle in the trivial sense", and "many principles resist refutation by isolated experimentation". With these caveats, revisibility embodies the pragmatist view that there is no guarantee for any statement held true that it cannot turn out to be false. In this general form, revisibility applies in different ways to statements at all levels, from framework principles to theoretical and observational statements.

In a second pragmatist move, Putnam's reconstruction takes the participants' perspective (and their normative judgments) into account. This leads him to complement revisibility by a notion of the *contextual apriori*, nicely expressed by his remark that "there *are* necessary truths in physics, but they can be revised if necessary. . . . [However,] scientists were perfectly correct to assign a special status to these statements. . . . It is the task of the methodologist to explain this special status, not to explain it away" (1965, pp. 88–92). More of a classical pragmatist than Quine, Putnam's criticism of the empiricist dichotomy between analytic and synthetic statements follows Dewey's rule that, wherever we find reasonable distinctions, we should neither replace them by dichotomies nor fail to make them. Consequently, unlike Quine, Putnam does not conclude that there is no important distinction to be drawn within given bodies of belief just because each belief can be revised. Rather, his reconstruction stresses that revisibility only makes sense in practice when appropriate conditions for revision are provided (1962a, p. 42).[4] Where this is not the case, we take it for granted that the statements in question constitute objective knowledge and, if they contain extralogical vocabulary, even knowledge of the most abstract structures of the world. The complement to fallibilism in Putnam's pragmatism is a healthy confidence in the claims we have no specific reasons to doubt.[5]

When Putnam looks at inquiry from the perspective of a participant, he excavates a core of central assumptions that participants take for granted when they make and exchange factual claims. From this perspective, the anti-realist reductions of empiricism fail to do justice to the fallibilist attitude with which inquirers develop their theories. The central assumptions Putnam excavates are these: (1) normally, terms used descriptively in public practices of making and exchanging empirical claims refer; (2) statements at all levels in a system of empirical knowledge state facts, and are taken as objectively true and revisable as long as they are in use; (3) descriptively used terms can preserve reference over dramatic differences in theory and belief; (4) there is a publicly shared environment in which applications of terms and theories take place. The *referential principles* are (1)–(3). The *environmental principle* is (4).

We begin our reconstruction in section II by showing how the connection posited in (2) between objective truth and revisibility emerges from Putnam's rejection of the analytic-synthetic distinction and his discussion of the framework assumptions that are taken for granted in the formation of empirical judgments. After this, we will show in section III how the other principles emerge from considerations regarding changes in the epistemic conditions governing the application of empirical terms.

II. FRAMEWORKS AND CONTEXTS OF REVISION

In "The Analytic and the Synthetic", Putnam says "overworking the analytic-synthetic distinction is [a] ... root of what is most distorted in the writings of conventional [logical positivist] philosophers of science" (1962a, p. 33). This said, he warns against the "somewhat newer danger of denying its existence altogether", which he attributes to the effects of Quine's "Two Dogmas" (Quine 1951).[6] Thus, Putnam should be seen as reworking the distinction into a tenable view. He was so successful that the resulting position remains one of the centerpieces of his philosophy.[7] In view of the importance of the issue for understanding Putnam's epistemology, it deserves somewhat extended attention.

Putnam's discussion starts from a qualified endorsement of the holism expressed in the second, anti-verificationist and anti-reductionist argument of "Two Dogmas". The endorsement concerns Quine's metaphor that our system of knowledge is like a field of force within which there are multiple and changing justificatory dependencies between beliefs, and is combined with the idea of general revisibility. Putnam gives a special twist to this idea by splitting it up into three theses that present the system of knowledge not as a rigid, determinate unit but as a systematic, flexible and malleable whole (1962, pp. 40 ff.). The three theses are (1) the underdetermination of theory choice by experience: our beliefs face the tribunal of experience collectively and revision can come anywhere; (2) revisions are not merely local but may have more or less severe repercussions in the whole system, including changes in the meanings of fundamental terms and statements (this could be called *systematicity of knowledge and belief*); (3) statements in our conceptual system fall on a continuum extending from clear analytic cases ("All vixens are foxes") to clear synthetic cases ("There is a red balloon over there").

These theses support an important consequence: if our beliefs lie on a continuum, and if revision can strike anywhere, and if the effects of revisions are not local, then the same belief may be located at some place on the continuum at a given time (say, be fairly analytic) but, as a consequence of some revision elsewhere in the system, find itself at a different place at some other time (say, become quite synthetic). Not only the truth-value, but also the *epistemic status* of a belief in a given system of beliefs is contingent on empirical knowledge, which means that the epistemic status of a given belief is determinate only relative to a fixed body of belief.

This consequence allows Putnam to account for the revisibility of framework principles, like those of geometry. To describe their special status, Putnam takes the inside view and puts the use and function of such beliefs on display in order to make the differences with typically "synthetic" beliefs visible. First and foremost, framework principles in Putnam's sense are "included in the body of knowledge" and "thought to be *true* by someone whose knowledge that body of knowledge is" (1962b, p. 240). From the point of view of justification, they are "employed as auxiliaries to make predictions in an overwhelming number of experiments, without themselves being jeopardized by any possible experimental results" (1962a, p. 48). Accordingly, "one is not expected to give much of a reason for that kind of statement" (1962b, p. 240) because, in the context of their being so employed, "the human mind [can] not conceive their falsity" (1965, p. 88). Moreover, Putnam claims that "holding them immune from revision...was good methodology" (1965, p. 92). Another important aspect of framework principles is their role with respect to the extralogical terms they contain. The concepts articulated in framework principles are fundamental and, like the primitives of geometry, "can only be defined in terms of each other", insofar as "the use of these notions rest[s] on a particular framework of assumptions" (1965, p. 89). Thus framework assumptions come in (use-structuring) systems.

For all that, framework assumptions are revisable, given suitable circumstances. In the case of Euclidean geometry, Putnam remarks, "a statement that was necessary relative to a body of knowledge later came to be declared false in science" (1962b, p. 241). However, "The revision of framework principles is (a) possible . . . but (b) quite a different matter from the revision of an ordinary empirical generalization" (1965, p. 88). The special character of their revisibility-conditions accounts for the normative role of framework principles, while their actual revision is part of ordinary justificatory practices.

Putnam's general idea of how the statements in a framework that once were correctly held unrevisable can become the subject of evaluation and (with good reason) even be rejected as empirically false is that first the statements have to become synthetic, that is, change their status. Then they can be subjected to normal reasoning procedures for synthetic beliefs in general (and possibly be revised). Framework statements "can be overthrown only if someone incorporates principles incompatible with those statements in a successful conceptual system. . . . [They] are simply not abandoned in the face of experiment *alone*. They are abandoned because a rival theory is available" (1962a, p. 46).

Given Putnam's distinction between using experimental evidence and judging alternative conceptual systems, talk here of abandoning or overthrowing framework principles is exaggerated and, if taken as endorsing Kuhnian or Popperian epistemologies, perhaps misleading. In fact, since the status of framework principles is context-bound, what Putnam is suggesting is that, likewise, these principles are replaceable only if there actually is an adequate system in place allowing us to replace them. This suggestion leaves room to use statements of the older system within the limits and idealizations expressible by the new system, as when an architect uses Euclidean principles rather than factoring in the relativistic curvature of physical space (say, by requiring that his numbers be physically precise to the hundredth decimal place).

Putnam's main point is that the revision of framework principles is not an affair of canonical testing by empirical evidence, and this is what singles out those principles as enjoying a special status among our factual beliefs. Accordingly, the revision of framework principles requires alternative theoretical systems within which the candidates for revision can appear as empirical. Moreover, and in spite of not being subject (contextually) to ordinary empirical testing, if no alternative is in the field, framework principles – subject to revision and used as extralogical premises in explanations and justifications – have to be regarded as factual. They are, as Putnam says, "empirical in the sense of being about the world" (1963a, p. 109). This latter point leads him to reject as well the conventionalist view of framework principles as "stipulations" and the instrumentalist view of them as a "mere *systematization of the relations*" (1963a, pp. 108 and 95) – both understood as opposed to factual statements. Putnam counters the reductionist tendency to consider framework principles nonfactual just because the justification of their revision is not reducible to simple empirical arguments. He objects that the assumption of the objectivity of framework principles is presupposed by their revisibility since, if they can be seen to be false, then they have to have been held to be true, and thus held to state facts. This argument uses the epistemological presumption of general revisibility and the semantic principle that a true (extralogical) sentence is held to state a fact. Framework principles in use are factual assumptions on a par with other empirical assertions of the system, and their adoption can be supported by reasons internal to the practice of empirical belief fixation.

This idea is manifest in Putnam's explanation of why framework principles could be called "synthetic". Even before they are revised they are not analytic, in the sense of being true in virtue of the meanings of the terms involved alone, because the function of framework principles is not merely linguistic, but tied to their having systematic import. Given the same evidence, whether we assume one set or another of framework principles can make a difference to the factual claims we are able to assert or infer, and the relations among the various members of a given set of framework principles will usually yield lawlike generalizations – that is, further synthetic statements. Framework principles are not analytic because they are factually consequential. By contrast, analytic statements in a body of knowledge are "unverifiable in any practical sense, unrefutable in any practical sense, . . . true because they are accepted as true, and because this acceptance is quite arbitrary in the sense that the acceptance of the statements has no systematic consequences beyond, . . . e.g. that of allowing us to use pairs of expressions interchangeably" (1962a, p. 69). Also, when Putnam says that framework principles are " 'synthetic' to the extent that they are revisable in principle" (1962a, p. 59), this, taken together with his view on the revisibility conditions for framework principles, brings out an important aspect of "synthetic". That framework principles have the contextual status they have is connected to a significant fact, albeit a quite unempiricist and nonphysicalist one; namely, the historical and social fact that there are no adequate alternatives in the field.[8] This is important epistemologically because part of the justification of framework principles consists in the evaluation of available alternatives. In such a judgment, alternative framework systems play an evidential role in determining the merits of the existing framework. Whether there actually exist such alternatives is a not matter of stipulation or convention, which is why the acceptance of framework principles is not arbitrary. But, since there may already be such alternatives, and ones better in context than the present system, the accepted framework principles are also not absolutely necessary. By emphasizing the actual existence of alternative systems ("specific doubt" again), Putnam's treatment here cuts a nice middle ground between conventionalism and general skepticism.

Putnam sums this up by saying, "I *am* suggesting that each of us has an *empirical justification*, in a good sense of the term, for accepting the explanatory scheme" in question (1969, p. 447). The anti-antirealist insights stemming from Putnam's pragmatic transformation of the apriori into a contextual notion for systems of belief obeying the continuum thesis (c) is that framework principles in the right conditions constitute genuine knowledge, that doubting them requires knowledge and the obtaining of adequate facts, and that their truth-value therefore does not depend only on the state of the doubter/knower and the system of beliefs.

In sum, Putnam's criticism of the analytic-synthetic dichotomy yields the following conclusions. Nonlogical framework principles, the empiricists' paradigmatic candidates for "true by convention" or "nonfactual" assumptions, are and must be capable of being treated as factual beliefs if they are to do the work they actually do in normal practices of belief fixation. This capacity does not derive from their having a certain place in an inferential or justificatory network, but from their being taken as either true or false. Framework principles constitute beliefs whose correctness is not entirely determined by the system of which they are a part. Being able to defend the correctness of framework principles is not only a matter of coherence, convenience, custom or other instrumental virtues but also a matter of empirical information obtained in the application of statements of the system at large. And finally, the same statement may play the role of an unquestioned assumption in one context, and that of an empirical claim in a different context. For nonlogical statements of the framework, this means that their factuality and correctness is not a consequence of having or lacking a certain epistemic status (e.g., being counted as synthetic) but is generally presupposed for their having any function in a body of knowledge at all.[9]

As we remarked at the outset, Putnam's leading idea is general revisibility in the context of our inductive practices of empirical belief fixation. The result of his reflection on revisibilty, as applied to framework principles, is that they do convey factual information and they are revisable precisely for that: for being capable of stating facts and of being mistaken, like every other factual belief we may have. Put differently, we can say that background statements, when taken for granted, are taken to be *true* and subject to ordinary referential semantics. Thus we arrive at referential principle (2) for framework assumptions: they state facts, and are taken as objectively true and revisable as long as they are in use.

In the next section, we review how Putnam makes a related case for empirical terms, with the result (3) that occurrences of the same term in different theoretical and background contexts can (given adequate conditions) be treated as co-referential; that is, be subjected to being evaluated with the apparatus of ordinary referential semantics as well.

III. THEORY-CHANGE AND CONTINUITY OF REFERENCE

Putnam's reflections on conceptual change concern our use of empirical concepts. He shows that taking them as referential – as referring to certain things and not others – cannot be understood in verificationist terms. Rather, he argues that the decision to take a term as referring to something and as referring to the same thing on two occurrences depends on the results of actually applying it to a local environment and on how we judge the sameness and difference of those results. In particular, Putnam's analysis of the use of terms in statements that are considered revisable takes issue with two views associated with verificationism, respectively, the criterial view and holistic conventionalism. Putnam addresses the work of Malcolm for the first (Putnam 1962c) and of Feyerabend for the second view (Putnam 1963a). On the first, criterial view, each concept "F" is taken to be associated with a criterion or rule of language that determines when to say whether an arbitrary object is correctly called "F". On the second view, a whole network of beliefs or theory is used for the same purpose. On the first view, changing the criterion means changing the meaning of a term, on the second, changing the theory means changing the meanings of what we might call the theory's *eigenterms*. The main difference between the two views is that the first takes knowledge of the criteria to be a special sort of knowledge ("knowledge of meaning"), whereas the second takes the theories themselves to be largely empirical but requires a special type of justification for their acceptance ("convention", not confirmation). We look first at Putnam's response to the criterial view, and then quickly apply the lesson there to holistic conventionalism.

Putnam's counterstrategy is based on treating criteria as first and foremost part of a system of empirical statements (in fact, if they formulate at least sufficient conditions, they are to be considered as relying on laws), and on treating the use of general empirical terms as, broadly speaking, inductive. As empirical, the statements used in criteria can become subject to revision. The general idea is that criteria are descriptions of standardized situations in which the term in question can be taken to apply to an object or feature. When we (contextually or historically) change the criterion for a term but continue using it in a fact-stating practice, we no longer treat the criterial descriptions as marking relevant similarities that objects or features must meet in order to be considered as correctly described by the term specified. Nevertheless, the objects or features described by the criterion are still accessible to us after a change and are available as standard samples of the term in question (now regarded as merely *indicated* by the former criterion). The relevant similarities generated by the new criterion get anchored by finding that sufficiently many samples also satisfy the new or contextually more relevant measure to a satisfactory degree (i.e., within the contextually accepted margin of error).[10]

This idea is integrated into Putnam's picture of general revisibility by treating theoretical terms as "law-cluster terms" (1962a, p. 52 and 1963c, passim). This move sets the statements first used as "definitions" or criteria on a par with other statements containing the term. If, for example, the term "A" was introduced as denoting an object iff it satisfies the cluster F, G, H, and it is an empirical fact that such objects are always L, M, N, then it is an empirical fact that both descriptions are co-extensional under relevant initial conditions XYZ (and the relevant ceteris paribus clauses). Thus, if we need a description of some A's for whatever purpose, we have the choice to use either of the descriptions as long as the relevant conditions for applying them are fulfilled and everything is more or less normal. If we successfully use the second, "nondefinitional" description, this will, as a matter of fact, yield an object of which "A" is true. But then, in this context, it will be an empirical truth, if any, that the object determined by L, M, N also shows F, G, H. Both descriptions simply switched their relative places on the continuum of epistemic statuses, and this is a consequence of a pragmatic attitude toward using alternative means for an end. Treating "A" as a *different term* just because it was applied under a different but extensionally equivalent description would be arbitrary in such a case. Once this is accepted, however, it is possible that, under initial conditions different from XYZ, only L, M, N are satisfied and F, G, H either not applicable or *false*. This would mean that we find out that F, G, H is *false* of some objects and events that satisfy L, M, N. The question whether to apply "A" in the latter case is clearly open (in the former, clearly unclear), and deciding it will depend on whether the phenomenon in question can be reasonably identified with other things already determined for "A". Thus the empirical extension for "A" *develops* in inductive steps of judgment from application to application, judgments that involve normative attitudes and a lot of know-how acquired in the ongoing practice of inquiry. The extension is not simply determined by some one criterion given in advance. But in case we do decide to identify the results already obtained for "A" with this new case, it would be false that *all* A's are F, G, H, hence the statement initially used without restriction (as a "definition" of the class of all A's) would have been *revised*. Whether we do decide to view the revision of criteria as a change in empirical knowledge about the class of all phenomena denoted by "A" will usually depend on the historical and social situation. It depends on whether in practice we can reasonably defend lumping together the results of applying "A" as sufficiently similar; that is, it will be a question to be decided by scientific practice itself. Whatever way the decision goes, though, it will have been decided neither by one nor by the other criterion alone.

In view of the unforced character of the decisions involved, Putnam succinctly says "That criteria may be over-ridden when good sense demands is the sort of thing we may regard as a 'convention associated with discourse' . . . rather than as something to be stipulated in connection with the individual words" (1963c, 328). In cases of revision or override, the former criterion would nonetheless still be a useable way to access those elements of the extension of "A" of which it is true. Although it would not *determine* the extension of "A", it would *indicate* some A's. Putnam puts this as follows: "with the development of new scientific theories it is constantly occurring that sentences that did not previously 'have a use' . . . acquire a use – not because the words acquire *new* meanings, but because the old meanings as fixed by the core of stock uses determine a new use given the new context" (1960, p. 377). So the standard samples as determined in the old context are taken as candidates for the application of the new theory, satisfying (or not) the new descriptions in a contextually determinate way.[11]

Since any of the statements occurring in our system of empirical knowledge might turn out to be false (general revisibility), Putnam generalizes as follows: "our 'criteria' are good but not perfect indicators. The accepted criteria are often modified in the course of time . . . [and] the changes in the accepted criteria reflect the fact that we have more and more knowledge" (1962c, p. 311). Putnam takes it that investigators normally regard their ways of determining reference to be empirical and therefore inductive, revisable and fallible. Regarding those ways as an absolute warrant would mean not to let terms refer to anything that does not exactly obey given criteria, and to hold that the objects of reference are either captured correctly by those criteria or don't exist. The ascription of such absolute warrants, however, "does not do justice to [investigators'] probable intelligence. . . . In all likelihood, they knew perfectly well that their criteria were *crude* ways of detecting what they were talking about" (1962c, p. 312). In an apt expression of Gary Ebbs (2001), criteria are *cues* to motivate a decision, but not *general means to bring a decision about*.[12] Referential decisions are underdetermined by the successful application of criteria in a situation.

On the other hand, in cases where theories have undergone significant changes, we may have definite reason to worry about continuity in the use of concepts. If we have specific questions about the similarity of the results of their application to things we usually call "A", we may suspect that what is supposedly being referred to seems to have changed too much. Putnam illustrates this with the example of an (imagined) change from a criterion embodying an etiological pattern to diagnose multiple sclerosis to a virological criterion. "On [our] view the question of interest is . . . what, if anything, *answers* to our notion of multiple sclerosis. When we know what answers to our criteria . . . *that* – whatever it is – will be the 'extension' of 'multiple sclerosis'" (1962c, p. 311). We need to examine whether Putnam's "that" stands outside the practice of inquiry. His redescriptions of the situation in terms of "natural kinds", "underlying conditions" and the like certainly suggest that it did.[13] Perhaps we may need a finished theory of the universe in order to know what we are talking about and whether we are actually stating empirical facts when we take each other to do so. At least we appear to need a total extension that is fixed independently of use (as opposed to developing in use) in order to be able to state empirical truths. But do we?

According to Putnam's remark, the extension of "multiple sclerosis" is not determined by some one set of criteria in advance (or in the end),

but is developed inductively from the referents that we contextually determine using this or that criterion. Perhaps we do so in an open-ended
use of the term, as his account of the "acquisition of new senses" by the
terms we use in an ongoing practice of inquiry indicates. Thus Putnam's
picture of a contextually successful use of concepts that is open to changes
in the associated criteria actually requires much less than a fixed extension for a practice-transcendent "that". As long as we do not "know what
answers to our criteria", "the use of the term is based on the supposition
that there is *something* . . . for which our *'criteria'* are good but not perfect
indicators" (1962c, p. 311). This is enough for a minimal commitment that
is not anti-realist but also not (metaphysically) realist. That commitment
denies the verificationist principle (more generally, the principle of semantic determinism) that epistemic application conditions and current theory
taken together fix the reference of a given term, so that changes in the
former entail changes in the latter. For Putnam, by contrast, our ordinary
representational vocabulary and the fact that we take ourselves to be talking about the world cannot be explained away or overridden by epistemic
substitutes. Questions about referential continuity are relevant to questions
about conceptual continuity, not because they can be derived from theoretical or epistemic principles concerning continuity through change, but
precisely because they cannot be. When we look at holistic conventionalism, which regards theories as criteria, in the sense of algorithms for the
application of its *eigenterms*, the same argument applies *mutatis mutandis*.
So it too fails.

Putnam buttresses these reflections on reference with a continuity rule:
'don't multiply references beyond necessity' for co-reference.[14] This is not
a methodological maxim for observers of the practice but a rule of thumb
for participants who generally take the claims of others at face value. If our
practice of applying referential semantics to others' discourse is to work,
what we actually do in taking their claims at face value is best described
as working on the assumption that they referred, and that, if they used the
same word as we do, generally we can treat occurrences of it as co-referential
with our word. This is (and should be) the standard attitude toward others'
language use in a practice that allows for all sorts of revisions, including
conceptual change. This rule is clearly nonepistemic in that our success in
applying it is not derived from our estimate of the similarities of our and
the others' specific beliefs concerning the denotation of the term, nor from
anything else.

Putnam's continuity rule, as we said, is a rule of thumb for participants in
certain practices, and it reflects a standard attitude. In virtue of the former,

it is not unconditional, and in virtue of the latter, it does not issue in some "big truth" about our practice. It should not be overblown into a general maxim or global methodological requirement. It simply calls for there to be good reasons in specific and locally well-defined cases if we decide that occurrences of the same term are *not* to be treated as co-referential. Here are some of the implicit conditions of the application of the rule. (i) Users of a term assume that the statements they make in using the term are mutually relevant to the claims they are entitled to make, and that the change in beliefs associated with a term are reflective of a (self-correcting) learning process. (ii) Users of a term can rely on some continuity in the practice of theorizing; that is, the same term used by both as representing a certain kind of quantity, magnitude, classifier, etc. (iii) Users of a term can make a case for (or at least give a good account of) redescribing the entities referred to by others such that each can consider the description as a reasonable extension of their use.

These conditions are trivially satisfied in the case of users of a term in more or less contiguous ongoing practices. In these conditions, the standard attitude appears to participants as the natural attitude. It results in our fully applying referential semantics to others' claims and holding them responsible on this basis. Nevertheless, if one or more of these conditions appears to fail, this may give us reason to revise our decision to apply the rule of thumb *in this case.* Such a revision could result in our not any longer unqualifiedly applying referential semantics to the others' statements, uses of a term or whole set of beliefs.[15]

The "realist" outcome of Putnam's arguments in this section can be summed up in the thesis that concepts may remain invariant across even radical changes in belief. If they do remain invariant, taking them to be so is an interpretative decision, that is, a pragmatic affair. What we normally take to be invariant in processes of empirical belief fixation is the factor relevant for the factual claims we can use the term for, that is, its reference. Taking the concepts to be so invariant enables us to perform the evaluative and epistemic practices constitutive of our taking some of our beliefs to constitute factual knowledge. As a consequence, neither the existence nor the properties of the objects of reference are entirely dependent on the epistemic conditions we use to regulate the employment of the terms used to refer to them. Neither referentiality nor factuality derives from epistemic sources alone.

This rather lengthy discussion of Putnam's writings between 1959 and 1965 has brought to light important connections between his fallibilism (the principle of general revisibility), his pragmatic perspective and his realism.

Concerning the latter we have seen how Putnam's rejection of forms of verificationism leads to a sort of anti-antirealism that supports referential semantics as a central presupposition of public practices of inquiry. That referential apparatus involves the three referential principles we mentioned at the outset. (1) Normally, terms used descriptively in public practices of making and exchanging empirical claims refer. (2) Statements at all levels in a system of empirical knowledge state facts, and are taken as objectively true and revisable as long as they are in use. (3) Descriptively used terms can preserve reference over dramatic differences in theory and belief. Particularly for the last to work in a public practice of making and exchanging claims, there must be some shareable domain of things to which the terms apply so that we can see whether the results obtained are similar in relevant respects. Thus, Putnam's pragmatic fallibilism also presumes the environmental principle (4) that there is a publicly shared environment in which applications of terms and theories take place, the results of which underwrite the correctness or incorrectness of our claims. This doesn't mean that there must be some one uniquely specifiable domain of things for all contexts of making and exchanging claims, but that for each such context there has to be some assumption of shared objects. What is important for the success of mutual interpretation is the publicity of the objects under investigation, not the uniqueness of the way they are specified. Therefore, the assumption of publicly available objects of investigation does not depend on there being canonical ways of specifying the objects. Thus Putnam's pragmatic perspective in these early works includes what we could call a *minimal realism in use*.

Even if we accept the connection between general revisibility and referential semantics, however, we might be tempted to ask further whether that representational apparatus can be given independent justification and anchoring. The instability of science, the historical fact of the overthrow of successive theories, for example, might challenge our reliance on truth and reference for treating empirical claims. This sort of worry leads Putnam to his explanationist defense of a more substantive realism, to which we now turn.[16]

IV. ON NO MIRACLES AND (SOME) SCIENTIFIC REALISM

Putnam's arguments in favor of scientific realism in the 1970s take the form of arguments against miracles. "The positive argument for realism is that it is the only philosophy that doesn't make the success of science a miracle.

That [(1)] terms in mature scientific theories typically refer..., that [(2)] the theories accepted in a mature science are typically approximately true, that [(3)] the same term can refer to the same thing even when it occurs in different theories – these statements are viewed by the scientific realist not as necessary truths but as part of the only scientific explanation of the success of science" (1975d, p. 73). Thus Putnam begins to shape the referential principles (1)–(3) that underlie inquiry into a specifically realist doctrine that links practice with success and truth. As he says, "*practice is primary*; ... we judge the correctness of our ideas by applying them and seeing if they succeed" (1974a, pp. 268–269).[17] If they are correct, they succeed, and the truth of our beliefs is the "contribution of linguistic behavior to the success of total behavior" that accounts for the reliability of certain forms of learning (1976a, pp. 102ff.). A second formulation of the argument comes from *Meaning and the Moral Sciences* (1978). Here, Putnam says that realism is "an over-arching empirical hypothesis" (p. 20) that explains two things: "scientists act as they do because they *believe* (1) and (2), and ... their strategy works because (1) and (2) are *true*" (p. 21). This pictures science (and learning in general) as an activity that issues in publicly assessable knowledge claims. It expresses the idea that only representational success explains empirical success, for otherwise the reliability of theory-laden methods of public assessment would remain a "miracle".

At the time Putnam called the referential principles (1)–(3) "internal realism" (1976b, p. 130),[18] because he assumed, seemingly in line with the pragmatic perspective, that it constitutes "*science's* explanation of the success of science" (1992b, p. 352). But while it is correct that these assumptions correspond to what Putnam had taken to be presuppositions of the inductive practices of inquiry, we shall see that, from the outside perspective, where the practices of gaining empirical knowledge are treated as an object of study, they acquire an entirely different character.

To understand the catalytic role of these 'no miracles' reflections for Putnam's development more fully, it is useful to add another line of thought that, coupled with a certain picture, motivated his search for *arguments* in favor of realism. We saw that his endorsement of general revisibility and the contextual apriori entail the possibility that theoretical claims may turn out to be false and certain theoretical terms may come to be seen as nonreferential. But if scientific progress involved some sort of *general* representational failure, Putnam now argues, then the very "communicability of scientific results" and the practices of their public evaluation (1975c, p. 237) – in short the *publicity* of science – would become a miracle.[19] However, claims whose correctness cannot be subjected to public scrutiny for lack of shared content can scarcely be regarded as objective in any interesting sense (or taken at face value). This gives rise to another explanationist strategy, the Peircean one of deriving the concept of an objective reality from the fact of failure itself (Peirce 1868). The central thought is that our capacity to recognize beliefs as fallible would be a miracle if their correctness depended only on internal factors, like thoughts, beliefs and will. Thus the only explanation for the failure of our beliefs, collectively, is that there is something outside thought, but connected with it, that is responsible for our beliefs' correctness. Now, identify the environment we apply our theories to with the external factor (the one that is "independent of our will"), and we are left with external reality (as opposed to, say, our collective system of beliefs) as the explanans. So casting familiar practices and their results as miracles goes right along with converting the local environments (the fourth, environmental principle) into a global "external reality". This step takes the open-ended, commonsense notion of an environment with which our instruments, theories and perceptions interact and replaces it with a theoretical concept that is supposed to capture the essence of the conditions of objective truth in general. It generates a *picture* of objective knowledge, later called by Putnam "metaphysical realism" (1981, p. 49). Apart from embracing the possibility that our best theories could fail to be objective (now in the sense of "not accurately reflecting reality"), it assumes that there is some fixed, uniquely structured world of theory-independent entities ("reality") to which all true theoretical statements must correspond. Theoretical terms from all theories are linked to these entities in a determinate way, and all theoretical change reflects changes in knowledge about this reality. This reality is, as it were, the deep-structure of the world in which we live. Since our theories reflect it pretty accurately, when we act on the basis of what our theories say, we are bound to be successful. We shall refer collectively to the no-miracles argument coupled with referential principles (1)–(3) plus the picture of an external reality that grounds judgments of objectivity as the *explanationist defense* of scientific realism.

Principles (1)–(3) have an ambiguous status in Putnam's philosophy at the time. On the one hand, without the realist picture, they seem to underwrite a quite natural account of the communicative basis of scientific inquiry as a public activity dealing with fallible factual claims. This basis consists, quite simply, in taking each other's claims at face value wherever reasonable and thus subjecting them to the norms of deductive and inductive inference, which in turn are essential to regarding others' empirical statements as evaluable in fallible practices of acceptance. One of Putnam's achievements was to show that the verificationist attempt to treat reference

as determined from epistemic sources fails to do justice to many important features of this practice (underdetermination, general revisibility, anti-
absolutism, etc.). But at the time of the explanationist defense Putnam was
tempted to go beyond the pragmatic treatment of objectivity that emerges
from the presupposition of general revisibility. The picture added to the
three referential principles tries to go further by holding that what *really*
accounts for the correctness of our claims is a definite way the world is.
Thus the role of the realist picture is to distinguish between beliefs that are
objectively right and those that are merely intersubjectively acceptable.

However, the referential principles that we need to invoke if we take each
other at face value and as subject to the norms of fallible inquiry run into
well-known problems when they become entangled with the realist picture
and the denial of verificationism. The classical difficulty is the coupling of
independence, externality and connectedness that issues in a problem of
access. If we take a given theoretical statement and, in the pursuit of our
aims, want to know whether it corresponds to reality, we need access to the
"real" state of affairs. But if the state of affairs is independent of beliefs or
cognition, we fall into a regress, since with respect to whatever cognition we
use to gain access, we will need to know that *it* too corresponds with reality.
Similarly, if we demand that the truly objective entities our terms refer to
are *independent* of all cognition and we want to determine the referent of a
particular term, we will need cognitive contact with it, which means that
we take the referent, not as independent, but *as observed* or *as described*.[20]
As Putnam frequently stressed, the referential principles cannot tell us how
to *establish* referential connections but presuppose them.[21] The problem of
access turns precisely on the question of how to have this presupposition
in the picture. So, if our cognitive access to reality is neither immediate
nor guaranteed (e.g., by epistemic criteria), and reference and truth consist
in a determinate correspondence to mind-independent reality (to which
we don't have such access), then we seem incapable of providing reasons
for the belief that our terms refer or that our statements are true in this
correspondence sense.

This presents us with the following situation. The referential principles alone account for the public and communicative character of scientific
practice, without either verificationism or the realist picture. The role of
the realist picture was to explain the objective revisibility (and independent confirmability) of the factual beliefs dealt with in these practices. But
the picture, by opening up the problem of access, blocks any defense of
the referential principles that depends on direct access to the referents of
our terms. Thus, accepting the picture to explain the objectivity of our

claims actually weakens our prima facie reasons to believe in the referential principles. However, if we were to abstain from assuming those principles, we would cease to regard our claims as referring and being true (or false), and then we could hardly regard ourselves as engaged in "discourse" at all. Similarly, without the realist picture, our "discourse", it seems, would be merely a socially shared activity, but not an objectively evaluable practice concerned with empirical knowledge. It thus comes to seem that we need to restore our confidence in the referential principles *with* the realist picture. In that case, however, we need a line of argument that avoids any form of immediate access. Putnam's flirtation with the explanationist defense can be seen as just such an attempt to find an *indirect* argument for the referential principles *with* the realist picture.[22] Does it work, or even, could it work?

V. WHY THE EXPLANATIONIST DEFENSE DOESN'T WORK

The expression "success of science" is ambiguous. It could mean the (instrumental, predictive, empirical) success of scientific theories – which is what the referential principles are about – or it could mean the success (e.g., reliability) of scientific methods in producing empirically correct statements. With respect to both, we can have prima facie doubts about the actual threat of miracles (and the corresponding comfort of explanations).

Seen from the pragmatic perspective of reasons that bring us to accept a theory, the very idea of an explanation of the "success of science" in the first sense seems puzzling.[23] Of course, acceptance is underdetermined by evidence, and theories can be accepted but turn out to be false. But when we accept a theory as true, the most compelling reason is that the theory is successful, and when we accept an alternative, one of the reasons why it is in the field as a serious candidate is that it is at least as successful as the theory to be replaced. Both in the process of acceptance and in the process of revision, success is a *condition* rather than a *result* of taking theories to be true. Our practice of theory acceptance, in requiring success as an entitlement, pragmatically excludes that we might take an unsuccessful theory to be true. But then the best explanation of the success of theories in mature sciences is that these are just the theories we admit.[24] In this sense of "success" there is nothing in the success of our theories that requires explanation. However, this also seems to extend to a defense of the strength of *methods*. For we often take the procedures of empirical sciences as our standard, so our practice entails that we expect the methods of science to be more successful than other methods.[25] But then it is pragmatically incoherent to ask for an explanation of the success of science as if the latter were not to be expected ("a miracle").

One might respond, as Putnam (1981, p. 39) does to van Fraassen, that we could not require success for theories or methods if they could not have it (or only happened to have it). Realists would add that only theories which correspond to a mind-independent reality succeed, and the others don't. At this point the realist moves outside the normative participant's perspective to what Putnam calls the "God's Eye point of view" and insists that we take up the "challenge" of explaining success. At the same time, the realist tries to stand inside our practices in order to take scientific successes seriously. These retrograde motions entangle the explanationist defense in problems that run deep.[26]

First, the problem of access returns with a vengeance when we compare ordinary explanatory practices in science and the explanationist defense. Among the requirements on explanatory, empirical hypotheses is that, in principle, they be independently testable and that they generalize. This prevents a hypothesis from being just a shortcut for summarizing some particular experiment or pattern of observations, and thus is crucial for our treating the proposed hypothesis as factual. In terms of Putnam's early philosophy of science, a factual element requires that the parameters in question be part of a law *cluster*, a system or structure of law-like connections that work in sufficiently independent ways to be mutually confirmable. In view of this, the content of the explanationist defense is peculiar. Since the defense encompasses *all* reality and *every* theory that is to have *any* empirically ascertainable content, it follows there is nothing left for it to generalize to. Moreover, whatever access we propose to the parameters in question (to "reference", "reality", etc.), depends on using our referential principles along with the realist picture of a mind-independent world. But then, according to the usual standards, the explanationist defense is not a proper explanatory, empirical hypothesis after all. The explanans does not generalize and it cannot count as factual insofar as it employs parameters that are not accessible without assuming that very hypothesis; that is, it is not independently testable. Indeed, the explanationist defense seems trapped in a vicious circularity.

But perhaps that is unfair. Precisely since the explanationist defense ranges over all science and takes all of science as its evidential base it needs to cover only *one big situation*. What else should it generalize to? So, it cannot have been intended to be empirical or scientific in the sense of confirmable. Perhaps when supplemented with the realist picture the referential prin-ciples are framework assumptions – very general, unstated, unproblematic but needed as background. Then, as Putnam so convincingly argued in his early writings, they would indeed be factual. However, there are (at least) two reasons why they cannot count as framework principles. One is obvious: they fail the test of not needing reasons, since the explanationist defense is offered as just such a reason! The second is that there are viable alternatives, and so they fail the test of being *required* as auxiliaries in our empirical justifications.

As to the second, it is clear that the fact (if it is one) that our theories are true and their terms refer does not make them successful at any task, unless "success" is *defined* as representational success. But then the defense is obviously circular, as then the truth and reference of our theories explains the truth and reference of our theories (their representational "success"); hence Putnam's insistence on practice rather than representation as primary, and his emphasis that the successes in question involve application of theories to empirical circumstances and observing whether the results are, relative to the expectations warranted by the theory, positive or negative. But this clarification of the explanandum gives rise to a perfect symmetry between realism and a form of antirealism, namely instrumentalism.[27] As Putnam later recognized: "when we try to make the vague claims of the metaphysical realist precise, we find that they become compatible with strong forms of antirealism" (1992b, p. 353). In our context, this can be seen as follows. Suppose "success" involves applying a theory to certain empirical circumstances and observing whether the results accord with the theory. Then, if we have positive results, this warrants saying that in the given circumstances (under the assumed interpretation) our theory was reliable. Thus the hypothesis that our theory is reliable *in general* explains why, under these particular circumstances, we were successful. By contrast, the realist would say that our theory's correspondence with reality explains its success because the mechanisms described by the theory work as the theory says and, if they do, the observed result must obtain. Now, in all cases where the realist can invoke this explanation in terms of correspondence to reality – namely, the cases where the theory actually does explain the result of an application – the instrumentalist can invoke his explanation of the result in terms of the general reliability of the theory. Actually, we find that wherever there is some specific success and a satisfactory explanation based on the realist picture, we can reinterpret "truth" in an instrumentalist manner, and the result is an explanation that is perfectly acceptable from an instrumentalist point of view.[28] But then it is false that realism is the only, or, in view of the symmetry, even the best explanation of success. In any event, the realist suggestion that, because they have no alternative, the referential principles, when combined with the realist picture, are framework principles does not work.

VI. WHY THE EXPLANATIONIST DEFENSE COULDN'T WORK

This brings us to a second reason against regarding the realist picture as necessary in scientific reasoning. These considerations will bring us in contact with Putnam's more recent work, as this last effort to revive the explanationist defense forces us back to the participant's perspective, and thus backfires on the realist. How could a semantic picture help us understand the success of scientific practice, a historically situated and practical process?[29] Whatever is responsible for particular scientific success is not some semantic property of our theories but a feature of the environment in which they have been employed. For example, the bridge holds up because it is statically sound, not because of the truth of our theory describing the bridge as statically sound. Likewise, no additional account of truth or reference is needed to explain the success of scientific activities insofar as they are explicable at all. From the perspective of our explanatory use of theories, truth adds no more than disquotation;[30] the statement in our theory "the bridge is sound" is (empirically) true iff (in fact) the bridge is sound. In general we can say that wherever scientific practice results in a good explanation for some given success, the explanation does not get better (simpler, more acceptable, more cogent) by adding the referential principles and the realist picture.

This argument might be seen as question begging insofar as it supposes that semantic reasons are *nonsubstantive*, and therefore are the wrong kind of reason (aren't we smuggling in an analytic-synthetic distinction?). But this charge overlooks the scope of the explanationist defense. Scientific (first-level) reasons provide local and specific grounds for holding a certain belief. The explanationist defense works globally, supposedly applicable to all scientific reasoning, and unspecifically. (In parallel with Peirce's famous "paper-doubts", one could call it a "paper-reason".) Once we take specific instances, for example, by saying that some particular theoretical statements refer (are true, correspond to mind-independent reality) and we "disquote" (i.e., read the statements as making factual claims), then we are simply adding some empirical data (the theory's laws and its results) to our explanation of a certain success. None of these statements speaks of mind-independent reality as such, while each of them, if accepted as true, is taken to state an empirical fact. When actually used in the explanation of given successes, the specific instances of the explanationist defense result in ordinary, empirical explanations. So, taken globally, the referential principles with the realist picture do not add explanatory power to science, and when taken in specific instances, the principles simply convert specific theoretical and observational statements into factual claims. The realist picture drops out, and we have a more or less reliable ordinary, first-order explanation involving "just more data".

With Putnam, we conclude that the metaphysical realism of the explanationist defense is not needed for an explanation of any empirical successes of science. In its explanatory work, science takes care of itself. This rules metaphysical realism out as part of the framework principles presupposed in scientific explanation. Thus the three referential principles need not be understood in terms of a mind-independent reality and our relation to it. In view of this, we conclude that the explanationist defense of scientific (or metaphysical) realism is a failure.

Earlier we noted that, under the assumptions of metaphysical realism, the problem of access stands in the way of any direct reason to believe that our claims have the referential features they seem to have when we use them to state facts. Therefore, it seemed, we needed an indirect reason under that assumption. Now we see that the most promising indirect reason fails. In this situation, there are three obvious moves: (*a*) rejecting the referential principles, (*b*) rejecting the realist picture, or (*c*) rejecting anti-verificationism. Putnam's early pragmatism allots a central role to the referential principles (*without* the realist picture) in our public practices of making and exchanging factual claims. For him, our use of these principles simply embodies the communicative attitude of taking each other's claims at face value, and that means if we take them as true, then we take them as stating facts. This was part of his motivation to look for an indirect argument instead of just resigning before the problem of access. So, (a) is not a plausible option given Putnam's pragmatic outlook. The fact that our attempts to ground the picture of a mind-independent reality have forced us out of the "God's Eye point of view" back into the perspective of our practices already indicates that the realist picture lacks coherence. That impression deepens once we realize that instrumental success in science involves interacting with the environment just as much as reference through indication does. Moreover, if success counts as relevant to our knowledge (confirmation, information, etc.), then success is as much a cognitive way of accessing the world as reference. Thus, the problem of access begins to look like a red herring. This will be the starting point of Putnam's recovery of our ordinary notions of representation and reality. He will also find independent reasons that seriously undermine the realist picture, so it is fair to say that the failure of the explanationist defense leads him to that recovery. Nevertheless, for quite a while, Putnam combined (b) and (c), and steered what he called a "moderately verificationist course" by identifying truth with warranted assertibility under epistemically ideal conditions.[31] He has frequently stressed that he considers this attempt as flawed and now rejects this conception of truth (1994d, pp. 242ff. and 1992b). At one point, he even portrays his former self as "simply past[ing] together elements of early modern realism and elements of the idealist picture" (1999, p. 18). The suggestion is that, in spite of having independent reasons against the picture of a mind-independent but fixed and unique reality, he was still worrying about the problem of access – the one verificationism is geared to – posed by the very picture in which he had no more deep faith (1999, pp. 3–20).

Once this flirtation was over, however, Putnam jettisoned the realist picture, remarking that "the attempts at clear formulation never succeed in capturing the content of 'metaphysical realism' because there is no real content there to be captured" (1992b, p. 353). At the same time, Putnam preserves a version of the referential principles for our fallible practices involving empirical claims, just as he had characterized them in his earlier writings. Putnam's current work aims at providing a better understanding of those principles as natural assumptions, neither explanatory nor problematic, and thus not in need of any special assurance or license for their use. Developing this position is what he calls "rejecting 'realism' [read: the realist picture] in the realistic spirit" (1990a, p. 42) by "the recovery of our ordinary notion of representation (and of a world of things represented)" (1994b, p. 300). It moves from miracles to a reality beyond miracles, our practices themselves. The explanationist defense of realism withers away, as do the miracles, and something better results from the interaction between the pragmatic outlook Putnam had developed in his early work and his fling with realist metaphysics. (This is why we called his reflections on the defense "catalytic".) Putnam's considered position is thus aptly called "pragmatic realism".

VII. PRAGMATIC REALISM

In his more recent work, Putnam has begun to reflect on the pragmatic perspective of his early work and on pragmatism itself. Thus we see a number of articles dedicated to the study of philosophers in the pragmatist tradition, and above all to the work of the later Wittgenstein. Moreover, Putnam's interest in these studies is not merely exegetical but systematic, as becomes most apparent in his (1995). We would like to close this essay with a perspective on some of the elements of Putnam's current, complex view. That view presents us with a multifaceted dissolution of the metaphysical realist picture and its attraction, while at the same time preserving the commonsense realism that participants rely on when they regard the claims they make as fallible. Putnam characterizes this program as follows: "preserving commonsense realism while avoiding the absurdities and antinomies of metaphysical realism . . . is something I call pragmatic realism . . . it is a view that takes our familiar commonsense scheme, as well as our scientific . . . and other schemes at face value" (1987, p. 17). Thus Putnam's reaction to the failure is not to give up the referential principles (1)–(3) but to revert to the participant's perspective and from there to deepen his reflection on their use in our practices of evaluating empirical claims. In the course of this reflection he dismantles the metaphysical realist picture and recovers the environmental principle (4), the commonsense idea of a publicly shared environment, as its pragmatic counterpart. We shall approach Putnam's current position by discussing its central elements, the first of which is the *participant perspective*.

The first conclusion Putnam draws from the failure of the explanationist defense is to insist that questions about the objectivity of our knowledge-claims can be discussed usefully only from the perspective of participants in ongoing practices of belief-fixation, because the results reached there are the only paradigms of empirical knowledge that we have. "The heart of pragmatism, it seems to me . . . was the insistence of the supremacy of the agent point of view. If we find that we must take a certain point of view, use a certain 'conceptual system' . . . then we must not simultaneously advance the claim that it is not really 'the way things are in themselves'" (1987, p. 70). The central point of Putnam's subsequent arguments is to show that this decision to abjure the God's Eye point of view is *not* equivalent to abjuring claims to objectivity, but rather shows the opposite. It shows that the picture of objectivity the metaphysical and scientific realists wanted to see our practices aiming at is neither operative nor needed, given the normative resources used in inquiry. This brings us to a second element of Putnam's current position, *access and the independence of word and object*.

From the perspective of practices in which we use a language to make and evaluate empirical statements, we find that there is no *other* access to whatever we can come to regard as real than through making statements and taking them to be, if true, then descriptions of reality. Putnam puts the point as follows: "*Given* a language, we can describe the 'facts' that make the sentences of that language true in a 'trivial' way – using the sentences of that very language" (1987, p. 40). Thus, from the standpoint of the practices of empirical inquiry, there simply is no *global* problem of access. When we come to take a statement to be true, we succeed in stating a fact. Putnam provokes the metaphysical realist by saying just this: "There are 'external facts', and we *can say what they are*" (1987, p. 33). When Putnam complements this statement by reaffirming the participant's perspective in saying, "what we *cannot* say – because it makes no sense – is what the facts are *independent of all conceptual choices*" (1987, p. 33), he points to a fresh approach to the problem of access. From the fact that we approach the world by making (true/false) statements it certainly does not follow that we have (can have) no access to it. Rather, we should conclude the opposite, that we access any "reality" that can play a role in helping us to determine whether a given statement is correct. From the perspective of participants who use language to make and evaluate empirical statements, the apparently astonishing claim that we have no access to "unconceptualized" reality is a triviality, for it "does not mean that reality is hidden or noumenal; it simply means that you can't describe the world without describing it" (1992a, p. 123).[32]

From this perspective, the metaphysical realist picture defended in the explanationist defense, the view that our claims have to "correspond to mind-independent reality" in order to be objectively evaluable, arises from conflating the "(platitudinous) idea that language can represent something which is itself outside of language" (1994b, p. 300) with the epistemological concern that in order to be justified in applying ordinary referential semantics, we have to be *certain* that there is something in the world that is connected (in the right way) to the descriptions we use. But the epistemological concern disappears when we realize, for example, that "according to our descriptions themselves, the word 'quark' is one thing, and a quark is quite a different thing" (1992a, p. 123). This difference is not between the "undescribed" or "neutrally accessible" on the one side and the "contaminated" on the other. Because we know how both the word and the object reached by disquotation can be described, there is usually no reason to believe that the respective entities (word and object) are necessary for either the existence or the specific properties of each another. According to our practices themselves, just as facts about spelling are not relevant to facts about quarks, in general, the fact *described by using* a certain linguistic expression in assertoric discourse and the fact *of using* this expression are, as Putnam says, "independent" in any sense we can understand, without involving anything "outside" the describable (1994b, p. 301).[33] This brings us to a third element, *referential semantics and standards of fallible inquiry*.

According to Putnam's current view, applying referential semantics to beliefs that can claim to be objective is not a case of backing up our claims with a sort of guarantee. Rather, when we apply ordinary referential semantics to a class of statements, we regard them as having truth-values that do not depend on the mere fact of our acceptance, but on the result of a fallible *evaluation* (1992a, p. 77). Thus, "to say that truth is objective . . . is just to say that it is a property of truth that whether a sentence is true is logically independent of whether the majority of the members of the culture *believe* it to be true. . . . this is . . . simply a feature of our notion of truth" (1988, p. 109). So the problem of objective knowledge is the local problem of determining the truth-value of statements used to make empirical claims. The problem is not about comparing statements with reality as such (whatever *that* is). The problem is just that we do not know in advance, or by the mere fact that a statement is used on a certain occasion, or by the fact of just accepting the sentence, which of the two possibilities (true or false) is the case. But if one of a pair of contrary statements is taken to be true, its contrary cannot be *simultaneously* true. This means that in a language to which we apply referential semantics, for every answerable question there is *just one right answer* in the language. The metaphysical realist picture conflates this with the idea that there is a single descriptive basis that yields right answers for *all* answerable questions.

Choosing a particular way of describing a situation may amount to a "convention" or a matter of expedience, since it is not determined by the norms of referential semantics itself; still, this sense of convention "is not the view that, in some inconceivable way, it's all *just* language" (1987, p. 36), because when we want to know whether a given empirical statement (as opposed to its contrary) is to be taken as true, "the *answer* does not thereby become a matter of convention" (1987, p. 33). It is not a matter of convention because inquiry is inductive and open-ended. Recall Putnam's pragmatic criticism of the criterial or conventionalist ploys with respect to the semantics of empirical terms. From our perspective as participants in fallible practices of evaluation, talk about the "independence" of the world just amounts to the idea that the result of evaluating a certain statement in a situation is not (or rather, must not normally be) determined by consensus or convention. Rather, making a decision as to truth or falsity involves using referential semantics in a publicly shared environment in view of all the knowledge we can bring to bear on the question. With regard to this sort of decision, Putnam's work involves an increasing generalization of his earlier rejection of criterial views, resulting in his rejection of "algorithmic" pictures of the procedures of application in favor of the view that every evaluation in context involves "general intelligence" rather than specific knowledge of assertability-codes (1988, p. 75).[34] What enters into the determination of the truth-value of a given statement can vary enormously from context to context, and always involves trade-offs and judgments of reasonability. Consequently, what is meant by "independence" is not some unique characteristic running through all those cases of settling on a truth-value. In this approach to objectivity, using ordinary referential semantics (with disquotation) is, as Putnam succinctly remarks, "necessary for *logical* reasons, not for *descriptive* reasons" (2001a, p. 11). He explains this by the observation that "If . . . statements are . . . fully governed by norms of truth and validity . . . [then they are, AM/AF] subject to the standards of fallible inquiry" (2001b, IV, 2). Thus, Putnam recovers the referential principles (1)–(3) from a thorough examination of the requirements of our fallible procedures of inquiry by way of deflation: they are not descriptive but normative. Still, we need to understand how Putnam integrates deflationism (cf. 1999, pp. 52–59; 2001b, IV; and 2001a, pp. 9–14) into his pragmatic epistemology. This will bring us to his combination of *contextual evaluation and general revisibility*.

The task is set when Putnam says "deflationism about truth – as long as it involves . . . a verificationist account of understanding – adopts the most disastrous feature of the antirealist view. . . . What is wrong in [this kind of, AM/AF] deflationism is that it cannot properly accommodate the truism that certain claims about the world are (not merely assertable or verifiable but) *true*" (1999, pp. 55–56). Putnam has in mind *contextually unproblematic* statements like "there is a table in front of me" when uttered or thought while putting down one's cup. This might suggest that Putnam is reintroducing a substantive notion of truth,[35] one where ordinary language provides the version of the world as it "really is".

We think not, however; rather we think Putnam is making a methodological point. In contexts where truth is at issue we take various statements as factual. This means we take them as true, although capable of being false. "The fundamental features of our cognitive situation (are): that we are *fallible* (knowledge claims are defeasible), and that *we have the right to claim to know, in certain situations, at certain times, and for certain purposes*. . . . Without genuine knowledge claims, there is nothing to be fallibilistic about" (1998, pp. 254 and 262). Such unproblematic, contextual judgments often reoccur in several contexts (cf. Fine's "local judgments of truth"

[1996a]). Indeed, because of their familiarity (as opposed to their "thinness"), they work much like contextually a priori statements and, as a moving part of reasoned judgment, are essential to taking *any* claim as true (Putnam 2002, pp. 17ff.). Consequently, if statements evaluated with their help are to be objective, we must regard these contextual judgments themselves as *capable of objectivity* (not merely assertability). But this does not make them true substantively (describing how it "really is"). As with the contextually apriori, as context shifts they can be revised (without change of meaning) and thus lend themselves to neither a substantive nor a verificationist reading.

This treatment of objectivity supplements the principle of revisibility with a *principle of contextual evaluation* according to which evaluations of truth are always made in a context of specific reasons and conditions. A corollary is that one cannot divide statements into "unproblematic" or "problematic" independently of context. Of course, this does not mean that we cannot (or need not) make the contextual distinctions required for reasoned evaluations (cf. 2002, p. 22). Putnam's pragmatic epistemology thus embodies two general norms governing objectivity. First, every evaluation involves commitment to judgments of reasonableness that involve distinctions between unproblematic and problematic statements for the case at hand. Second, the result of an evaluation is expressed in terms of truth and falsity, or related oppositions of (objective) correctness. Thus the semantic categories and the contextual allocation of status are neither descriptive, nor gratuitous, nor reducible, nor substantive. Rather, Putnam regards them as methodologically normative with respect to objectivity. This brings us to *commonsense realism, pluralism and the environment.*

That this picture of objectivity and inquiry from the participant's perspective is not only satisfied by one but *many* descriptions is the basis of Putnam's pluralistic "commonsense realism". It starts from observations like "we may partly describe the contents of a room by saying that there is a chair in front of a desk, and partly describe the contents of the same room by saying that there are particles and fields of certain kinds present" (1994d, p. 243). At another place, Putnam says more generally that "the same situation, in a perfectly commonsensical sense of 'the same situation', can be described as involving entirely different numbers and kinds of objects" (1992a, p 120). It is important to see that the notion of *the same room, the same situation* or *same state of affairs* Putnam uses does not reimport the problem of direct access to a reality that wears its identity for users of various ways of describing it, as it were, on its sleeve, an unproblematic "given". Seeing how, though, is a delicate matter, and it involves us in another round of reflection. What is at issue is the recovery of (4), a publicly shared environment, without identifying it with "unconceptualized", "mind-independent" or "external" reality.

The idea underlying Putnam's view is the notion of a publicly shared environment as the normal domain in which evaluations of truth take place. He starts from the premise that we are "creature[s] with a certain kind of normal environment, and with a certain history of individual and species interaction with this environment" (1994c, p. 289). While this could still invite the impression that we are dealing with a *given*, that impression fades when we consider Putnam's pluralism and his deflationist way with the global problem of access. Recall that the problem of access for two descriptions that are used simultaneously in a situation is solved by disquotation, and thus each of the users of a description has access to the situation. The question then becomes what is involved when we regard the situation as *shared*. Concerning this Putnam says, "access to a common reality does not require incorrigibility . . . [and] access to a common reality does not require access to something *pre-conceptual*. It requires, rather, that we be able to form *shared* concepts" (1995, p. 21).

This is somewhat enigmatic, but we can try to make it clearer by expanding on the possibilities Putnam indicates. We take him to say that sharing the situation does not depend on assuming either that we share a "neutral" description we agree on (e.g., "as it really is") or that we have direct access to the fact that the situation is shared. When Putnam speaks of our forming shared concepts, we take him to be employing his noncriterial view of concepts. This suggests that the publicity of the situation among users of different descriptions can be seen as the result of the same interpretative skills and practices that are at work in our use of inductive concepts as they are exhibited *within* each of the different descriptive practices. They "form shared concepts" by finding a way of approximating the extensions of the other description in extensions of their own, and by finding that, once this is done, the respective inductive developments of these extensions harmonize in sufficiently good measure in this type of context.[36] What is required for this possibility is that there be a sufficient covariance in truth-judgments by each of the users of the different descriptions in what each of them regards (in their own ways) as the same sort of situation as the ones described by the (respectively) same statement on other occasions. In this light, Putnam's pluralism is committed to the view that "all situations have many different correct descriptions, and that even descriptions that, taken holistically, convey the same information may differ in what they take to be 'objects'" (1994b, p. 304). Thus someone describing the contents of a room in terms of chairs and someone describing it in terms of clouds of fermions can "share the concept" by taking the description of the room as containing three chairs to indicate the situation consisting of such-and-such clouds of fermions, and vice versa.[37] One needs to be careful here, however, because the mutual reinterpretability of the descriptions in question does not imply that both descriptions are pragmatically equivalent through all contexts of application. If I want to know where my son has put the chair, I will not (in fact, must not) call up Fermi-Lab to find it; and if I want to know whether what is in the cup is coffee or muddy water, a redescription in terms of "H_2O, give and take some impurities" won't help me solve my problem. Still, this is compatible with saying that, if there is a beverage in the cup at all, then the chemical description will not say that, in fact, there is nothing or that there is a piece of platinum. Recall that the question was not how to produce good overall translations, but to find out whether Putnam's presupposition of a shared environment smuggles in the metaphysical realist's picture. If our reading is correct, it does not. What is required for "sharing" a situation and considering it as shared is the elaboration of an overlap in respective partial extensions (of the respective correlated concept-signs) as applied to the environment (as parsed by each version into *their* relevant parameters). It does not rely on shared descriptions. Since the partial extensions are accessible, in ordinary inductive ways, to the users of either description, there is also no supposition of direct access. Finally, since in case the correlated descriptions disagree this can produce a revision of one of the descriptions by way of the other, Putnam's view requires no incorrigibility. Thus access to a situation *as shared* is not through neutrality or direct intuition, but through common inductive practices involving communication and cooperation. To this effect, Putnam cites Dewey by saying that "the whole interaction is *cognitive*" (1994c, p. 289).

After his deflationary recovery of the three referential principles, Putnam can thus claim to have reclaimed the fourth, the presupposition of a publicly shared environment, from its identification with the mind-independent, external reality in the metaphysical realist picture. Instead of being "unconceptualized", the environment contributing to the determinacy of our evaluations of empirical statements appears as richly conceptualized and multiply accessible, but not predetermined by our evaluative practices. This brings us to the final element in Putnam's current view that we want to feature: *ontological anti-reductionism and conceptual relativity.*

The last step in Putnam's deepened reflection concerns the *ontological* idea contained in the metaphysical realist picture of a uniquely structured domain as the basis of the objectivity of our claims. In order to address this question, he draws ontological conclusions from the views developed so far (commonsense realism, pluralism and objectivity). They imply that the several descriptions that may be applicable in a particular case, while perhaps ordered into better and worse when it comes to answering different questions, are on a par with respect to objectivity. Each of them can be taken at face value, as stating facts if taken to be true. Putnam accordingly regards his pluralist, commonsense realism as "a view that takes our familiar commonsense scheme, as well as our scientific . . . and other schemes at face value" (1987, p. 17). At the same time, via disquotation, each makes different ontological assumptions that we, if we take them at face value, accept as a matter of course. This has two related consequences. The first consequence is that, in each such case of multiple describability, we have a choice of an acceptable way of describing the situation that is not dictated by the situations themselves. This amounts to choosing a set of ontological categories for organizing the situation. Putnam consequently says (with Kant and Goodman), "It is *we* who divide up 'the world' – that is the events, states of affairs, and physical, social, etc., systems that we talk about – into 'object', 'properties', and 'relations', and we do this in a variety of ways" (1994d, p. 243).

The full ontological force of Putnam's pluralism comes to light in view of the anti-reductionist conclusion he draws from applying referential semantics to multiple descriptions each of which has an equal title to objectivity. Given such multiple descriptions, the objects, properties and relations taken for granted in each are as real as the objects, properties and relations taken for granted in the others. Thus, "the statement that there are electrons flowing through a wire may be as objectively true as the statement that there is a chair in this room or as the statement that I have a headache. Electrons exist in every sense in which chairs (or sensations) exist. . . . Here I *am* a 'scientific realist'" (1982a, p. 495). In other words, "commonsense tables and chairs and sensations and electrons are *equally real*" (1987, p. 12).

Putnam is now in a position to subvert the heart of the metaphysical realist picture itself: the idea that our standards of objectivity presuppose the notion of a fixed, uniquely structured reality. The argument takes as given that we do use various contextually equivalent ways of describing the world to make empirical statements. We evaluate them according to the logical norms of referential semantics and the epistemological standards of a fallible methodology. Since the descriptions are not ontologically equivalent, the only way in which the ontological component of the metaphysical realist picture can be understood is as the *epistemological* thesis that there is one among the descriptions that is the best in all contexts. That unique one would then serve as a reduction base for deciding the truth-values of any of our empirical statements. Putnam has a number of arguments against this epistemological thesis, one of the most effective of which is his "companions in the guilt" argument (1982b; 1990a, pp. 135–142; 2002, p. 23). Roughly, suppose one disqualifies all claims that are not reducible to fundamental science as "subjective". This would likewise affect the normative notions at work in scientific methodology itself, and thus make scientific practice itself "subjective". But this is a *reductio* of the view that objectivity is grounded in an epistemologically unique basis.

Putnam's treatment of conceptual relativity is designed to show the same *reductio*. Here he focuses on cases whose structure inverts that of the cases used in his pluralist arguments. The general structure relevant to conceptual relativity is that "There are ways of describing what are (in some way) the 'same facts', which are (in some way) 'equivalent' but also (in some way) 'incompatible'" (1987, p. 29). The example Putnam often uses is where three individuals of some sort (say, particles) can be redescribed in a way that counts not only individuals but also all nonrepetitive combinations of these as "objects" (i.e., it counts "mereological sums"). In every situation in which objects are grouped according to one of the versions and counted, there is a correlate in the other version. If one of the versions is applied to a situation, say the initial one, and yields a clear result ("3"), then the other version yields an equally clear result ("7"). (In general, if there are n objects in the first version, then there are (2^n-1) objects in the second.) In each version there is only one right answer to the question of how many objects there are. Likewise, the correctness of the result does not depend on how many objects users of each version think there are in a situation. If we take any (scientific) statement referring to any sort of object that is held to be true of a certain situation or physical system, there will be a corresponding statement about the same physical system that groups the elements of the situation according to the norms of mereology, and this latter will be true of the situation iff the former is. The same holds for inferential relations between sets of scientific statements; truth is preserved. Thus both versions are equivalent in expressive power, are fully interpretable in one another and preserve explanatory relations as well as predictive power under transformation. As Putnam says, "the two schemes are in practice thoroughly equivalent" (1992a, p. 116).[38] But each time the objects of a situation are counted, the result of one version expressed in a sentence like "there are three objects on the table" contradicts the result on the basis of the other expressed in a sentence like "there are seven objects on the table", so that there is no way of joining them in one overarching conception of what objects *really* are. Since knowledge claims remain unaffected by such a decision, for Putnam this means that our knowledge claims do not require any such ontological decision at all. For all we know, the truth-condition for the empirical statement "there are three electrons interacting with the slit" *is* a situation with three individuals if and only if it is one with seven mereological objects. Certainly these descriptions cannot be taken as falsifying each other in any environment-related sense. Moreover, this equivalence is itself the outcome of judging the result of simultaneously applying the respective descriptions to situations in the environment (i.e., a result obtained *within* a practice of making and evaluating empirical statements).

Putnam suggests that similar cases of conceptual relativity are available in standard scientific practice (often referred to as "dualities"). For example, he points to the field/particle duality in quantum mechanics and the geometrical duality between taking points as particulars or as limits of extended structures. Each case generates a surface contradiction in the description of ontological commitments (fields or particles, points or lumps), while both descriptions applied to empirical circumstances are factually equivalent in the mentioned sense. In these cases one could say (although Putnam does not put it like this) that the subject matter of inquiry can be *multiply constituted* from different bases without this having any effect on the available knowledge or the determinacy of the claims that are exchanged. The phenomena of conceptual relativity could thus be understood as instances where a body of empirical statements (or theoretical structures) can be embedded in different (i.e., nonconjoinable) background ontologies without loss or gain.[39]

Putnam's use of conceptual relativity subverts realists who want to defend the picture of a uniquely structured realm of underlying reality as a precondition for the objectivity of our claims. The symmetries between the descriptions in cases of conceptual relativity show that the determinacy of our claims does not depend on the supposition that the question "Which of the two ontologies should we prefer?" be answerable in a definitive or nonarbitrary way. Indeed, there can be neither empirical nor even practical reasons to prefer one to the other. If there were reasons at all, they would have to be conventional (i.e., social reasons). Thus the realist must be prepared to say that the objectivity of our claims is grounded in one fixed, uniquely structured realm, *and* that this realm is chosen by social convention! That *reductio* shows that our practices of making empirical claims and taking them to be objectively correct descriptions of a publicly accessible environment do not presuppose any such superthing. Each claim does presuppose a variously accessible, richly conceptualized and sometimes multiply organizable local environment for its evaluation, an environment that, for all these reasons, can be common to many differently predisposed human beings. This is, roughly, where Putnam started his development, which in many ways has been a "journey from the familiar to the familiar" (1994b, p. 300).

Notes

1. Putnam calls this way of situating his philosophical stance explicitly the "supremacy of the agent point of view" (1987, p. 70), and connects it with the pragmatist and Kantian traditions. The expression "participant perspective" was used in Ebbs (1992) in his illuminating analyses of Putnam's views, where it refers to his earlier as well as his later position. In a somewhat different theoretical context, this expression (which calls to mind Dewey's critique of the spectator's perspective) had been in use since the 1970s in the writings of Habermas to distinguish between philosophies produced from the "observer" and "participant" standpoints, where only the latter are able to capture normative elements of the practices at issue in philosophical analysis. A descendant of the latter notion, exploiting its Kantian and pragmatist undertones, has been employed in characterizing Putnam's method (again, early and late) as "presupposition analysis" in Mueller (2001). In this chapter, the term is used generically.

2. Putnam places his current position within the broader framework of a pragmatist philosophy, whereas his earlier writings served to undercut empiricist strategies of explaining knowledge and meaning. So we could conjecture that, according to Putnam, a thoroughly pragmatist point of view is the strongest anti-empiricist stand to take, all things considered. This, in turn, ties in nicely with his recent focus on the weaknesses of reformed empiricism of the Quinean sort and what has come to be called "naturalism".

3. In fact, there is one exception in Putnam's early writings, and this concerns his views on mathematics and logic. In his early writings in the philosophy of mathematics, he decided to follow a "realist" strategy in accepting universals as mathematically real. Realism in these discussions, however, was opposed to nominalism, not to a broader anti-realist point of view. But nominalism and (epistemic) realism are not incompatible, which is why this sense of "realism" will not play a role in our account. (For an early assessment of his own writings in this sense of realism, see 1975a, p. vii. For later remarks to the same effect, see 1992b, pp. 348 ff.) Over time, and because of his conceptual relativity, Putnam's position on the ontological import of mathematics has moved away from this early Quinean stance; for this development see 1994d, pp. 259–260; 1999, p. 179; 2001b, lecture III.

4. Keeping track of this latter point provides one way of understanding the ever-growing differences between Putnam and Quinean naturalism. For these differences see Putnam 1994d, p. 248, and 1992b, p. 402.

5. In his recent work (1998), Putnam explicitly makes the point that this extends to knowledge claims in general.

6. Quine's position on the issue is further expanded in his (1935) and (1954).

7. This can be seen by the correspondences between the themes he develops at this early stage and claims in his later work, e.g., "'Two Dogmas' Revisited", "Analyticity and Apriority: Beyond Wittgenstein and Quine", and "Convention: A Theme in Philosophy" (all in 1986), as well as 1992b, pp. 391–393, and 1994d, pp. 249–252.

8. In the case of what is nowadays referred to as "folk psychology", he says: "The acceptance of [a] conceptual system, or explanatory scheme, is justified, as is the acceptance of many an empirical hypothesis, by the joint facts of explanatory power and no real alternative" (1969, p. 447).

9. At this point, we can already see that Putnam's reconstruction not only contextualizes the distinctions between analytic and synthetic statements, a priori and empirical claims, conventional and factual elements in the acceptance conditions of beliefs, but also by doing so makes it difficult to see a dramatic difference between internal and external, or, more important, between the procedures guiding decisions in normal or revolutionary changes.

10. A related conception was proposed in Fine 1967. If we conjoin the idea that the semantics of empirical concepts depends on the results of their application to empirical circumstances over time with the idea of "rigidity", we get the Kripke-Putnam theory of natural-kind terms. Applying the semantics of rigidity to live empirical concepts is criticized in Fine 1975, anticipating some of the reasons that led Putnam increasingly to distance himself from Kripke's views on the matter. A more detailed analysis of Putnam's pragmatic account of the semantics of empirical concepts can be found in Mueller 2001, chaps. 8–10.

11. As Putnam will say later, this way of reconstructing concept-use treats the fact that theories are regarded as successors or competitors and the fact that their basic vocabulary refers to a sufficient amount of shared objects as two ways of making the same point (1988, p. 11).

12. Soames attributes to N. Salmon the related idea of law clusters as groups of individually sufficient, but neither jointly nor individually necessary, conditions for the application of a term and develops that notion (Soames 1999, pp. vii and 170ff.).

13. Consider, for example; "the use of the word 'temperature' rests upon the empirical fact that there exists a single physical magnitude . . . which is normally responsible for differences in 'felt warmness'" (1963b, p. 128).

14. Cf. 1963b, p. 130. This is inspired by the results of Ziff's work on semantics and Harris's work on discursive appropriateness and paraphrasability (yielding a pragmatic notion of linguistic synonymy), which Putnam transposes into reference. In fact, it works as a sort of master argument in Putnam's criticism of Feyerabend, conventionalism, and Malcolm. He refers to the principles we are going to discuss in 1959, pp. 209ff.; 1962, pp. 52ff.; and 1962c, pp. 318ff.

15. It should be obvious that by deflecting attention from the question of continuity of beliefs toward continuity of practice and reference, Putnam accomplishes two things: he changes the burden of proof, and he converts what seemed to be a

global issue into a variety of *local* questions. Where it seemed that we should *justify* the continuity of reference through conceptual change, it now appears that what has to be proven is the *dis*continuity under such conditions.

16. There was a second motivation behind Putnam's turn to metaphysical realism; namely, his political engagement at the time. "The . . . concerns for a better world, the desire to make my philosophical activity a part of that concern, and the involvement with Marxism . . . led me to an increasingly strong metaphysical realism, simply because that position seemed more consistent with Marx's 'dialectical materialism' as I interpreted it" (1992b, p. 350).

17. The quote continues: "in general, and in the long run, correct ideas lead to success, and ideas lead to failures where and insofar as they are incorrect. Failure to see the importance of practice leads directly to failure to see the importance of success."

18. History had it that the term "internal realism" applied to whatever doctrines Putnam came to hold *disputing* the viability of the explanationist defense. At first, Putnam did not take issue with this "mistake" of his interpreters and in 1981 even used the expression to refer to his own view. As soon as he did, "internal realism", like a character in a serial that begins to be a prison for the author's creativity, was put to rest. Putnam came to share Gary Ebbs's impression (1992) that the character was by now preventing rather than enhancing understanding. The definite burial of the term can be found in his 1992b and 1999, part 1 (the 1994 Dewey lectures). "Pragmatic realism" inherited the fortune. It surfaced, to the best of our knowledge, first in 1987 (p. 17), and then, more prominently, in 1988 (p. 114).

19. Although skeptical worries about this latter possibility work, at the time, as a supplementary motivation for Putnam's beginning to take an explicit position on the issue, we submit that he never seriously entertained, and does not now entertain, the idea that it could be coherent to be convinced that we are engaged in making empirical claims *and* that versions of (1)–(3), applied to the terms and statements used by us to make the claims, are false. The background reservation is just the thought that we cannot make sense of claims that are empirical but empty (i.e., do not refer at all) or totally indeterminable (do not refer in an evaluable way). The dramatized version of the skeptical worry is the "disastrous meta-induction": "What if *all* the theoretical entities postulated by one generation . . . invariably "don't exist" from the standpoint of later science? . . . *just as no term used in the science of more than fifty* (or whatever) *years ago referred, so it will turn out that no term used now . . . refers.* . . . But what happens to the notion of *truth* in theoretical science if none of the descriptive terms refer? Perhaps all theoretical sentences are "false"; or some convention for assigning truth-values when predicates don't refer takes over" (1978, p. 25).

20. The step according to which the described entity *just is* the objective entity is obviously subject to the same difficulty, since its warrant could only consist in *another* cognition of the entity in question.

21. This is how we understand his consistent emphasis that the outcome of his anti-verificationism, namely his (and Kripke's) theory of reference and his semantic externalism, does not provide necessary and sufficient conditions for

(or reductions of reference to) something else (e.g., causality), but *presupposes* it. See 1974b, p. 286, and 1978, p. 58, where he says that he would rather call the "causal" theory of reference the "social co-operation plus contribution of the environment theory of the *specification* of reference". The same idea recurs later in 1992, pp. 23, 165, 211, and passim. See his 1990b for his repudiation of Kripke's metaphysical reading of reference. Mueller 2001, chap. 10, stresses the pragmatic character of Putnam's externalism.

22. We want to emphasize (and this speaks for continuity in his outlook) that Putnam himself repeatedly stresses that his experiment with a more substantive version of realism than the one required by his pragmatic outlook was rather uncomfortable for him. See 1988, pp. xii and 107, where he describes his relation to scientific realism as an "approach-avoidance conflict", and 1999, where he speaks of having been caught in "antinomies" he saw no way to reconcile, and began "recoiling" from one extreme to the other (see esp. pp. 12–16).

23. This line of argument is in Williams 1986.

24. With a Darwinian twist, this is van Fraassen's way of defusing the success argument (1980, pp. 39–40). Of course, saying that it depends on us (is one of our norms) to only admit theories we regard as successful does not at all mean that we *make* the theories successful.

25. This is not scientism, but simply a fact of about how science enters our lives. Thus, Putnam's division of linguistic labor (cf. 1975c, pp. 227ff.) stresses that we often defer to scientists to improve our reasoning in the process of making certain decisions about reference. The reason is not the technocratic one, that scientists are more competent about fixing extensions of our terms, but the fact that the right scientists know a lot about, for example, gold and how to find out whether something is gold (cf. 1988, pp. 22–26).

26. The dialectic of the inner and outer is elaborated for both realism and anti-realism in (Fine, 1996a, chaps. 7 and 8; see especially chap. 8 for some criticisms of the explanationist defense that we draw on below).

27. In spite of Putnam's dismissal of instrumentalism (1981, pp. 38–39), this is quite in line with the epistemological aspect of his model-theoretic argument (in 1976b and 1977); see 1992b, pp. 345–355.

28. Compare Putnam 1976b, pp. 126–129 as well as 1994b, 302–304 on the upshot of his model-theoretic argument. See also the "metatheorems" in Fine 1986 and 1996a, pp. 180–186.

29. This nagging question accompanies Putnam's reflections on the explanationist defense from early on, in his 1978 and 1981.

30. See Levin 1984 and Williams 1986; also Putnam 1999, pp. 55–56.

31. See the discussion of "truthmongers" in Fine 1996a, chap. 8 for a critique of this identification that connects it with a general form of behaviorism.

32. In an interesting twist, Putnam turns the grammaticality of the claim that we have no access to reality as it is against those (like Rorty) who want to say that there is nothing but discourse: "if we agree that it is *unintelligible* to say, 'We sometimes succeed in comparing our language and thought with reality as it is in itself', then we should realize that it is also unintelligible to say 'It is *impossible* to

stand outside and compare our thought and language with the world'" (1994b, p. 299).

33. See also 1992b, pp. 355, 366–368.

34. See, too, his discussion with Rorty on the nature of assertibility-conditions in (1995, pp. 32–38). For a connection with the "unforced judgments" that are at the heart of social constructivism, see Fine 1996b.

35. Recall an earlier Putnam, "*as* thinkers we are committed to there being *some* kind of truth, some kind of correctness which is substantial and not merely 'disquotational'" (1981, p. 21), and more adamantly in 1994a, chaps. 13 and 16. The dismissals of disquotationalism in these articles now have to be qualified. In his 2001a, Putnam therefore chooses to specify his view as a sort of disquotationalism (rather than 'deflationism', which he associates with verificationism).

36. This does not mean, of course, that they generalize in the same directions everywhere else – i.e., allow for global mutual or even only one-way reduction ("perfect extensional translation"). It seems to be precisely one of the points of Putnam's pluralism that they do not, but that this does not prevent users of such descriptions from developing local agreements of truth. The idea of comparing theories by means of locally overlapping extensions was explored in Fine 1975.

37. Putnam clearly notices this means that, in these cases, we ought to abandon the usual notion of synonymy as a constraint on successful interpretation, since the correlated sentences are not *synonymous* in any straightforward sense, in spite of the fact that they can make an equivalent contribution to the *communicative success* of their users; see his 1992a. It would be hasty, though, to sum this up in the fashionable turn of phrase that Putnam "overcomes representationalism", as his construction makes and requires the clear distinction between sign and object presupposed in ordinary referential semantics, and the outcome of his construction is that, while the users of various descriptions may be referring to different objects, they can still represent the same situation (much like a live-TV report and a flight-number-space-time matrix can represent the same plane).

38. For a more detailed account of this see Putnam 1980.

39. A useful discussion of these questions can be found in Case 1997. For an account of the parallelism between producing conceptual relativity and revising redescriptions in fallibilistic practices of evaluation see Mueller 2002 and Mueller, forthcoming.

References

Case, J. (1997). "On the Right Idea of a Conceptual Scheme". *Southern Journal of Philosophy* 35:1–18.

Ebbs, G. (1992) "Realism and Rational Inquiry". *Philosophical Topics* 20:1–33.

(2001). "The Very Idea of Sameness of Extension across Time". *American Philosophical Quarterly* 37:245–268.

Fine, A. (1967). "Consistency, Derivability, and Scientific Change". *Journal of Philosophy* 64:231–240.

(1975). "How To Compare Theories: Reference and Change". *Nous* 9:17–32.

(1986). "Unnatural Attitudes: Realist and Antirealist Attachments to Science". *Mind* 95:149–177.

(1996a). *The Shaky Game: Einstein, Realism, and the Quantum Theory.* 2nd ed. Chicago: University of Chicago Press.

(1996b). "Science Made Up: Constructivist Sociology of Scientific Knowledge". In P. Galison and D. Stump (eds.), *The Disunity of Science: Boundaries, Contexts, and Power.* Stanford, CA: Stanford University Press, pp. 231–254.

Levin, M. (1984). "What Kind of Explanation Is Truth?" In J. Leplin (ed.), *Scientific Realism.* Berkeley: University of California Press, pp. 124–139.

Mueller, A. (2001). *Referenz und Fallibilismus.* Berlin/New York: DeGruyter.

(2002). "Putnams pragmatischer Kognitivismus". In M. Willaschek and M. L. Rater (eds.), *Hilary Putnam und die Tradition des Pragmatismus.* Frankfurt: Suhrkamp, pp. 65–87.

(forthcoming). "Conceptual Relativity, Semantic Contextualism and Fallibilism". *Teorema.*

Peirce, C. S. (1868). "Some Consequences of Four Incapacities". In *Philosophical Papers* 5.264–314.

Putnam, H. (1959). "Memo on 'Conventionalism'". In Putnam 1975, pp. 206–214.

(1960). "Minds and Machines". In Putnam 1975b, pp. 362–385.

(1962a). "The Analytic and the Synthetic". In Putnam 1975b, pp. 33–69.

(1962b). "It Ain't Necessarily So". In Putnam 1975, pp. 237–249.

(1962c). "Dreaming and 'Depth Grammar'". In Putnam 1975b, pp. 304–324.

(1963a). "An Examination of Grünbaum's Philosophy of Geometry". In Putnam 1975, pp. 93–129.

(1963a). "How Not To Talk About Meaning". In Putnam 1975b, pp. 117–131.

(1963b). "Brains and Behavior". In Putnam 1975b, pp. 325–341.

(1965). "Philosophy of Physics". In Putnam 1975, pp. 79–93.

(1969). "Logical Positivism and the Philosophy of Mind". In Putnam 1975b, pp. 441–451.

(1974a). "The 'Corroboration' of Theories". In Putnam 1975, pp. 250–269.

(1974b). "Language and Reality". In Putnam 1975b, pp. 272–290.

(1975a). *Philosophical Papers I. Mathematics, Matter and Method.* Cambridge: Cambridge University Press.

(1975b). *Philosophical Papers II. Mind, Language, and Reality.* Cambridge: Cambridge University Press.

(1975c). "The Meaning of 'Meaning'". In Putnam 1975b, pp. 215–271.

(1975d). "What Is Mathematical Truth?". In Putnam 1975, pp. 60–78.

(1976a). "Reference and Understanding". In Putnam 1978, pp. 97–122.

(1976b). "Realism and Reason". In Putnam 1978, pp. 123–138.

(1977). "Models and Reality". In Putnam 1983, pp. 1–25.

(1978). *Meaning and the Moral Sciences.* London: Routledge and Kegan Paul.

(1980). "Equivalence". In Putnam 1983, pp. 26–45.

(1981). *Reason, Truth, and History.* Cambridge: Cambridge University Press.

(1982a). "Three Kinds of Scientific Realism". In Putnam 1994a, pp. 492–498.

(1982b). "A Defense of Internal Realism". In Putnam 1990, pp. 30–42.

(1983). *Philosophical Papers III. Realism and Reason.* Cambridge: Cambridge University Press.

(1987). *The Many Faces of Realism.* LaSalle, IL: Open Court.

(1988). *Representation and Reality.* Cambridge, MA: MIT Press.

(1990a). *Realism with a Human Face,* Cambridge, MA: Harvard University Press.

(1990b). "Is Water Necessarily H_2O?". In Putnam 1990a, pp. 54–79.

(1992a). *Renewing Philosophy.* Cambridge, MA: Harvard University Press.

(1992b). "Replies. " *Philosophical Topics* 20,1:347–408.

(1994a). *Words and Life.* Cambridge, MA: Harvard University Press.

(1994b). "The Question of Realism". In Putnam 1994a, pp. 295–312.

(1994c). "Realism without Absolutes". In Putnam 1994a, pp. 279–294.

(1994d). "Rethinking Mathematical Necessity". In Putnam 1994a, pp. 245–263.

(1994e). "Comments and Replies". In P. Clark, and B. Hale (eds.), *Reading Putnam.* Oxford: Blackwell, pp. 242–302.

(1995). *Pragmatism. An Open Question.* Oxford: Blackwell.

(1998). "Skepticism". In M. Stamm (Ed.), *Philosophie in synthetischer Absicht.* Stuttgart: Klett-Cotta, pp. 238–268.

(1999). *The Threefold Chord. Mind, Body, and World.* New York: Columbia University Press.

(2001a). "Concluding Remarks and Reply to Juergen Habermas". Manuscript. Published in German as "Antwort auf Jürgen Habermas," in M. Willaschek and M. L. Rater (eds.), *Hilary Putnam und die Tradition des Pragmatismus.* Frankfurt: Suhrkamp, 2002, pp. 306–321.

(2001b). "The 2001 Hermes Lectures, held in Perugia (Italy)". Manuscript.

(2002). "Pragmatism and nonscientific knowledge". In J. Conant and U. Zeglen (eds.), *Hilary Putnam: Pragmatism and Realism.* London/New York: Routledge, pp. 14–24.

Quine, W. V. O. (1935). "Truth by Convention". In Quine 1976, pp. 77–106.

(1951). "Two Dogmas of Empiricism". In Quine 1980, pp. 20–46.

(1954). "Carnap and Logical Truth". In Quine 1976, pp. 107–132.

Soames, S. (1999). *Understanding Truth.* Oxford: Oxford University Press.

van Fraassen, B. (1980). *The Scientific Image.* Oxford: Clarendon Press.

Williams, M. (1986). "Do We (Epistemologists) Need a Theory of Truth?" *Philosophical Topics* 14:223–242.

5 | Putnam on Skepticism

YEMIMA BEN-MENAHEM

INTRODUCTION

In *Reason, Truth and History* (1981), Hilary Putnam offers two rejoinders to the skeptical conjecture that we might all be 'brains in a vat.' The first is that the 'brains in a vat' hypothesis is self-refuting: were we brains in a vat, we could not possibly be expressing a truth when we said we were brains in a vat, hence the 'brains in a vat' hypothesis must be false. This argument rests on the conception of meaning developed in "The Meaning of 'Meaning.'" The second rejoinder is considerably simpler: "Internalist philosophers dismiss the 'Brains in a Vat' hypothesis. For us, the 'Brains in a Vat World' is only a *story*, a mere linguistic construction, and not a possible world at all" (1981, p. 50). These rejoinders reflect two different strategies for confronting skepticism Putnam adopted over the years, one in his earlier writings, the other in more recent works. *Reason, Truth and History* is thus Janus-faced: the apotheosis of the first strategy, it also ushers in the second. This essay will examine the shift from one strategy to the other, demonstrating the continuity in their underlying motivations. Putnam's conception of meaning,[1] I will show, played a major role in these developments, taking Putnam from the thesis that skepticism is false to the thesis that it is senseless. To substantiate my claims, I explore Putnam's responses to skepticism about scientific truth, skepticism about meaning, and skepticism about necessary truth. This will entail comparison of his early and later arguments for realism; his early and later objections to the indeterminacy of meaning; and the different positions he endorsed on the question of necessary truth.

The change of strategy that is the subject of this chapter can be characterized as follows. Putnam's earlier arguments against skepticism either attempt to refute particular forms of skepticism directly or make the case for particular nonskeptical positions. His later work, by contrast, undercuts even prima facie claims as to skepticism's intelligibility. Exposing the emptiness of skeptical doubt, the latter strategy lays bare its violation of the basic conditions for coherent thought and meaningful discourse. On this view, skepticism cannot be upheld in earnest as a philosophical position, or even intelligibly formulated. As we shall see, this strategy of repudiating skepticism is first introduced in the above quotation, in the context of the verificationist semantics Putnam was espousing at the time but rejected a short time later. The strategy itself, however, survived this change in his outlook on semantics.

Adopting the repudiation strategy streamlines the entire project of overcoming skepticism. Instead of having to demonstrate that this or that skeptical argument is invalid because of some insurmountable flaw, the opponent of skepticism can dismiss it forthwith; it is ipso facto discredited. Any more specific arguments then proffered in response to particular versions of skepticism are intended more as reiterations of this fundamental insight in the language of the particular area in which the skeptical doubt was raised, than as counterarguments in the traditional sense.

Understood in this way, Putnam's later strategy against skepticism is nonetheless still compatible with a number of very different positions. Philosophers as diverge as Kant, Peirce, Carnap, Wittgenstein, Quine and even Hume have all been seen as denying the cogency of skepticism rather than attempting to refute it directly.[2] Further distinctions must therefore be made to bring out the unique thrust of Putnam's position. Putnam perceives himself as closer to Kant than to Hume, to Wittgenstein than to Carnap, to Peirce than to Quine. Indeed, his identification with the Kant-Peirce-Wittgenstein legacy rather than the more hard-line empiricism-cum-naturalism associated with the others becomes exceedingly salient over the years. The change in Putnam's attitude to skepticism reflects the growing impact of these philosophers on his thought.

On the basis of his explicit references to skepticism, it does not seem to have been of particular concern to Putnam prior to *Reason, Truth and History*. However, a closer look reveals that from early on, establishing a foothold for knowledge and truth has been one of Putnam's most persistent philosophical endeavors, and skepticism, or, rather, a broad spectrum of skeptical positions, the target of ongoing critique. Putnam has persistently sought to forge an alternative to the skeptical positions associated with instrumentalism, conventionalism and relativism in the philosophy of science, and meaning variance and the indeterminacy of meaning in the philosophy of language.

We should note at the outset that the skeptical positions Putnam critiques in his earlier writings fall short of full-blown skepticism about the external world or knowledge in general. Thus, it is not so much classical

Pyrrhonism that Putnam addresses at this time, but the homegrown forms of skepticism then in vogue in the English-speaking world. These strains of skepticism threatened, in their different ways, to undermine all claims to truth, knowledge and trustworthy communication. Putnam's realism, intended to counter these nonrealist positions, provides a detailed critique of each variant in its turn. By the time Putnam writes *Reason, Truth and History*, however, much has changed. His novel theory of meaning in place, he is now in command of a powerful tool that enables him not only to come up with a more compelling strategy, but also to extend his critique to more wide-ranging forms of skepticism. In other words, as Putnam's critique of skepticism becomes more radical, more radical forms of skepticism become vulnerable to it.

Section I of this paper charts Putnam's change of strategy as reflected in his work on realism. It construes the transition from realism to internal realism as a manifestation of growing disenchantment with the analogy between realism and scientific theories. Section II explores the connections between Putnam's conception of meaning and his arguments against skepticism, focusing in particular on the 'brains in the vat' argument. Section III compares Putnam's earlier and later responses to Quine's indeterminacy thesis, and to meaning skepticism in general. Section IV examines the implications of Putnam's change of strategy for his understanding of the notion of necessary truth.

I. REALISM AND EXPLANATION

One of Putnam's earliest concerns was the defense of scientific truth against skeptical positions that see scientific theories as no more than useful fictions. Hence realism. Putnam viewed his early realism as a philosophical theory analogous, in important respects, to a scientific theory, and argued for it on the basis of its superior explanatory power. In his recent writings, however, realism is no longer defended on these terms. Instead, its defense hinges on the indispensability of the notions of truth and objectivity, and their constitutive role in intelligible discourse.

"Realism," Putnam used to say in the 1970s, "is the only philosophy that does not make the success of science a miracle."[3] Briefly, the idea is as follows. Electrons figure in our explanation of the workings of electrical equipment, and genes figure in our explanation of hereditary diseases. Realists understand the success of predictions derived from theories employing these notions straightforwardly in terms of the existence of electrons and genes. By contrast, nonrealists, suspicious of 'theoretical entities,' maintain that such notions are merely fictitious constructs that happen to work. But how can such 'as if' notions, or the theories employing them, be of any explanatory value? And how can the phenomenon of success, the fact that such fictions yield successful predictions, be explained? Realism, Putnam therefore concludes, provides the only explanation for the success of science.

Putnam elaborates on the argument from success to highlight its analogy with hypothetico-deductive arguments as they figure in science.[4] The claim here is that scientific practice is based on assumptions that make sense from a realist point of view but are unjustifiable from a nonrealist perspective. For example, scientists will typically conjoin several theories to derive new predictions. This procedure is understandable if each of the conjoined theories is considered to be true, for truth is preserved under conjunction.[5] But utility, simplicity, economy, beauty and other attributes cited by nonrealists as surrogates for truth in the evaluation of theories lack this characteristic, that is, are not preserved under conjunction. Thus even the commonplace practice of conjoining theories cannot be justified on the nonrealist premise. If the claim that science presupposes realism is accepted, the following hypothetico-deductive argument is forthcoming: (1) Scientific practice is based on realist assumptions; (2) scientific practice is successful. Conclusion: realism should be accepted as the explanation of the success of science. Arguments of this kind, known as inferences to the best explanation, are widely used in both scientific and everyday contexts.[6] Realism thus becomes a scientist's philosophy of science in two senses: it is, as a matter of fact, the view scientists tend to presuppose, and it is the position that best accords with the received canons of scientific reasoning.

As a number of writers have noted, the argument from success has several (somewhat interdependent) limitations. First, it is precisely the inference to the best explanation of the kind in question that opponents of realism find unconvincing. They are unlikely to be persuaded by another, albeit more general, argument of the same kind. Second, the claim that scientific practice rests on realist assumptions, and would be inexplicable without them, has been challenged by adducing nonrealist grounds for the same procedures. Third, despite the formal analogy with hypothetico-deductive explanations within science, the more general argument for realism does not meet the standards of scientific explanation in terms of its putative empirical import: it does not yield new scientific predictions unavailable to its opponents.[7]

My aim in surveying Putnam's argument from the success of science, and the objections that have been raised against it, is not to settle the dispute, but to point to the centrality of the notion of *scientific explanation* in this controversy about realism. As described above, the controversy turns on the question of whether realism is an explanatory theory satisfying the desiderata of scientific explanation. The parties to the dispute seem to presuppose that philosophy is on a par with science in terms of its goals, and analogous to science in its methods. This conception has been challenged by a number of philosophers, most radically by Wittgenstein. Even without fully embracing Wittgenstein's descriptive and therapeutic understanding of philosophical activity, and even without totally banning philosophical explanations, as Wittgenstein did, some find the analogy between ordinary scientific inferences to the existence of particular entities, such as electrons and genes, and the grand philosophical inference to realism, rather strained. Giving up this analogy, however, does not in itself refute realism. That there is no quasi-scientific inference to realism qua explanatory theory does not imply that science can do without our ordinary notions of truth, reference and existence, or consistently replace them with nonrealist substitutes. It simply means that realism is not a scientific theory. I would venture to say that Putnam's later writings sustain this conclusion.

If realism is no longer taken as a scientific theory, the way we argue for it must change accordingly. Indeed, as of about 1980, Putnam's support for realism pivots on the irreducibility of realist notions of truth and reference to other notions rather than on the explanatory force of realism. This change of strategy parallels the transition from realism to internal realism, but Putnam does not make the connection between the two moves explicit. Closer inspection of a number of key aspects of these transitions will help fill in the gaps. The last two papers included in *Meaning and the Moral Sciences* (1978) are of crucial importance here. The last paper, "Realism and Reason," Putnam's 1976 presidential address to the Eastern Division of the American Philosophical Association, marks the debut of internal realism. In it, Putnam distinguishes between metaphysical realism and internal realism, developing the first of a series of model-theoretic arguments against the former. In the penultimate paper, "Reference and Understanding" – the last paper in which Putnam is committed to unqualified realism[8] – the argument from success reaches its pinnacle. In later years, though still mentioned from time to time, it gradually loses its prominence. The two papers, I believe, are doubly linked: on the one hand, extending the argument from success as far as it will go facilitates recognition of the flaws in metaphysical realism; on the other, once the language–world relation is viewed from the internal perspective, the argument from success is no longer required.

"Reference and Understanding" makes two moves that seem to pull in different directions. First, it generalizes the argument from success: realism explains not only the success of science, but also the success of human behavior in general. Moreover, "the notions of truth and reference may be of great importance in explaining the relation of language to the world" (1978, p. 100). At the same time, the paper casts off the traditional realist semantics of truth conditions. Its point is that these seemingly incompatible moves are not only compatible, but even complementary, concluding:

> (1) that the notion that one learns one's native language by learning what the truth conditions are for its various sentences has no presently intelligible sense, at least for a realist; (2) that it does not follow that the realist's notions of truth and reference are not important for the discussion of language – but their importance is for the explanation of the contribution linguistic behavior makes to the success of total behavior, not to a theory of understanding. (Ibid., p. 116)

Readers have been perplexed by the relation between the realist conception of meaning Putnam developed in "The Meaning of 'Meaning'" (MoM), and his later disavowal of metaphysical realism (more on this below). Let me emphasize, therefore, that Putnam's reservations about truth-condition semantics in "Reference and Understanding" do not constitute a break with MoM. MoM puts forward a realist account of meaning – "meanings just ain't in the head" (1975, p. 227) – that is, construes meaning as anchored in external reality rather than determined solely by ideas, images, or concepts in speakers' minds; this realist conception, however, need not be grounded in traditional views about realist semantics. In particular, it does not assume that realist semantics must be given in terms of truth-conditions. For one thing, individual speakers may have very limited knowledge of the truth-conditions of their utterances, even when these utterances make perfect sense. This is implied by "the division of linguistic labor," a feature of Putnam's conception of meaning that makes it inherently social. The causal account of reference at the base of MoM enables Putnam both to anchor language in reality, as realists seek to do, and to forgo knowledge of truth-conditions as a prerequisite for meaningful discourse. "Reference and Understanding" thus draws conclusions already latent in MoM. A further surprising application of MoM sets the stage for the repudiation of the skeptic's 'brains-in-a-vat' scenario in *Reason, Truth and History*. Before turning to this argument, we must first consider Putnam's argument against metaphysical realism.

The crux of Putnam's model-theoretical argument(s)[9] against metaphysical realism is as follows. Metaphysical realism rests on the claim that reality is independent of human cognition and representation. Hence truth is a nonepistemic relation obtaining between this independent reality and certain human representations of it. The analogy that comes to mind is the satisfaction relation that obtains between formal theories and their models. As is well known, however, theories rich enough to be of any interest to us as comprehensive theories of 'the world,' will have an infinite number of models.[10] The unique correspondence relation alleged to ground the metaphysical realist's notion of truth thus disintegrates into a multitude of different – and potentially conflicting – relations. Regardless of epistemic considerations, that is, regardless of whether we can ever come to know the truth, the model-theoretic argument does away with the concept of 'the' truth about reality. I want to stress that the problem is not merely that independent reality is a myth, but that it turns out to be an incoherent myth.

Why is this argument lethal to metaphysical realism yet benign from the internal perspective? The root of the problem, as we just saw, is the alleged language – world correspondence. Once we yield to the temptation to construct a 'theory of correspondence' so as to include the correspondence relation itself in our comprehensive theory of the world, the model-theoretic considerations with regard to the nonuniqueness of the satisfaction relation come into play. Internal realism resists the temptation, declining to construct a theory about how representations represent reality. This restraint enables internal realism to avoid being drawn into presenting reference and truth in a way that leaves them vulnerable to the model-theoretic multiplicity argument. Construing Putnam in Wittgensteinian terms (and thereby pushing him somewhat further in the direction of Wittgenstein than he finds comfortable), I would suggest that the relation between a representation and what is being represented is an *internal* relation. As such, it cannot and need not be scientifically explained, or reduced to other (external) relations. Internal realism does not reduce the notions of truth and reference to other 'more basic' notions, nor does it see them as 'redundant.' Rather, it sanctions confidence in the notions of truth and reference as they are ordinarily used. That 'Hilary Putnam' refers to Hilary Putnam and 'book' refers to books is taken for granted, and so it should be. Admittedly, even the simplest sentences could be rendered problematic.[11] One could worry about 'Hilary Putnam wrote more than ten books' – do we count collections of essays? And so on. But the point is not that from the internal perspective language becomes completely transparent, or decontextualized. Rather, it is that the internal realist eschews the perverse model-theoretic reinterpretation of language that Putnam lays squarely at the door of the metaphysical realist.

To return to skepticism: the remarkable lesson of the model-theoretic arguments is that the skeptic and the metaphysical realist are in the same boat! In fact, it is in the context of characterizing the metaphysical realist that Putnam first brings up the 'brains in a vat' scenario:

> The most important consequence of metaphysical realism is that *truth* is supposed to be *radically non-epistemic* – we might be 'brains in a vat' and so the theory that is 'ideal' from the point of view of operational utility, inner beauty and elegance, 'plausibility', simplicity, 'conservatism' etc., *might be false*. 'Verified' . . . does not imply 'true,' on the metaphysical realist picture, even in the ideal limit. (1978, p. 125)[12]

According to Putnam, in allowing that our best theory of the world might in fact be false, the metaphysical realist goes a fair distance toward skepticism. From the moment Putnam makes this connection, these diametrically opposed positions, metaphysical realism and skepticism, are jointly targeted by his internal realism. Both positions admit the possibility of a gap between reality as it is and reality as represented by an ideal theory, a possibility declared unthinkable by the internal realist. Despite its skeptical appearance, then, the model-theoretic argument is employed by Putnam as an argument *against* skepticism. The significance of this point can hardly be overstated; the literature is replete with ironic attempts to rescue Putnam from his own 'skeptical' argument.[13]

The idea that even the best theory may be false has been very dear to realists. That truth and verification are to be kept apart is built into the realist notion of truth, and to keep them apart, it seems, the possibility of ideal verification short of truth must be acknowledged.[14] Furthermore, it is the idea that our theories can be false – that reality can resist, so to speak, our endeavors to comprehend it – that gives content to the realist notion of objectivity. If we could 'make' our theories true by fiat, as some nonrealists seem to suggest, the big difficulty would be to explain why so many of our theories turn out to be false. Indeed, in my view, realism is more closely tied to understanding scientific *failure* than to explaining its success.[15] Though Putnam gives up on the possibility of failure only in the limit case of the ideal theory, he is giving up on an idea that is constitutive of traditional realism.

How do these considerations impact on Putnam's argument from success? Interestingly, when first introducing the distinction between metaphysical realism and internal realism, Putnam points to the argument from success as the hallmark of internal realism:

> In one way of conceiving it, realism is an empirical theory.... it explains ... the ... mundane fact that language-using contributes to getting our goals, achieving satisfaction, or what have you. ... [A] 'correspondence' between words and sets of things (formally, a *satisfaction relation*, in the sense of Tarski) can be viewed as part of an *explanatory model* of the speakers' collective behaviour. ... let me refer to realism in this sense – acceptance of this sort of scientific picture of the relation of speakers to their environment, and of the role of language – as *internal* realism. (1978, p. 23)

At this point Putnam is obviously still committed to the argument from success. It seems to me, however, that this commitment is but a vestige of his earlier understanding of realism, and is bound to clash with the internal perspective. If my description of the transition to the internal perspective is an accurate reconstruction, internal realism should no longer be seen as an explanatory theory. If, in particular, in view of the model-theoretic argument, the concept of an independent reality to which true representations correspond is paradoxical, it remains paradoxical when used as a quasi-scientific explanation of success. Certainly, insofar as the best theory of the world is concerned, the inconceivability of its turning out to be false also implies that its truth cannot and need not be explanatory or explained, at least not in the ordinary sense of scientific explanation. As indicated above, I see the idea that truth and reference are to be taken at face value as the main thrust of internal realism. Truth and reference can neither explain the superphenomenon of human success, nor be explained by a superscientific theory. Taken at face value, they are irreducible to other notions and do not play the explanatory role assigned to the theoretical concepts of science.

The difference between legitimate and illegitimate uses of explanatory arguments is the difference between local and global explanatory contexts. Electrons, genes and their like come to be accepted as real when the theories in which they figure gain sufficient explanatory and predictive import. It is conceivable that these theories will be refuted or deemed useless and implausible, in which case our belief in the entities in question will eventually die out. But our coming to accept 'reality' as a whole as 'real' is an entirely different matter. The very awkwardness of the last sentence indicates that the difference between the explanatory power of entities such as genes, or the theories in which they figure, and that of reality, or realism, is a matter of principle, not degree. Putnam is aware of this difference. It is, after all, precisely the presumption of a global model of the correspondence between language and the world that his critique of metaphysical realism seeks to discredit. And it is precisely the presumption of a global suspension of judgment that, on his view, gets the skeptic into the sort of trouble that ensnared the metaphysician. It would be only natural, I think, if at this point the global argument from success were to be similarly subjected to critique, and discounted as an argument for internal realism. But, as we saw, no such process seems to have been under way in the 1976 address quoted above. Over time, however, internal realism seems less and less like a scientific theory. Rather, in the spirit of pragmatism, it is woven into the fabric of thought and life.

The skeptic, in turn, is not merely portrayed as violating the canons of scientific method, but as purporting to doubt that which cannot reasonably be doubted. Putnam responds to Strawson's query about "whether the nonexistence of the external world is really a coherent idea" as follows:

> I will offer reasons for thinking the answer is "no, it isn't," or at least that we have not been so far enabled (by the sceptic or, for that matter, by his familiar opponent, the traditional epistemologist) to give it a coherent sense.[16]

This formulation is typical of Putnam's recent writings, and illustrates the difference between his earlier and later responses to skepticism. One aspect of this change of attitude is a shift in the burden of proof. The skeptic's insatiable and unsatisfiable demand for further justification places the entire burden on his opponent, while Putnam's response suggests that doubts must be reasonable, and it is up to the skeptic to show that his doubts meet the minimum requirements of sense and reason. Further, the response to Strawson raises the question of fallibilism. Can one reject skepticism as sweepingly as Putnam does here, while still acknowledging human fallibility? Setting this question aside for the moment (but see section IV), let me note that the themes that have occupied us in the last few paragraphs can be traced back to Peirce: the convergence of truth and ideal verification, the ensuing dissipation of reality 'in itself,' the role of the demand that doubts be reasonable in rebutting skepticism, and finally, the marriage of anti-skepticism and fallibilism, are all at the core of Peirce's pragmatism.

A recurrent confusion regarding Putnam's internal realism is generated by the tendency to associate it with Carnap's distinction between internal and external questions. For Carnap (1956), internal questions are factual (i.e., scientific) questions, formulated within a language whose grammar is given in advance, whereas external questions concern the linguistic framework itself. Thus, external questions are ill-conceived if taken as questions about *truth;* frameworks, neither true nor false, are only more or less convenient, and are sanctioned ipso facto by Carnap's principle of tolerance. For Putnam, on the other hand, realism is not an optional framework we can replace with another at our convenience. Now Putnam does adopt a no-fact-of-the-matter stance on a number of ontological issues, such as the 'real' nature of numbers, the 'essence' of a chair, and so on.[17] But affirming the reality of physical objects and fellow human beings is not a matter of discretion. In the parlance of those who insist on using the framework metaphor, the physical world is an irrevocable framework. Here Putnam allies himself with Wittgenstein rather than Carnap. Neither Carnap nor Wittgenstein would have endorsed Putnam's earlier realism or the argument from success on which it is based. Both might have welcomed his change of strategy. But whereas Carnap adopts a conventionalist attitude to frameworks, Wittgenstein is apprehensive that we might be overstepping the limits of sense in presuming to look noncommittally 'beyond' this or that framework. Putnam has come to share this Wittgensteinian concern.

I noted the symmetry between skepticism and metaphysical realism. The skeptic is happy to denounce metaphysical realism, but tends to forget that negations of nonsensical statements can be just as meaningless as the original statements. This, essentially, is Putnam's response to Rorty in "The Question of Realism":

> But if we agree that it is *unintelligible* to say, "We sometimes succeed in comparing our language and thought with reality as it is in itself," then we should realize it is also unintelligible to say, "It is *impossible* to stand outside and compare our thought and language with the world." . . . While I agree with Rorty that metaphysical realism is unintelligible, to stop with that point without going on to recover our ordinary notion of representation is to fail to complete that journey "from the familiar to the familiar" that is the true task of philosophy. (1994, pp. 299–300)[18]

II. REALISM AND MEANING

One of the issues of contention between realism and nonrealism was, we saw, how to make sense of scientific practice. The influential writings of Kuhn and Feyerabend in the 1960s presented a more unsettling challenge to a realist conception of meaning. Kuhn and Feyerabend maintain that different theories (paradigms) represent different worlds, and are therefore "incommensurable." The idea is dazzlingly simple: scientific terms get their meaning holistically, from the theories (paradigms) in which they are used. When theories change, the meanings of the terms change accordingly. To the extent that reference is determined by meaning, such changes in meaning bring into play changes in reference. Thus, if one theory asserts that mass is conserved while another denies it, the term 'mass' not only has different meanings in these theories, but also different extensions. The upshot of adopting this seemingly benign conception of meaning is that the two theories, though clearly incompatible by commonsense standards, are rendered compatible, for they no longer speak of the same entity. The consequences for the rationality of science are disastrous: if different theories do not describe the same world, rational assessment of their comparative empirical merits is ruled out. Scientific assertions and predictions can only be evaluated within isolated conceptual spheres. This is as extreme as relativism can get. It is no wonder that Kuhn portrays scientific change as religious conversion.

Couched in meaning-theoretic terms, the argument for incommensurability is not a direct argument against realism: it does not presume to directly refute the existence of such philosophically contentious entities as physical objects and 'theoretical' entities. No direct argument, however, could be more devastating for the realist. The holistic-relativistic theory of meaning, which is based on the above fairly intuitive assumptions, was thought by many philosophers of science to be incontrovertible.[19] Although the point is not made explicitly in these terms by Kuhn and Feyerabend, the incommensurability argument implies that there can be no realist theory of meaning worthy of the name, no theory of meaning that sanctions even the elementary realist premise that different theories can speak of the same world. To make sense of realism, therefore, the realist was called upon to come up with an alternative.

Putnam's response to this challenge was to turn the incommensurability argument into a *reductio ad absurdum* of the assumptions underlying the holistic-relativist conception of meaning. In particular, the assumption as to the immediate connection between meaning (in the sense of theoretical content associated with a term) and reference had to be reconsidered. Once we let the meanings of terms vary without thereby altering their references, the different theories–different worlds argument for incommensurability is blocked. The goal of providing an alternative account of reference that would give it intertheoretic stability is achieved by the causal theory of reference. On the causal theory, as long as they keep track of the causal links between themselves and the entities they refer to, speakers can refer to the same objects through even radical theoretical change. Such keeping track involves tracking both the formation of the initial causal link between speakers and (a token of) the entity in question, and the causal chains between speakers who subsequently use specific terms with the intention of referring to the very entities their interlocutors and predecessors referred to in using the said terms.

Just as the Kuhn-Feyerabend conception of meaning does not, in itself, constitute an argument against realism, so Putnam's realist alternative does not, in itself, constitute a vindication. But if the challenge posed by the Kuhn-Feyerabend conception was to come up with a theory of meaning adequate for the articulation of realist ideas about the language-reality nexus, this challenge has been successfully met. As we shall see, such meaning-theoretic considerations loom large in the ensuing debate about other forms of skepticism, while the role of direct arguments diminishes.

Having disarmed the skeptical threat of meaning-theoretic relativism by severing the connection between theoretical change and change of reference, Putnam takes steps to consolidate his new conception of meaning in MoM, perhaps his best-known paper. Although skepticism is mentioned in the introductory paragraphs, it is certainly not the paper's main target. Nevertheless, the conception of meaning it outlines is at the heart of Putnam's critique of skepticism.

Putnam faults traditional theories of meaning for being mentalistic rather than externalist, and individualistic rather than social. Their mentalism is manifest in their construal of meanings as functions of speakers' mental ideas, representations and so on, upon which external reality does not intrude. The causal theory of reference ensures that speakers can have different ideas about a particular entity, and thus be in different mental states, while still referring to the same entity through causal chains terminating in that entity. MoM makes the complementary, though more radical, claim that speakers can be in identical (types of) mental states while referring to different entities. Putnam uses the Twin Earth (TE) thought-experiment to make this claim. TE resembles Earth down to the smallest detail, except that the liquid functioning as water, and called 'water' on TE, is not H_2O, but a different chemical compound. The word 'water,' Putnam contends, has different meanings on the two planets. But since there is no reason to ascribe different mental states to individuals using the term 'water' on Earth and their counterparts on TE (at least not prior to the emergence of chemistry), we have a clear example of people whose mental state is the same ascribing different meanings to a given word. One need not, however, travel as far as TE to find such examples. Putnam relates that he is unable to tell a beech from an elm, and his mental image of the two is the same; yet, because they refer to different trees, the words 'elm' and 'beech' differ in meaning for him, as they do for other competent speakers of English. That one can refer to elm trees without being able to identify them illustrates Putnam's "division of linguistic labor": since meanings are social rather than individual, it is unnecessary for each speaker to have the relevant knowledge, and it suffices that experts do.

The assumption underlying the TE example is that words like 'water' always refer to the stuff we call 'water' in the actual world. Though it is neither analytic nor a priori or irrevisable that water is H_2O, nothing other than H_2O can be considered water from our present point of view. And it is our present point of view that counts in the allocation of meaning.

Taken together with the causal theory of reference, Putnam's conception of meaning provides the realist with the arsenal needed to counter relativism. Moreover, it replaces the mentalistic account, on which to know what meaning(s) speakers assign to a term we must look into their minds, with an account that makes meaning responsible to external reality; hence externalism, as this conception has come to be known. But take note: nothing in this *externalist* account of meaning is incompatible with Putnam's *internal* realism! Nothing in MoM presupposes the metaphysical realist's concept of reality in itself, reality that is completely independent of how we perceive and describe it. As we saw, the internal realist has no qualms about the notions of reference and reality employed in MoM; indeed, he takes them for granted. Thus, when, at the end of 1976, Putnam begins to dissociate himself from metaphysical realism, the externalist conception of meaning developed in MoM remains unchallenged, serving as a bond between his earlier and later writings. This bond is manifest in *Reason, Truth and History*, where Putnam explicitly targets 'brains in a vat' skepticism.

Putnam's argument that the 'brains in a vat' hypothesis (BVH) is self-refuting is directly based on his externalist theory of meaning. On this theory, we saw, in order for someone to be referring to water, (s)he must be referring to the stuff we call 'water' in the actual world, and have some kind of causal connection, possibly indirect, with that stuff. Brains in a vat, however, cannot meet these conditions. The most ordinary words, such as 'hand,' 'tree' and 'people,' do not denote for them what they denote for us. And the same goes for 'vat.' Thus, were one of them to utter the sentence "I am a brain in a vat," the word 'vat' would not refer to the vat it would have to refer to to make the sentence true. The sentence is therefore false. The self-referring BVH turns out to be paradoxical – for all X, if BVH is true for X, it will be false when uttered by X with reference to itself. Hence, BVH must be false for X.

As long as we accept Putnam's theory of meaning, the argument against BV skepticism is valid from both the metaphysical realist and the internal realist perspectives. In itself, it presupposes neither of these positions. Admittedly, realists of the two persuasions differ as to how they conceive truth, reference and causality; we could, perhaps, capitalize the metaphysical realist notions, and speak of Truth, Reference, Causality and so on, to indicate the difference.[20] But the (lower-case) nonmetaphysical understanding of these notions is quite sufficient to sustain the argument against BVH. Putnam suspects, though, that metaphysical realists might be inclined to a "magical theory of meaning" rather than the MoM account.[21] On the 'magical' view, causal chains are unnecessary; words (representations, intentions or what have you) magically point to their referents without the mediation of speakers' interactions with those referents. Whether the words 'tree' and 'vat,' as used by brains in a vat, refer to trees and vats depends only on whether the right magical relation holds between the words and their referents, not on whether the speaker ever came into contact with the referents. Revisiting the model-theoretic argument, Putnam shows that it works against such magical theories of reference in the same way it worked against the magical language – world correspondence presupposed by the metaphysical realist. In both cases, model-theoretic considerations speak against the uniqueness of the alleged relation. In both cases, the assumption that the relation obtains is undermined if the relation is not in fact unique.

Internal realism, in turn, remains as impervious to this new use of the model-theoretic argument as it was to the previous use, for it declines to posit a theoretical reference relation, be it construed magically or otherwise. This imperviousness receives its strongest formulation in another presidential address (to the Association of Symbolic Logic, December 1977), where, having developed yet a third version of the multiple-interpretation argument, Putnam concludes:

> To adopt a theory of meaning according to which a language whose whole use is specified still lacks something – namely its 'interpretation' – is to accept a problem which *can* only have crazy solutions. To speak as if *this* were my problem, "I know how to use my language, but now, how shall I single out an interpretation?" is to speak nonsense. Either the use *already* fixes the 'interpretation' or *nothing* can. (1983, p. 24)

But here we have been rushing ahead of Putnam's intentions at the time. Putnam wrote the paper from which this quotation is taken, as well as the sentence quoted in my introduction, in which he describes the 'brains in a vat' world as "just a *story*," from a verificationist point of view. That is, at this point in the evolution of his views, he construes 'internal realism' as hardly distinguishable from Dummett's verificationism. On the internal perspective, it will be recalled, the world can only be described from within a scheme of representation. Verificationism, wherein 'the truth' is replaced with that which is warranted by our justification procedures, is, of course, one way of discounting reality 'in itself.' As Putnam put it:

> 'Truth' in an internalist view, is some sort of (idealized) rational acceptabil- ity – some sort of ideal coherence of our beliefs with each other and with our experiences *as those experiences are themselves represented in our belief system* – and not correspondence with mind-independent or discourse-independent 'states of affairs.' (1981, p. 50)

The verificationist phase was short-lived. In the preface to the book just quoted (written, it would seem, after the rest of the volume was completed), Putnam makes it clear that he is not proposing a reduction of truth to rational acceptability:

> But the relation between rational acceptability and truth is a relation be- tween two distinct notions. A statement can be rationally acceptable at a time, but not true; and this realist intuition will be preserved in my account. (1981, p. x)

Giving up reductive verificationism, however, is not much of an impedi- ment to the internal perspective. The crucial point regarding representation 'from within,' expressed in the italicized clause in the above quotation – *as those experiences are themselves represented in our belief system* – remains re- markably stable in Putnam's thinking.[22] As we saw, the point can be made in Wittgensteinian terms, independently of any particular semantic theory; indeed, it can be made from a vantage point that jettisons semantic theories altogether.[23] And it is precisely this minimal internal perspective, devoid of grand semantic theories, that mandates Putnam's intimation that the skeptic has left himself no way to confer meaning even on his own words.

In the transition to the internal point of view, the emphasis shifts from proving skepticism wrong to unmasking its meaningless. Again, this shift is gradual. As Putnam recognizes in the 'brains in a vat' chapter of *Rea- son, Truth and History*, the MoM account of meaning can be used to show that skepticism is senseless rather than false: "'We are brains in a vat' says something false (if it says anything)" (1981, p. 15). Indeed, in imputing *incoherence*, we generally worry about meaninglessness rather than falsity. Naturally, the question of what it takes to justify a charge of meaninglessness is more involved, and receives more detailed unpacking as such claims gain salience in Putnam's subsequent writings.

Let me take stock of the anti-skeptical arguments reviewed thus far:

1. Both the skeptic and the metaphysical realist make the untenable assumption that the best theory of the world could be false. Let us call this the falsity assumption. Its untenability is demonstrated by the first model-theoretic argument, denying a unique truth-grounding correspondence between language and reality.

2. Assuming the MoM account of meaning, the skeptical 'brains in a vat' scenario is self-refuting. To the extent that metaphysical realists wish to commit themselves to its feasibility, perhaps for the purpose of upholding the falsity assumption, they too are guilty of self-refutation.

3. A skeptic (or metaphysical realist) attempting to rescue the 'brains in a vat' scenario by means of a 'magical' theory of meaning impervious to (2) faces another round of the model-theoretic argument, this time against the purported unique 'magical' reference relation.

4. Internal realists reject the falsity assumption, and, if they subscribe to MoM, endorse argument (2).

Arguments (1)–(4) make up what I called Putnam's first strategy – the refutation of skepticism. Arguments (1) and (3), which employ model-theoretic considerations, are *reductio* arguments against (at least some versions of) metaphysical realism. We also saw the launch of the second strategy, namely:

5. Internal realists can take a shortcut, dismissing as unintelligible both the 'brains in a vat' hypothesis and the meaning-skepticism that follows from the model-theoretic arguments.

III. MEANING AND SKEPTICISM

To illustrate Putnam's change of strategy vis-à-vis skepticism in yet another philosophical domain, it will be useful to have a second look at a passage quoted a few paragraphs back.

> To adopt a theory of meaning according to which a language whose whole use is specified still lacks something – namely its 'interpretation' – is to accept a problem which *can* only have crazy solutions.... Either the use *already* fixes the 'interpretation' or *nothing* can. (1983, p. 24)

I want to point out that Putnam's rejection of a traditional form of skepticism – that is, skepticism about the existence of the external world – leads him to reject a very recent form of skepticism – skepticism about meaning. The connection is evident in his mobilization of meaning-theoretic considerations to strike down BV skepticism. Arguing against meaning-skepticism thus becomes an essential part of Putnam's polemic against traditional skepticism.

The notion of meaning-skepticism immediately calls to mind two celebrated arguments: Quine's indeterminacy of translation and Wittgenstein's rule-following paradox. Both have been read skeptically as well as nonskeptically. On the skeptical reading, each of the arguments points to a failure of language to definitively pin down some entity: a meaning, an interpretation, a series of correct applications, and so on. By contrast, nonskeptical readings construe these arguments as directed only against philosophical positions that make the mistake of reifying such entities, or postulate mechanisms that pin them down unequivocally. The nonskeptical camp insists that our understanding of language and communication is not impeded if these reifying philosophies are renounced. As they see it, Quine's indeterminacy argument and Wittgenstein's rule-following paradox evince *iconoclasm* rather than skepticism. Meaning as a reified entity is but an idol worshipped by some philosophers, an idol that must be smashed. But we need not worry that anything of real value will be damaged in the process.

Putnam's response to Rorty's anti-realism, quoted at the end of section I, highlights the contrast between skepticism and iconoclasm. In Rorty's protest against the metaphysical drive to represent reality in itself, Putnam "detects the trace of a disappointed metaphysical realist impulse" (1994, p. 299). The iconoclastic awareness that nothing of real value has been lost when idols are smashed is reassuring – the notions we are left with are the very notions we need to make sense of the world. This reassurance, which sustains Putnam's internal realism, is also behind his perseverance in the face of meaning-skepticism.

Putnam certainly favors the iconoclastic, anti-skeptical reading of Wittgenstein, but is inclined to read Quine as a skeptic. Admittedly, Quine himself originally gave his indeterminacy argument a skeptical gloss, while moving toward iconoclasm in later years. Putnam's skeptical reading of Quine is manifest early on, in the analogy he draws between Quine's conception of meaning and geometric conventionalism. "The Refutation of Conventionalism" draws a parallel between Grunbaum's argument for the conventionality of the metric of space-time, and Quine's argument for the indeterminacy of translation.[24] In both cases a no-fact-of-the-matter

argument is put forward. Quine's thesis that there may be equally warranted yet incompatible translations of the same sentences is likened to the
conventionalist thesis that there are empirically equivalent yet incompatible
physical theories.

The controversy over conventionalism in the physical sciences began
with Poincaré's celebrated claim regarding the conventionality of geometry.
A number of different geometries, Poincaré argues, are empirically equivalent in the sense that each of them can be used as the geometric basis for a
physical theory that explains the entire body of physical fact. In other words,
geometry is underdetermined by experience. In the wake of the development of the theory of relativity, this position generated vigorous debate.
The focus of the controversy was the uniqueness of the definition of the
four-dimensional metric of space-time. While realists maintain there is
one uniquely correct definition of the metric, conventionalists point to a
variety of possibilities for such a definition, and to the discretion scientists
enjoy when choosing between the various alternatives. Poincaré's argument
has been developed into a general argument for the underdetermination of
scientific theory by observation, the classic plea for such strong underdetermination being Quine's "Two Dogmas of Empiricism." Characteristically,
there is a skeptical undertone to the no-fact-of-the-matter position evinced
by the conventionalist in confronting the realist's attempt to single out a
unique truth.

One of Putnam's objections to conventionalism is that the range of possibilities is only apparent: as further methodological considerations come
into play, a uniquely reasonable choice typically emerges. Now there is
a twofold connection between Quine's indeterminacy of translation thesis
and the conventionalist thesis that science is underdetermined by fact. First,
underdetermination of theory by fact serves as an argument for the indeterminacy of translation: it is precisely the sentences that are underdetermined
by observation that, on Quine's view, are most likely to receive incompatible translations. And second, as Putnam shows, the two arguments have a
common structure: translation is underdetermined by the linguistic dispositions of speakers in the very way scientific theory is underdetermined by
observation.

Having laid bare the similarity between conventionalism and Quine's
indeterminacy thesis, Putnam critiques both theses along similar lines. The
problem, he says, is that "conventionalism is at bottom a form of essentialism" (1975b, p. 162). Picking a particular set of essential conditions, both
arguments legislate that these conditions constitute a definition of the concept in question – the metric in Grunbaum's case, translation in Quine's.

Since more than one 'metric' or 'translation' meets these conditions, underdetermination sets in. But surely, Putnam observes, underdetermination of
this kind is a by-product of the narrow definition the conventionalist settles
for. In reality, for a metric or a translation to be sufficiently reasonable, a
broader set of desiderata must be satisfied, narrowing down the number of
feasible alternatives. In science, the desiderata are simplicity and coherence
with a body of scientific truth. With regard to translation, Putnam's point
is subtler: his demand is not merely that translation be simple, but that it
preserve intersentential links such as inference and explanation.

Quine's narrow criteria of adequacy ensure that sentences accepted as
true by the community are not translated into sentences considered false,
but are unable to guarantee the satisfaction of Putnam's desiderata. In other
words, Quine expects of translation only the preservation of *truth*, not the
preservation of what we ordinarily conceive as *meaning*. Quine's point is,
of course, that it is precisely this fact about 'meaning' – the fact that it is
underdetermined by truth-preserving translations – that tells against the
ordinary notion of meaning. Putnam retorts that there is nothing wrong
with the ordinary notion of meaning, Quine's constraints on translation are
simply too weak to capture it. We should not be surprised, therefore, that a
multitude of incompatible 'translations' meet Quine's minimalist standards.
Putnam illustrates his point (1975, pp. 168–169) by designing a 'translation'
that correlates (1) "The distance from the earth to the sun is 93 million
miles" with (2) "There are no rivers on Mars," while correlating all other
sentences with themselves. This bizarre 'translation' satisfies Quine's criteria but disrupts explanatory linkages. Consider, for instance, (3) "It takes
8 minutes for light from the sun to reach the earth." Whereas (1) figures in
the explanation of (3), the 'translation' of (1) plays no role in explaining the
'translation' of (3). Being unacceptable by Putnam's criteria, these 'translations' cannot establish Quine's indeterminacy thesis. Such Pickwickian
'translation' may indeed be indeterminate, but true-to-life translation is as
determinate as one would want, in the context of ordinary human communication, with its characteristic vagueness and imprecision.

Let us compare this objection with a passage on indeterminacy from
Reason, Truth and History:

> One can understand the assertion that a translation fails to capture exactly
> the sense or reference of the original as an admission that a better translation
> scheme might be found; but it makes only an illusion of sense to say that
> all possible translation schemes fail to capture the 'real' sense or reference.
> Synonymy exists only as a relation, or better, as a family of relations . . . which

we employ to equate different expressions for the purpose of interpretation. The idea that there is some such thing as 'real' synonymy, apart from all workable practices of mutual interpretation, has been discarded as a myth. (1981, p. 116)

Here it is no longer a circumscribed failure to take into account some relevant constraint on translation for which Putnam faults Quine, but rather the far more serious failing of having created an "illusion of sense" where no sense is really present. The passage goes straight to the heart of the clash between the iconoclast and the skeptic. If there are no such entities as 'real' meaning, 'real' synonymy, and so on, what loss has, in fact, been incurred when we assert that the 'real' notion has eluded us? Putnam is willing to do without 'real' meaning and synonymy, but stresses that this renunciation does not amount to meaning-skepticism insofar as human communication is concerned. It is questionable, in my opinion, whether Quine was indeed bemoaning the inaccessibility of the 'real' thing when he put forward the indeterminacy thesis. Although a number of his formulations support the skeptical reading, others suggest that his target is a specific philosophical theory – the "myth of the museum," as he calls it. On this reading, it is Quine's opponent, the believer in Platonic meanings, who worships an idol, whereas Quine is with Putnam in the iconoclast camp. "The word 'Meaning' is indeed bandied as freely in lexicography as in the street, and so be it. But let us be wary when it threatens to figure as a supporting member of a theory" (Quine 1995, p. 83).

Putnam's move from refutation to iconoclasm is another example of the pragmatic turn we should be familiar with by now. Its basic thrust is that meaning-skepticism is unreasonable even before getting down to specific counterarguments. The iconoclastic move is all the more significant in view of Putnam's own model-theoretic arguments, which can easily be taken to advance an indeterminacy at least as radical as Quine's. To be precise, we must recall that Quine's thesis comprises two quite independent indeterminacies, the first denying the uniqueness of sentence-to-sentence translation, the second denying the uniqueness of reference. As we have seen, Putnam's refutation touches upon the former thesis, narrowing down the number of translations by adding constraints; his model-theoretic arguments, on the other hand, strengthen the case for the indeterminacy of reference. Quine's "inscrutability of reference" arises due to the elusive nature of individuation, the lack of decisive fact as to whether '*gavagai*' means 'rabbit,' 'undetached rabbit part' or 'manifested rabbithood.' Putnam's model-theoretic arguments point to the more extreme erosion of reference resulting from possible permutations of language that preserve sentences' truth-values while shifting the references of their component terms.

Putnam and Quine make different use of the indeterminacy of reference: Quine sees it as having ontological ramifications, whereas Putnam uses it as a *reductio* argument against metaphysical realism and 'magical' theories of reference. Indeed, he uses it against theories of reference in general, insofar as they presume to characterize the language – world relation from a 'neutral,' language-independent viewpoint. Internal realism, we saw, is a partisan view from within our own language, and thus need pay no attention to reference-shifting permutations. To the internal realist, "'rabbit' refers to rabbits" is unproblematic, or, as van Fraassen (1997) puts it, constitutes a 'pragmatic a priori.' There are further differences between Putnam and Quine with respect to the assumptions underlying their respective philosophies of mind and views of language, the most significant being Quine's commitment to behaviorism, a position Putnam has repeatedly rejected. Despite these differences, the gap between their positions on meaning should not be overstated. Both seek, first and foremost, to dislodge what they see as a mythic theory of meaning, on which meanings are well-defined Platonic entities, inhabiting an abstract sphere of disembodied ideas or the minds of individual speakers, and unequivocally determining reference. Both Putnam and Quine seek to replace this picture with a description of linguistic practice that construes neither meanings nor the meaning–reference relation in this traditional way. Moreover, both take human communication as a given. In promoting indeterminacy, they do not question our communicative success, but rather the adequacy of the mythic theory often invoked to explain it. To the extent that meaning-skepticism alleges a failure of communication, namely, failure to capture the 'real' meanings of utterances, it is endorsed by neither Putnam nor Quine.

IV. MEANING AND NECESSITY

My last example of Putnam's change of strategy will focus on his evolving views as to necessary truth. Over the years, Putnam entertained a number of different positions on the status of truths traditionally considered necessary truths, including the narrower class of logical truths. Let me mention a few of them. In his work on quantum logic, Putnam advances the view that logic is empirical. In "It Ain't Necessarily So," he replaces the traditional conception of necessity *tout court* with a softer notion of relative necessity – necessity within a particular body of belief. "Analyticity and

Apriority" defends the view that some truths – and in particular, the law of noncontradiction – are indeed absolutely necessary. Finally, "Rethinking Mathematical Necessity" and subsequent papers put forward a new synthesis between the earlier concept of relative necessity and a position Putnam traces back to Kant, Frege and Wittgenstein, on which logic is constitutive of rational thought, and thus delineates the bounds of sense. Here Putnam's response to the concern that the basic laws of logic or arithmetic could prove false is that we are unable to make sense of this claim or the alleged alternative laws it envisions. "Rethinking Mathematical Necessity" thus rehabilitates the notion of necessary truth.[25]

Neither of these positions is in and of itself a defense against skepticism. My reason for drawing attention to Putnam's views on necessary truth is that, like his recent responses to skepticism, they bring to the fore the question of whether there is an intelligible alternative to the received view.

A number of questions arise regarding the connection between skepticism and the grounding of necessary truth. First, traditionally, the robustness of the laws of logic and arithmetic, or even of, say, the transitivity of temporal order, is conceived of as essentially different from the robustness of belief in the existence of physical objects and fellow human beings. The former truths, it is said, are necessary: the latter, only widely accepted but contingent facts. Indeed, the latter have been subjected to skeptical distrust far more frequently than the former. Should it be maintained that both sorts of belief are equally well substantiated by the emptiness of all purported alternatives, how are we to understand the traditional difference? Doesn't the sweeping application of the no-meaningful-alternative argument signal a breakdown of the necessary/contingent distinction, and not its rehabilitation, as we had been led to expect?

Second, emphasis on conceivability seems like a shift from logic to psychology. How much weight does Putnam assign to our ability (or lack of ability) to conceive of alternatives to the received view? Third, and most intriguing, once we accept a belief on the basis of the no-meaningful-alternative argument, can we nonetheless ascertain its defeasibility? The rejection of skepticism is in harmony with pragmatism, but the argument Putnam uses here could be seen as a betrayal of another key tenet of pragmatism, namely, recognition of the fact that we are fallible, and any of our beliefs might eventually prove false.

To get a handle on these problems, it is best to begin with Putnam's notion of relative necessity in "It Ain't Necessarily So." Putnam, considering conceptual revolutions such as the discovery of non-Euclidean geometries and their application in physics, argues (*a*) that such revolutions illustrate the revisability of necessary truths; and (*b*) that though these revolutions typically involve semantic changes, that is, new definitions of basic terms, they are never exhausted by mere semantic change. The former observation – the susceptibility of necessary truth to change – might be thought to suggest that necessary truths should be construed as ordinary empirical truths subject to refutation. Putnam does not go this route. Until the discovery of non-Euclidean geometries, he maintains, no experiment would have served to test Euclid's fifth postulate. Had we come across potential counterexamples, we would have saved Euclidean geometry by changing the laws of physics. But the immunity of this postulate turned out to be less absolute than once thought. Conceptual revolutions open up new vistas that make room for previously unforeseen alternatives. Hence the notion of relative necessity – necessity relative to a particular epistemic context.

The latter thesis – that conceptual revolutions are not exhausted by semantic change – is one of Putnam's strongest objections to conventionalism. On the conventionalist account, the robustness of 'necessary truths' reflects, not the unassailability of fact, but our commitment to rules we have created. Revision of 'necessary truths' is possible, but amounts only to substitution of one set of stipulations for another.[26] Putnam refuses to reduce the revolutionary shift from Newtonian to relativistic mechanics to a semantic change in the definition of a single term, namely, 'the metric.' Granted, scientific revolutions do introduce new concepts into our lexicon, but they are never solely about new definitions or meanings, and thus never solely about conventions. Our creation of new concepts, and our coming to accept new beliefs, go hand in hand. There is no way we can redefine terms such as 'straight line' or 'metric' that will not, ipso facto, lead to revision of beliefs previously thought of as necessary. Taken together, theses (*a*) and (*b*) lead Putnam to reject the traditional account of necessary truths without adopting either of its recent rivals – empiricism and conventionalism.

"Rethinking Mathematical Necessity" strengthens the notion of relative necessity. Putnam's earlier claim, that what is conceivable to us might have been inconceivable prior to a particular scientific revolution, could, perhaps, be taken psychologically, pointing to contingent failures of human imagination. The stronger thesis put forward now, at least with regard to logic, will not admit of such psychologism. Here, the argument is that logic, being constitutive of thought and meaningful discourse, must be in place before any claims to truth, knowledge and justification can be made. Thus, from Putnam's present perspective, as from Wittgenstein's, 'illogical thought' cannot be considered thought at all.[27]

The constraint on meaningfulness seems simple enough: to speak meaningfully of a conjectured possibility – a different world, a different logic, and so on – we must be able to flesh it out, to convey what the envisaged possibility would look like, how it would emerge, how it would function, and so on. 'Fleshing out' is not a binary notion, though, but a matter of degree. A world in which *modus ponens* fails may not be visualizable at all, while other worlds may lend themselves to richer or poorer descriptions. Wittgenstein entertains the possibility of wood being bought and sold, not by volume or weight, but by the area it covers. Is this description of an alternative to our own practice sufficiently 'fleshed out' to make sense? What would be required vis-à-vis fictional scenarios such as legends and science fiction? And what about the brains-in-a-vat scenario? Obviously, whether a possibility makes sense is itself a matter for negotiation, and a reasonable application of the 'fleshing out' criterion yields a vision of necessity that is flexible and admitting of gradation.

Putnam's use of the no-meaningful-alternative argument, we saw, seeks to bring out an analogy between attempts to deny necessary truth and the skeptic's denial of knowledge of the external world and other minds: both are rejected as meaningless. The skeptic will probably object that the solipsistic alternative she entertains makes perfect sense and needs no further 'fleshing out.' Indeed, her world looks, sounds, smells and feels every bit like the world experienced by the rest of us, whom she considers to be under the sway of the illusion of knowledge. Putnam may be right about the constitutive role of logic, but belief in external reality and other minds is far from being constitutive in the same way. I am unaware of any explicit response to this putative objection Putnam may have offered. It seems to me, however, that the skeptic's objection fails to grasp the place of practice in pragmatism in general and Putnam's philosophy in particular. The beliefs and attitudes the skeptic casts doubt upon may not be constitutive of reason, but they are constitutive of our actions, and indeed our lives. This line of reasoning will, of course, require further elaboration should we wish to pursue it in our efforts to defeat skepticism.

I now come to our last question, the relation between the rejection of skepticism and the avowal of fallibilism. Both these positions can be found in Peirce, and both are embraced by Putnam in his endeavor to make room for knowledge while avoiding the hubris of taking oneself to be beyond error. But a problem arises, a problem akin to that of the 'introduction paradox': the author of a work, though confident of the views expressed therein, nonetheless acknowledges the likelihood that some are erroneous. Is there a tension between the pragmatist commitment to fallibilism and the

dismissal of skepticism? To begin with, we must distinguish the global doubt
of the skeptic from more circumscribed doubts. Peirce insisted that scientific investigation must address specific questions against the background of
a relatively stable body of belief. He made this claim in the context of opposing the Cartesian notion that global doubt was a prerequisite of knowledge,
that all previously held knowledge had to be called into question before a
fresh start could be made. Indeed, it is precisely the feasibility of making
an utterly fresh start that Peirce was denying. Davidson makes a similar
point in "On the Very Idea of a Conceptual Scheme." Islands of doubt or
disagreement can exist in a sea of shared belief, but global doubt and total
disparity of belief are both incomprehensible. Fallibilism, though allowing
us to question each of our beliefs in turn, does not license the skeptic's
global doubt.

A second and closely related difference we must bear in mind is that between abstract and concrete doubt. The concrete doubt of someone facing
a problem, be it intellectual, moral or emotional, is existentially different
from the gesture of abstract philosophical doubt. A concrete doubt will
typically have reasons. I may doubt X's friendship because X keeps avoiding me, or because X has begun to act in ways that do not seem compatible
with wishing me well, and so on. The skeptic, of course, does not think such
reasons are necessary; on the contrary, it is the failure of her opponent to
provide satisfactory reasons for a given belief that sustains her doubt. Fallibilism need not mandate concrete doubt about each of the beliefs under
consideration, but does acknowledge the possibility that concrete doubts
will arise when reasons are given.

These differences between skepticism and fallibilism suggest that, generally, skepticism can be rejected while fallibilism is endorsed. Yet when it
comes to a specific belief, we might still worry that being skeptical about
it amounts to manifesting the very attitude evinced by the fallibilist. The
skeptic refuses to see the belief in question as constituting knowledge; the
fallibilist asserts that it might, like any other belief, eventually prove false.
Where exactly does the difference lie? Perhaps in their respective concepts
of knowledge. The skeptic's criteria for knowledge may be too stringent for
the fallibilist, who is willing to base claims of knowledge on evidence that is
good enough though less than perfect. The fallibilist is thus not being in-
consistent in urging that knowledge is corrigible. But this weakened notion
of knowledge will not cover cases falling under Putnam's no-meaningful-
alternative argument. On this argument, it is unintelligible to cast doubt
on beliefs that are constitutive of reason, for no alternative set of beliefs

has been sufficiently fleshed out to make sense to us. How can the fallibilist escape this predicament? Isn't he required to make sense of the possibility that the belief in question might turn out to be false? And if he cannot do so, as must be the case if Putnam is right, is he not just as unintelligible as the skeptic?

It appears that to uphold fallibilism while defending the unassailability of necessary truth, Putnam must soften fallibilism somewhat. When the fallibilist claims that we might be wrong about any one of our beliefs, including so-called necessary truths, he must not pretend he can doubt such truths. Indeed, given the no-meaningful-alternative argument, he cannot. But, learning the lesson of conceptual revolutions, he may still acknowledge the possibility that new conceptual horizons will enable us to make sense of that which we cannot conceive at present. The fallibilist's claim that necessary truth is not immune to doubt and revision can only be intended in this weaker sense. With regard to the issues addressed by classical skepticism, however, even this softened fallibilism sounds somewhat hollow.

On the issue of external reality and other minds, it seems, it is hardly possible to envisage that conceptual change, radical as it may be, will make a real difference. Hence we may want to restrict fallibilism in yet another way. Fallibilism will be applicable to beliefs and assertions, whereas general attitudes, which by their nature cannot be asserted or denied, will remain outside its scope. If I am right in construing Putnam's internal realism (see section I) as such a vital attitude rather than a quasi-scientific theory, then our embracing it expresses itself in our reaching out to reality, not in assertions that fall within the scope of fallibilism. Whether the modifications of fallibilism suggested here resolve the potential tension between fallibilism and the notion of the unthinkable advanced in Putnam's recent writings is a question that calls for further consideration.[28]

I opened this essay with a distinction between two strategies for defeating skepticism. Evidently, the no-meaningful-alternative argument I have elaborated upon lies at the heart of the second strategy – exposing the senselessness of skepticism. The inspiration of Wittgenstein is conspicuous. "Scepticism is *not* irrefutable, but obviously nonsensical (*offenbar unsinnig*), when it tries to raise doubts where no questions can be asked. For a doubt can exist only where a question exists, a question only where an answer exists, and an answer only where something *can be said*" (*Tractatus* 6.51). Similar dicta appear throughout Wittgenstein's later writings. For Wittgenstein, however, this attitude toward skepticism is closely tied to his descriptive-therapeutic conception of philosophy. It would take another essay to examine Putnam's vision of philosophy, but I will conclude this one by noting that on this central issue I do not see Putnam following in the footsteps of Wittgenstein.

Notes

1. I try to avoid the term 'theory of meaning,' which Putnam explicitly rejects (1983, p. xvii).
2. See, in particular, Strawson (1985) and Stroud (1984).
3. (1975, vol. 1, p. 73; 1978, chap. 2).
4. The argument, in this form, was first suggested by Richard Boyd; see, e.g., his (1984).
5. This idea can also be adjusted to apply to the notion of approximate truth.
6. The name originated with Gilbert Harman; see his (1965). For critique of the use of this inference as a defense of realism, see Fine (1986) and Ben-Menahem (1990).   .
7. Quantum mechanics is generally considered an exception, where realism and nonrealism do compete in the empirical arena, and are thus thought to differ in empirical import. I argued against this common misconception in my (1997), but will not pursue the matter here.
8. Whether Putnam's early realism was indeed a form of metaphysical realism is an interesting question. Although in at least one place (1978, p. 129) Putnam said it was, this is debatable.
9. Model-theoretic considerations are central to "Realism and Reason," "Models and Reality," and chapter 2 of *Reason, Truth and History*. I will not go into the nuances of the differences between the arguments presented in these papers.
10. Some, but not all, versions of Putnam's model-theoretic argument are based on the Lowenheim-Skolem theorem, according to which every formal theory rich enough to include arithmetic will have non-isomorphic models. Thus even the number of entities in 'the world' will differ from one model to another. For reasons I will not discuss here, this application of the Lowenheim-Skolem theorem is still controversial.
11. In a number of recent talks, Putnam has emphasized the context sensitivity of even the simplest of expressions. A sustained argument for context sensitivity can be found in Travis (2000).
12. Putnam remembers that this passage is a response to David Lewis's remark, intended as a defense of metaphysical realism, that surely our best theory could be false, for we might turn out to be brains in a vat.
13. Some of these attempts to counter Putnam's paradox are inspired by the very pragmatist considerations that motivate internal realism; see, e.g., van Fraassen (1997).
14. Putnam has wavered somewhat with respect to the relation of truth to verification, at times endorsing Dummett's verificationism, at times stressing the

irreducibility of truth to verification or any other nonrealist alternative. "Models and Reality" is perhaps the point at which he is closest to Dummett. *Reason, Truth and History* and *Representation and Reality* put more weight on the irreducibility of the notion of truth. Putnam consistently disagrees with Dummett, however, on holism. Dummett's conception of language is hierarchical; Putnam's, holistic.

15. Some nonrealist positions can account for success more readily than they can explain failure. The conventionalist attempt to ground truth in definitions or grammatical rules is one example, the relativist notion of truth within a particular context, paradigm, etc., another.

16. Putnam (1998, p. 239).

17. Putnam uses the term "conceptual relativity" in this context.

18. Putnam alludes to Wisdom (1938).

19. Frege knew better, of course; see Juliet Floyd's essay (Chap. 2) in this volume.

20. From the metaphysical realist point of view, causality itself, a relation that is 'in the world,' is supposed to single out the correct reference relation. But any relation so conceived will be vulnerable to the model-theoretic argument. See Putnam (1983, p. 24).

21. Strictly speaking, the metaphysical realist need not subscribe to a 'magical' theory of reference. Indeed, some metaphysical realists accept a causal theory of reference. However, in view of the analogy between the 'magical' theory of reference and the 'magical' correspondence between representations and the world that lies at the core of metaphysical realism, Putnam's suspicion seems well warranted.

22. A point McDowell has stressed both in interpreting Wittgenstein and in other contexts.

23. Wittgenstein also flirted with verificationism before his later position was fully formed.

24. Putnam compares Grunbaum (1962) and Quine (1960). See also Grunbaum (1973).

25. It would take another essay to review these positions and their interrelations in detail. Note, however, that there is no contradiction between the irrevisability of a few basic laws and the revisability of others, as in the case of quantum mechanics. Moreover, in quantum mechanics, sense has been made of such an alternative logic.

26. This is, roughly, Putnam's understanding of conventionalism. A fully accurate characterization of conventionalism, however, would call for additional elaboration.

27. On illogical thought in Putnam and Wittgenstein, see Conant (1992).

28. The problem of whether we can meaningfully acknowledge the possibility of a thought that is unthinkable by our lights, a thought lying beyond our horizon of intelligibility, resembles a much discussed difficulty arising from the *Tractatus*. Is there only a single category of utter nonsense, or are there also more benign forms of nonsense that must not be asserted but can be made use

of? This question, in turn, raises the question of whether, and in what sense, the propositions of the *Tractatus* are themselves nonsensical; see, e.g., Diamond (1991). Analogous questions can be raised with regard to the notion of limits of sense in Wittgenstein's later writings.

References

Ben-Menahem, Y. (1990). "The Inference to the Best Explanation." *Erkenntnis* 33:319–344.

(1997). "Dummett vs. Bell on Quantum Mechanics." *Studies in the History and Philosophy of Modern Physics* 28:277–290.

Boyd, R. N. (1984). "The Current Status of Scientific Realism." In *Scientific Realism*, ed. J. Leplin. Berkeley: University of California Press, pp. 41–82.

Carnap, R. (1955). *Meaning and Necessity.* 2nd ed. Chicago: Chicago University Press.

Conant, J. (1992). "The Search for Logically Alien Thought: Descartes, Kant, Frege and the *Tractatus.*" *The Philosophy of Hilary Putnam, Philosophical Topics* 20:115–180.

Davidson, D. (1984). "On the Very Idea of a Conceptual Scheme." In *Inquiries into Truth and Interpretation.* Oxford: Clarendon Press, pp. 183–198.

Diamond, C. (1991). "Throwing Away the Ladder." In C. Diamond *The Realistic Spirit.* Cambridge, MA: MIT Press.

Fine, A. (1986). "Unnatural Attitudes: Realist and Instrumentalist Attachments to Science." *Mind* 95:149–179. See also A. Fine, *The Shaky Game: Einstein, Realism, and the Quantum Theory.* 2nd ed. Chicago: University of Chicago Press, (1996), chapters 7 and 8.

Grunbaum, A. (1962). "Geometry, Chronometry and Empiricism." In H. Feigl and G. Maxwell (eds.), *Minnesota Studies in the Philosophy of Science III.* Minneapolis: University of Minnesota Press, pp. 405–526.

(1973). *Philosophical Problems of Space and Time.* 2nd enlarged ed. Dordrecht: Reidel. (*Boston Studies in the Philosophy of Science III*, ed. R. S. Cohen and M. W. Wartofsky.

Harman, G. (1965). "The Inference to the Best Explanation." *The Philosophical Review* 74:88–95.

Putnam, H. (1975) *Philosophical Papers*: Vol. I, *Mathematics, Matter and Logic*; Vol. II, *Mind, Language and Reality.* Cambridge: Cambridge University Press.

(1978). *Meaning and the Moral Sciences.* London: Routledge and Kegan Paul.

(1981). *Reason, Truth and History.* Cambridge: Cambridge University Press.

(1983). *Philosophical Papers*: Vol. III, *Realism and Reason.* Cambridge: Cambridge University Press.

(1994). *Words and Life.* Ed. J. Conant. Cambridge, MA: Harvard University Press.

(1998). "Scepticism." In Marcelo Stamm (ed.), *Philosophie in Synthetischer Absicht.* Stuttgart: Klett-Cotta, pp. 239–270.

Quine, W. V. O. (1960). *Word and Object.* Cambridge, MA: MIT Press.

(1995). *From Stimulus to Science.* Cambridge, MA: Harvard University Press.

Strawson, P. F. (1985). *Scepticism and Naturalism: Some Varieties.* New York: Columbia University Press.

Stroud, B. (1984). *The Significance of Philosophical Scepticism.* Oxford: Clarendon Press.

Travis, C. (2000). *Unshadowed Thought.* Cambridge, MA: Harvard University Press.

Van Fraassen, B. C. (1997). "Putnam's Paradox: Metaphysical Realism Revamped and Evaded." *Philosophical Perspectives II: Mind, Causation and the World*, pp. 18–42.

Wisdom, J. (1938). "Metaphysics and Verification." *Mind* 47:452–498.

6 | The Tale of Quantum Logic
TIM MAUDLIN

Like all good tales, this is a story about temptation. It all begins with Kant.

In the first Critique, Kant posed the fateful question: how is a priori synthetic knowledge possible? Among the items of undoubted knowledge to be accounted for: that the world as revealed by experience shall be in a Euclidean space; that it shall be governed by deterministic laws; that all substance is permanent, being neither created nor destroyed.

The detailed argumentation brought forward in support of these claims is famously obscure, but the general outlines of the position are easy to sketch. We can know a priori that the world of experience will conform to these principles, not because they are conditions on things as they are in themselves, but rather because they are conditions on how things must be presented to us and conceived by us and judged by us in order to constitute *experience*. Items of experience must be given to us in perception, and so are subject to the forms of perceptive intuition (space and time). Further, in order to judge that our perceptions are of objective things, the appearances of things must conform to certain rules. In short, a priori synthetic knowledge is possible because it is not knowledge of how things are, but knowledge of how the world as revealed by experience must be, in order to be a world revealed by experience.[1]

The progress of science was not kind to Kant. Had he been correct, it would have been impossible for empirical scientific inquiry ever to produce an account of the world that is not set in Euclidean space, governed by deterministic laws, with conservation of indestructible substance. Such an account might be logically possible, since it need not contain contradictions, but it could not possibly be taken seriously, much less be accepted by the scientific establishment. However, one by one, each of these principles has been questioned, or even overthrown, by empirical research. At this moment, it is not clear that there is anything that would count as a permanent substance in the physical world, and it is generally accepted (whether correctly or not) that the laws of physics are not deterministic. But the first and most spectacular fall was the Euclidean structure of space.

156

In 1915, Einstein produced the relativistic theory of gravity: the General Theory of Relativity. That theory postulates that the fundamental spatio-temporal structure of the world is not fixed (as all previous theories, including the Special Theory of Relativity, had supposed), but rather varies with the distribution of mass and energy. In the vulgar tongue, this result was often reported by saying that according to Einstein "space is curved" (non-Euclidean), and it is the curvature of space which produces gravitational effects.[2] Presented in these terms, the confrontation with Kant could not be more stark.

Kant, of course, need not have been bothered by the discovery of non-Euclidean geometry per se. Indeed, as Kant insisted that geometry was synthetic rather than analytic, he would have *predicted* that one could, as a purely formal exercise, produce a set of geometrical axioms that differ from Euclid's and still entail no contradiction. What Kantianism could not abide is the idea that such a non-Euclidean geometry be taken seriously as a scientific proposal for the geometrical structure of *space* – the very space in which appearances are given to us. And this is just what Einstein did propose.

The neo-Kantians tried to rise to the challenge. They insisted that no experimental results could *force* one to abandon Euclidean space: all the phenomena of nature *could be interpreted* as taking place in a Euclidean space, by means of hypotheses regarding the physical behavior of matter, especially of what we call "measuring devices". Since the geometrical structure of space (and indeed space itself) is not directly observable, there also must be some postulates connecting the observable behavior of things to the underlying spatial structure in order for conclusions about the latter to be drawn from observations of the former. And if push comes to shove, these postulates could always be denied in order to preserve the Euclidean structure of space.

This was one of the issues that the Logical Positivists cut their teeth on. Reichenbach's *The Philosophy of Space and Time* (1958) is the locus classicus of the positivist response. In that book, Reichenbach grants the neo-Kantian claim: one can always hang onto Euclidean space, and use it in one's physics come what may, by making appropriate adjustments *elsewhere* in the theory. In particular, by postulating various sorts of universal forces and causal anomalies, any set of phenomena can be embedded in a space of Euclidean metric and topology.[3] But the characteristic Reichenbachian counterresponse is that the Kantian strategy, while logically possible, entails *paying a price* in order to retain Euclidean space. The price is exactly universal forces (which cannot be directly observed) and causal anomalies (unexplained duplications of objects or periodic boundary conditions). The *physics* of these forces and anomalies is unnatural and unprecedented: they would never be proposed save for the obsessive desire to retain Euclidean space. Eliminating the forces and anomalies by passing to a non-Euclidean space makes the physics simpler and more natural. And therefore, according to Reichenbach, the price is one that is too high to pay. Overall considerations of economy militate in favor of Einstein over Kant.

This calculus of theoretical utility ought to sound familiar: it is exactly the approach that Quine urges in "Two Dogmas of Empiricism" (1953). But in that paper Quine goes Reichenbach one better, at least in principle, for he suggests that the very same calculus of theoretical utility might similarly militate in favor of the revision *of logic itself:*

> Any statement can be held true come what may if we make drastic enough adjustments elsewhere in the system. Even a statement very close to the periphery can be held true'in the face of recalcitrant experience by pleading hallucination or by amending certain statements of the kind called logical laws. Conversely, by the same token, no statement is immune from revision. Revision even of the logical law of the excluded middle has been proposed as a means of simplifying quantum mechanics; and what difference is there in principle between such a shift and the shift whereby Kepler superseded Ptolemy, or Einstein Newton, or Darwin Aristotle? (Quine 1953, p. 43)

Quine here takes his place in the great pantheon of Temptation: the apple hangs glistening before us. Kepler, Einstein, Darwin . . . all one has to do to become the next entry on this list is show how a revision in logic could substantially simplify an empirical theory. He even points to the theory: quantum mechanics. Who could resist? Reichenbach has shown the way, the overarching structure. All that is to be sought are the analogs of universal forces and causal anomalies, the unlovely theoretical posits that are forced on us by the adoption of classical logic and that may be avoided by the use of a nonstandard logic. Fill in the blanks and win immortality! It's an offer you can't refuse. And thereby hangs our tale.

PUTNAM'S FIRST THEORY

Hilary Putnam took a bite of Quine's apple – or rather, as we shall see, two bites. The first resulted in the 1968 paper "Is Logic Empirical?" reprinted in *Mathematics Matter and Method* (1975) under the title "The Logic of Quantum Mechanics". The second – arising from recognized shortcomings of the first – gave birth to one section of "Quantum Mechanics and the Observer" in 1981 (reprinted in *Realism and Reason*, 1983). The first follows Reichenbach's lead quite explicitly, and so will be straightforward to analyze. The second, coming after Putnam's rejection of "metaphysical realism", provides a thornier exegetical problem. We shall consider them in turn.

Ultimately, after some three decades of tinkering, Putnam sailed free of the Siren song: in his response to a paper of Michael Redhead, he both acknowledges some of Redhead's criticisms and indicates that there are also other reasons for dissatisfaction with his former views (Clark and Hale 1994, p. 280). So in a sense, this essay is only of historical interest. Still, the papers in which Putnam advocates quantum logic are probably much better known than the retraction, and in my view there are more fundamental grounds for complaint than those cited by Redhead. In addition, Quine's offer of immortality doubtless has a perennial appeal. So it seems worthwhile to reconstruct the outlines of Putnam's strategy, and to pursue a radical evaluation of it.

Before addressing the details of Putnam's argument in "The Logic of Quantum Mechanics", we should pause to remark on some quarrels he deftly sidesteps. Consider, for example, the following argument that a partisan of classical logic might offer:

> The classical logical particles are given by their semantics. In particular, the classical connectives are truth-functional connectives: appending a negation sign to a sentence produces a sentence which is true exactly when the original is false and false exactly when the original is true. Similarly for the binary connectives. The conjunction of two sentences is a sentence which is true exactly when the conjuncts are true and false when at least one conjunct is false; their disjunction is true when at least one disjunct is true and false when both disjuncts are false. Given these semantical properties, one can then show that certain *inferences* must be truth-preserving: the inference from a conjunction to one of its conjuncts or from a disjunct to a disjunction, for example. But it is not the inferences which define the logical particles, it is the semantics.
>
> Now there might be other ways of conjoining propositions to form other propositions which validate *similar* inferences in many circumstances, or there might be other features of sentences beside *truth* which one might be concerned with. And in these cases, there might be structures which look somewhat like classical logic, but are not. For example, if one were concerned with *theoremhood* rather than *truth*, then one would say exactly the same thing about conjunction (a conjunction is a theorem just in case each conjunct is a theorem) but not about disjunction (a disjunction can be

a theorem even though neither disjunct is). So certainly the valid inferences concerning theoremhood are not the same as the valid inferences concerning truth, but still one has not abandoned classical logic – one has simply changed the subject.

Or again (to take an example which is very close to "quantum logic"), consider the class of "location propositions" concerning the whereabouts of my three-year-old son Maxwell in the house. Each proposition specifies a location (dining room, first floor, kitchen, etc.). Let us suppose that such a proposition is *true* just in case Maxwell *is entirely within the location*. So we are here concerned with truth, not with any other feature of a proposition. Now I can, if I wish, introduce binary connectives on these propositions, symbolized by "∪" and "∩" with the following semantics: the proposition "A ∩ B" is true just in case Maxwell is the *intersection* of the location mentioned in A and the location mentioned in B, and "A ∪ B" is true just in case Maxwell is in the *union* of the location mentioned in A and the location mentioned in B. Now in *all* circumstances, the truth value of "A ∩ B" will be identical to that of "A & B" (where "&" is the classical truth-functional connective), so valid inferences remain valid whenever "&" is replaced by "∩" or vice versa. And in *most* circumstances the truth value of "A ∪ B" is identical to that of "A ∨ B", where "∨" is the classical disjunction, so a truth-preserving inference that uses one of these connectives will *usually* preserve truth if that connective is switched for the other. But not always. For when, as sometimes happens, Maxwell is standing with one foot in the kitchen and one foot in the dining room, "kitchen ∪ dining room" is true while "kitchen ∨ dining room" is false.

So if one likes, one can talk of 'the logic of "∩" and "∪"', and one can note that it is, in most circumstances, very like the logic of "&" and "∨". And in some circumstances, using "∩" and "∪" might be more convenient, for the purposes at hand, than using "&" and "∨". And there might even be circumstances in normal discourse in which the English word "or" is better rendered into formal language by "∪" rather than "∨". But none of this would constitute replacing or undermining classical logic: the classical connectives still exist, and the classical theorems are what they are.

It is here that the disanalogy with space becomes clear. Euclidean geometry is a perfectly good bit of mathematics, as are the various forms of non-Euclidean geometry. The geometries *per se* do not come into conflict with one another. It is only when one makes an assertion about *physical space* – that it has one geometry rather than another – that a conflict can occur and a choice must be made. Adopting one hypothesis (that space is Euclidean) forces one to abandon another (that space is non-Euclidean). But adopting the language of "∩" and "∪" does not, *per se*, require one to abandon the language of "&" and "∨". There is no analog to physical space (what would it be – "true disjunction"?) such that at most one of the connectives "⊔" and "∨" can be the correct theory of *it*. So while there might be non-classical connectives like "⊔", and while it might be convenient when discussing quantum mechanics to use those connectives, they cannot, in any proper sense, be said to replace or correct the classical connectives.

I have a good deal of sympathy for this objection (the author of it, after all, has a son of the same age and name as mine), and I think that it does provide a significant challenge for any account in which "quantum logic" is supposed to replace classical logic. Putnam addresses some of these issues in section 6 of "The Logic of Quantum Mechanics", where he concludes that our account of meaning is not precise enough to determine whether replacing classical logic with quantum logic constitutes a change of meaning of the connectives, and if so of which ones. In that section Putnam only considers accounts that tie the meanings of logical particles to the inference rules they occur in, not (as suggested above) to the semantics, but still his discussion shows that he is not committed one way or the other on the issue of whether the meanings of the connectives have changed. Furthermore, it is clear that Putnam's arguments do not rely on there being some thing of which the classical and quantum connectives are alternative and incompatible accounts. So classical logic is not to be *displaced* by the discovery of some sort of superior alternative. Rather, Putnam means to produce, first, an argument that the use of classical logic has *bad consequences*, and then a separate argument that quantum logic could be used as an alternative structure that retains the virtues of classical logic in everyday life. It is of critical importance in this argument that the bad consequences of classical logic be really bad: it is these that argue in favor of *abandoning* or *renouncing* classical logic rather than simply leaving it unused when doing physics. But, of course, bad consequences of classical logic – no matter how bad – could not reasonably motivate us to renounce it without some replacement that can pick up the slack: even a bad set of inference rules is better than none at all. So the structure of Putnam's argument is: (1) if you accept classical logic, then there are certain empirical phenomena that are problematic because the phenomena, together with the logic, force you to accept some unlovely postulates in your physics (the analogs of universal forces and causal anomalies); (2) there exists an alternative logic such that the same phenomena, when analyzed using this logic, no longer demand the unwanted physical postulates; and (3) in the realm of everyday life, the two logics agree, so abandoning classical logic in favor of quantum logic will not entail the loss of any of the virtues that classical logic has been recognized as possessing.[4]

What, then, are the undesirable consequences of using classical logic? It is easiest to use the very example that Putnam most often employs: the two-slit experiment. Electrons are fired, one by one, at a barrier that contains two slits. Each individual electron makes a determinate, localized mark on a screen to the far side of the slits. But the pattern formed by a large collection of such electrons shows the interference bands characteristic of wave phenomena: the exact width and placement of the bands is a function of the distance between the two slits. So somehow the location at which each individual mark is made is influenced by the fact that both of the slits are open.

There are two salient empirical phenomena: the particular localized mark of each electron and the interference bands produced by the collection of marks. In general, interpretations of the quantum theory that have an easy time with one of these phenomena have to do some work to account for the other. Let us start with the more standard accounts.

The standard interpretations have little trouble accounting for the interference bands, since the individual electrons are represented by wave-functions. These wave-functions are formally defined over the configuration space of the system, although in this case, since there is only one particle in question, the configuration space is isomorphic to physical space. Furthermore, the wave-function is *spread out* in configuration space: it is nonzero over an area wider than the separation of the slits. And the dynamics of the wave-function is relevantly similar to the dynamics of, say, a water wave: the wave-function "goes through" each slit, and the two "parts" recombine and interfere with each other, as do water waves. Where the standard interpretations run into difficulties is in accounting for the *individual localized marks* produced by the electrons.[5] This requires the so-called collapse of the wave-function: the interaction of the electron wave with the screen somehow results in the electron becoming "localized" somewhere or other on the screen, with the probabilities for various positions being derivable from the (pre-collapse) wave-function.

If we accept that the wave-function is *complete*, that is, that there are no more physical facts about the electron than are represented in the wave-function, and if we accept that it is the interaction with the screen that causes the wave-function to collapse, then we must conclude that *the mark on the screen does not reveal a particular location that the electron had before the interaction.* Insofar as the electron had a location before the formation of the mark, it was "spread out" all over the region of the screen, since the wave-function was. So the screen cannot properly be said to *reveal* or *measure* the preexistent position of the particle; rather, it plays a role in *producing* the localization itself.

Various problems attend any such interpretation of the quantum formalism. Most famously, there is the problem of determining the circumstances in which "wave collapse" occurs, since the collapses are not consequences'of the non-collapse (e.g., Schrödinger) dynamics. The Copenhagen interpretation tended to associate the collapses with "measurements", or with the interaction between the "system" and an "observer", but, as John Bell liked to point out, such talk is unprofessionally vague (see Bell 1990). Progress on this front has been made: mathematically precise theories of the nonlinear "collapse" dynamics have been proposed by Ghirardi, Rimini and Weber (1986) and by Philip Perle (1990). But none of these refinements changes the basic point: before it hit the screen, the electron did not have a precise location, and the mark produced is not the record of some preexistent fact.

What should we say about how the electron got from one side of the slits to the other? If we decide that we can only say that the electron is where (at least most of) the wave-function is, then the electron did not go through the upper slit (only half of the wave-function did), nor through the lower slit. It neither went through slit A nor slit B. It did, however, go through the *union* of slit A and slit B. So just as with the case of Maxwell, we could introduce a language in which "A ∨ B" is false but "A ∪ B" is true. Or if we decide to say that the electron is wherever some significant proportion of its wave-function is, then we could say that the electron went through both slit A and slit B. None of these various ways of talking is inherently superior to another, and none changes the basic facts according to the theory. In particular, no matter how we decide to speak, it is still the case that the mark does not reveal where the electron was just prior the time the mark was formed.

This feature forms one horn of Putnam's dilemma. Putnam finds the idea that a position "measurement" should *create* or *disturb* the very quantity that it is supposed to "measure" to be repellent. Here is how he discusses an analogous case concerning energy and distance:

In the first place, if distance measurement, or energy measurement (or both) disturb the very magnitude that they seek to measure, then there should be some *theory* of this disturbance. Such a theory is notoriously lacking, and it has been erected as an article of faith in the state of Denmark that there can be no such theory. Secondly, if a procedure distorts the very thing it seeks to measure, it is peculiar it should be accepted as a good measurement, and fantastic that a relatively simple theory should predict the *disturbed* values when it can say nothing about the *undisturbed* values. (Putnam 1975, p. 183)

Further, it is supposed to be a virtue of adopting quantum logic that one need no longer maintain that position "measurements" create the position of the particle or that momentum "measurements" create the momentum:

> Lastly, we must say something about 'disturbance by measurement' in this interpretation [i.e., in "quantum logic"]. If I have a system in 'state' S_z (i.e. 'the position is r_z'), and I make a *momentum* measurement, I must 'disturb' S_z. This is so because whatever result T_j I get is going to be *incompatible* with S_z. Thus, when I get T_j, I will have to say that S_z is *no longer true;* but this is no paradox, since the *momentum* measurement disturbed the *position* even according to *classical* physics. Thus the only 'disturbance' on this interpretation is the classical disturbance; we do not have to adopt the strange view that *position* measurement 'disturbs' (or 'brings into being', etc.) *position*, or that *momentum* measurement disturbs (or 'brings into being', etc.) *momentum*, or anything of that kind. (Ibid., p. 186)

Putnam cannot be faulted for failing to anticipate the theories of Ghirardi, Rimini and Weber or of Perle, but let us reconsider these complaints in light of them. In these "collapse" theories, there *is* a theory of the interaction of the system and the "measuring device", and it is derivable from that interaction that the basic calculational tool of quantum theory, Born's rule, should hold (or hold within experimental error). So the "lack of theory" complaint cannot be brought against these theories. It *is*, however, still the case that position measurements typically "bring into existence" position and momentum measurements typically "bring into existence" momentum (unless the system was in the appropriate eigenstate, in which case all theories agree that the eigenstate is revealed by the measurement). So if this feature is per se objectionable, then the objection apparently still stands. Of course, it is not so easy to say why this particular feature should be objectionable, if the theory accounts for all of our experiments and the basic principles of the theory do not seem terribly ad hoc, but let's leave the objection as stated.

Back to our two-slit experiment. We have seen that according to the collapse theories, the position "measurement" made by the screen brings into existence rather than reveals the position of the particle, and we have seen that Putnam finds this objectionable. Is there no way to avoid it? There is one obvious way: simply postulate that the electron does indeed have a definite localized position at all times, and that the position is revealed by the screen. In this case, each electron follows a completely determinate trajectory from the source to the screen, a trajectory that passes either through slit A or through slit B. But now the problem is: how to account for the interference bands?

The bands, as we have seen, depend on both slits being open, and the distance between the slits. But if the electron goes through only one slit, how can the fact that the other slit is open influence its trajectory? The obvious answer is that there must be something other than the electron that goes through *both* slits and that accounts for the interference bands. And we already have a candidate for that thing: the wave-function. So we might be brought to ask the following simple question: is there any way to use the wave-function not to *be* the electron but rather to *guide* or *determine the path* of the electron, so that a collection of electrons, shot through the two slits, will form interference fringes? And the answer to this question, as Putnam knows, is "yes".

The relevant theory was first discovered by Louis be Broglie and then refined by David Bohm: it now goes by the names "the pilot-wave theory", "the causal interpretation" and sometimes "Bohmian mechanics". If one wants a theory that delivers the results of quantum mechanics and in which position measurements always reveal preexistent positions, then Bohm's theory fits the bill. And Putnam, in 1968, was aware of Bohm's theory, although he didn't like it. He gives a somewhat detailed critical evaluation of Bohm's theory in "A Philosopher Looks at Quantum Mechanics" (1965). In this passage, "ND" stands for the "principle of no disturbance", that is, "The measurement does not disturb the observable measured – i.e. the observable has almost the same value an instant before the measurement as it does at the moment the measurement is taken" (p. 138 in Putnam 1975):

> In the literature of quantum mechanics, interpretations according to which the elementary particles have *both* position and momentum at every instant (although one can only know the position or the momentum, but never both at the same instant) are called 'hidden variable' interpretations. The falsity of ND has serious consequences for these hidden variables theories. They are required to postulate strange laws whereby each measurement disturbs the very thing it is measuring – e.g. letting a particle collide with a plate produces a speck on the plate, but at a place where the particle *would not have been* but for the presence of the plate. Actually, such a disturbance of the thing observed by the measurement need not be postulated in *every* measurement, but it does have to be introduced in a great many cases.... In the best-known hidden variable theory – that due to David Bohm – an unknown

physical force (the 'quantum potential') obeying strange laws is introduced
to account for disturbance by the measurement. (Putnam 1975, p. 140)

One might have wished for a more forthcoming criticism. The laws
introduced by the hidden variables theories are twice called "strange", even
though no account is given of exactly what makes them strange. In the case
of Bohm's theory, the quantum potential is derived in a very straightforward
way using classical Hamilton-Jacobi theory. Furthermore, the theory can
be presented without the quantum potential at all, by directly using the
"guidance equation", which specifies how the wave-function determines
the paths of the particles. Far from being "strange", the guidance equation
is the simplest equation one can write down that uses the wave-function
to determine a velocity field for the particles and that also satisfies various
desirable symmetries (see Dürr, Goldstein and Zanghì 1996).

It is true that according to Bohm's theory the presence and exact construction of a measuring device can affect the result of a measurement (see
Albert 1992, pp. 153ff.). But that influence is also completely *principled*
(rather than *ad hoc*): it is a consequence of the physical construction of the
device and the fundamental laws of physics. That is, the influence is not
put in in order to save quantum mechanical predictions, it is rather *derived*
from the basic physical laws. But, of course, if one has an objection to the
very idea that physical laboratory apparatus can have an influence on the
results of an experiment, then one will indeed find Bohm's theory – or any
adequate "hidden variables" theory – objectionable.

Putnam does go on (in 1965) to make arguments to the effect that
Bohm's theory runs into "insuperable difficulties" and that it must invoke
entirely different principles to account for other sorts of experiments. Without spending the time to go into these charges in detail, I will simply assert
that they are untrue. The complete physics of (nonrelativistic) Bohmian
mechanics is given by the Schrödinger equation and the guidance equation, and the theory makes the same predictions as "standard" quantum
mechanics for all experiments that have ever been performed. But it is true
that the principle ND is often violated, and that the presence of "measuring"
apparatus often has an influence on the "result of the measurement".

At this point, we have in place the major theses of Putnam's argument
for *rejecting* classical logic and embracing quantum logic in its stead. The
argument proceeds thus:

Thesis 1. If one insists on using classical logic, then when interpreting
quantum mechanics one will be forced to postulate either hidden variables
or a collapse theory.

Thesis 2. It is objectionable to introduce hidden variables (presumably because they must be governed by "strange laws" and because measurements can disturb the measured values).

Thesis 3. It is objectionable to introduce a real collapse of the wave-function (supposedly because it demands a 'cut' between the system and the observer, but also because measurements typically *create* the "measured" quantities).

Thesis 4. If one adopts quantum logic in place of classical logic, one is not forced into this dilemma: there is no need to postulate either hidden variables or a collapse of the wave-function.

Since my analysis of Putnam's position relies critically on this reconstruction, let me cite the relevant passage extensively. I trust that the argument outlined above will be clearly visible.

From the fact that 'a language which does not have a word V which obeys such-and-such patterns of inference does not contain the concept *or* (or whatever) in its customary meaning' it does not follow either that a language which is adequate for the purpose of formulating true and significant statements about physical reality *must* contain a word V which obeys such-and-such patterns, or that it *should* contain a word V which obeys such-and-such patterns of inference. Indeed, it does not even follow that an optimal scientific language *can* contain such a word V; it may be that having such a connective (and 'closing' under it, i.e. stipulating that for all sentences S_1, S_2 of the language there is to be a sentence $S_1 \vee S_2$) commits one to either changing the laws of physics one accepts (e.g. quantum mechanics), or accepting 'anomalies' of the kind we have discussed. If one does not believe (1) that the laws of quantum mechanics are false; nor (2) that there are 'hidden variables'; nor (3) that the mysterious 'cut between the observer and the observed system' exists; one perfectly possible option is this: to *deny* that there are *any* precise and meaningful operations on propositions which have the properties classically attributed to 'and' and 'or'. In other words, instead of arguing: 'classical logic *must* be right; so something is wrong with these features of quantum mechanics' (i.e. with complementarity and superposition of states), one may perfectly well decide 'quantum mechanics may not be right in all details; but complementarity and superposition of states are probably right. If these are right, and classical logic is also right, then either there are hidden variables, or there is a mysterious cut between the observer and the system, or something of that kind. But I think it is *more likely that classical logic is wrong* than that there are either hidden variables, or "cuts between the observer and the system", etc.' Notice that this completely *bypasses* the issue of whether adopting quantum logic is 'changing the meaning' of 'and', 'or', etc. If it is, so much the worse for 'the meaning'. (Putnam 1975, pp. 188–189)

And, in a passage that explicitly draws the analogy to Reichenbach:

> Now then, the situation in quantum mechanics may be expressed thus: we *could* keep classical logic, but at a very high price. Just as we have to postulate mysterious 'universal forces' if we are to keep Euclidean geometry 'come what may', so we have to postulate equally mysterious and really quite similar agencies – e.g. in their indetectability, their violation of all natural causal rules, their *ad hoc* character – if we are to reconcile quantum mechanics with classical logic *via* either the 'quantum potentials' of the hidden variables theorist, or the metaphysics of Bohr. (Ibid., p. 191)

Notice that the argument is not merely that quantum logic might be more *convenient* than classical logic in some settings, but that classical logic must be *banned*, since accepting it commits us to the Hobson's choice between hidden variables and collapses. Notice also that the force of the argument depends crucially on Thesis 4: that whatever is objectionable about hidden variables or collapses can be *avoided* if we adopt quantum logic. Ultimately, our gaze will alight on Thesis 4, but let me quickly review the first three theses.

I fully accept the first thesis. Here is the final paragraph from a paper I have written on the interpretation of quantum mechanics:

> We are not left empty-handed. Bohm's interpretation and the GRW theory still stand, and there are others that can survive the test. But we at least can be clear about the questions that must be asked of an interpretation. Is it an additional variables interpretation whose dynamics guarantee solutions to the problem of statistics and the problem of effect? Is it a collapse theory that leads to appropriate outcome states with the right probabilities, and whose fundamental terms all have clear physical significance? If the answer in each case is "no", then commit it to the flames, for it can contain nothing but sophistry and illusion. (Maudlin 1995, p. 14)

Of course, I did not explicitly add that I am assuming the validity of classical logic, but in my argument I used nothing but classical logic. We shall consider whether or not classical logic is really a culprit here when we get to Thesis 4.

Thesis 2 surely requires more defense than it is given, especially considering the intensive examination of Bohm's theory conducted in the last several decades. Similarly, Thesis 3 would have to be clarified in light of theories like the GRW theory, which postulate collapses but no "cut" between the system and the observer. These are not mere details, of course, since Putnam's argument ultimately relies on a *weighing of costs:* the cost of accepting hidden variables or a collapse theory as opposed to the cost of abandoning classical logic. But let us leave this haggling over costs aside for the moment and get to the critical question: whatever the costs of accepting hidden variables or collapses are, could adopting quantum logic allow us to avoid them? What exactly are we *buying* with our refusal to allow classical logic?

At long last, we have to confront the question of just what quantum logic *is*. Fortunately, all of the points that need to be made can be adequately handled with a toy model that displays all of the relevant features of quantum logic. Although we will not use the exact technical machinery employed in quantum mechanics, nothing at all will be lost in the simplification.

In quantum theory, the wave-function of a system is represented by a ray in a high-dimensional complex vector space called *Hilbert space*. But in order to illustrate quantum logic, we can stick to plain old Euclidean space – even a three-dimensional Euclidean space. So think of the quantum state of a system as represented by a vector in Euclidean space. *Propositions* in quantum logic are represented by *subspaces* of the Hilbert space – in our Euclidean model, you can think of a proposition as a straight line or a plane through the origin. The entire space is also a proposition – the tautological proposition, as we shall see. A proposition in quantum logic is *true* of a system just in case the vector that represents the system lies in the subspace that represents the proposition. So in our little model, the x-, y-, and z-axes all represent propositions, as do the x-y, y-z, and x-z planes. Similarly, the line x = y, z = 0 represents a proposition, and so on.

Now think of the vector that lies in the x-y plane and bisects the right angle between the positive x and y axes. According to our truth conditions, if that vector represents a system, then the proposition associated with the x-y plane is true (since the vector lies in that plane) and the proposition associated with the line x = y, z = 0 is true (since the vector lies on that line), but the propositions associated with the x- and y-axes are not true. Let's call the vector just described "V", the proposition associated with the x-axis "X" and the proposition associated with the y-axis "Y". Let us also call the proposition associated with the x-y plane "X-Y", and so on.

We are almost finished. Just as in the case of the Maxwell-location language described above, we are now going to introduce some connectives for our propositions. The connectives will be propositional functions: given some propositions as input, they will specify a proposition as output. The two connectives will be called "meet" and "join" and will be represented by "∧" and "∨", respectively. These connectives are similar to, but not identical with, the connectives "∪" and "∩" introduced in the Maxwell-location language.

The meet is, in fact, just like the connective "∩": the meet of two propositions (subspaces) is just the intersection of those subspaces. Thus, the meet of the proposition X-Y and the proposition X-Z is just the proposition X, since the x-axis is the intersection of the x-y plane and the x-z plane. In symbols, X-Y ∧ X-Z = X. The meet of X-Y and X is just X. And the meet of X-Y with the line $x = y$, $z = 0$ is just that line, since it lies in the x-y plane. The meet of X and Y is the point at the origin, which is the logically false proposition ø, since no vector can lie within it (so it cannot be true).

It is obvious that the meet connective will work semantically just like the classical conjunction. For suppose propositions A and B are both true. Then the vector that represents the system lies within the subspace associated with A and within the subspace associated with B. But then the vector must lie within the intersection of the two subspaces, so A∧B is also true. And conversely, if A∧B is true, then both A and B must be true (if the vector lies in the intersection, then it lies in each of the subspaces that intersect).

Things are not so simple for the join of two propositions. The join of two propositions is represented by the subspace that is *spanned* by the subspaces associated with the propositions being joined. This is *not* the same as the union of the subspaces, since it will include vectors that lie in neither of the subspaces being joined. But the idea is still quite intuitive. Consider all of the vectors that can be made by adding a vector from subspace A to a vector from subspace B, by normal vector addition. This new set of vectors constitutes the subspace spanned by A and B. So the x-y plane is spanned by the x-axis and the y-axis, since every vector in the x-y plane can be written as the sum of a vector on the x-axis and a vector on the y axis. Or, in symbols, X∨Y = X-Y.

The semantics of the join is *not* the same as classical disjunction: therein lies the main difference between classical and quantum logic. Of course, if A is true, then so is A∨B for arbitrary B: if the vector which represents the system lies in the subspace associated with A, then it lies in any subspace spanned by that subspace and another. But in the opposite direction, the semantics are not like disjunction. In particular, A∨B can be true even though neither A nor B is true. Suppose, for example, the vector which represents the system lies in the x-y plane but, like *V,* is parallel neither to the x- nor the y-axis. Then X∨Y is true even though neither X nor Y is.

Or again, consider the quantum proposition $X \vee Y \vee Z$. Since any vector in Euclidean 3-space can be written as the vector sum of a vector in the x-direction, a vector in the y-direction, and a vector in the z-direction, those three vectors span the whole space. So $X \vee Y \vee Z$ is a quantum tautology – it is made true by any state vector. Indeed, the join of any three non-coplanar propositions will be a tautology for this reason. But the classical proposition X or Y or Z is not a tautology: it is only true if the state vector lies in one of the three directions. It is here that quantum logic and classical logic come apart.

As has often been pointed out, unlike classical conjunction and disjunction, meet and join are not distributive. That is, although "A and (B or C)" always has the same truth value as "(A and B) or (A and C)", "$A \wedge (B \vee C)$" need not have the same truth value as "$(A \wedge B) \vee (A \wedge C)$". For example, let A be the proposition associated with the line $x = y$, $z = 0$, B be X and C be Y. Then $(A \wedge B) = (A \wedge C) = \emptyset$, so $(A \wedge B) \vee (A \wedge C) = \emptyset$. But $(B \vee C) = $ X-Y, so $A \wedge (B \vee C) = A$. If the system is represented by a vector that lies in the subspace associated with A, then $A \wedge (B \vee C)$ will be true while $(A \wedge B) \vee (A \wedge C)$ is false.

All of this, of course, is just *mathematics*, and if one wants to represent propositions and their truth conditions in this way, then there is nothing to stop one from also introducing the propositional functions "$\wedge$" and "$\vee$"; "$\wedge$" turns out to have exactly the semantics of the classical conjunction while "$\vee$" is not a truth-functional connective at all, and a fortiori not the classical disjunction. And it might be convenient at times to use meets and joins rather than conjunctions and disjunctions. But there is obviously no reason as yet to suggest that the quantum-logical join should or could *supplant* classical disjunction in the language of science.

While the distinction between the join and disjunction at the semantic level is perfectly clear, there are some rather subtle interconnections between quantum-logical joins and classical disjunctions that invite misunderstanding. Let's run though a simple example.

Suppose that the proposition we have been calling "X" and associating with the x-axis of our space is the proposition which says that a particle is at a particular location r_1, and the proposition "Y" is the proposition which says that the particle is at a different location r_2. Then if the vector that represents the system happens to lie along the x-axis, then the particle is at r_1, and an experiment designed to find the particle will be certain to find it at r_1, and similarly mutatis mutandis for a vector that lies along the y-axis and r_2. But what if the vector that represents the system happens to lie in the x-y plane, but is parallel to neither the x-axis nor the y-axis?

We already know in this case that "The particle is at r_1" is not true and "The particle is at r_2" is not true, and, as a consequence, the classical disjunction "The particle is at r_1 or the particle is at r_2" is not true. But the quantum disjunction (join) "The particle is at r_1 $\vee$ the particle is at r_2" *is* true. So what will happen if we *look* for the particle by, say, putting up a fluorescent screen and seeing where a flash occurs?

Using the usual technique for deriving predictions from quantum states, one would say that if "The particle is at r_1 $\vee$ the particle is at r_2" is true, then an experiment designed to locate the particle will be certain to "find" it either at r_1 or at r_2, where the "or" is the classical disjunction. That is, the truth of the join of the propositions implies the truth of a classical disjunction regarding the result of a "measurement". This is an implication from a proposition using a quantum connective to a proposition formulated with a classical connective – it is an inference that cannot even be formulated if the classical disjunction is unavailable. A fortiori it cannot be an inference which could in any way suggest that the classical connective is *expendable*.

Furthermore, securing the inference from the premise to the conclusion requires solving the "measurement problem" – the basic interpretational problem in quantum theory. Indeed, the measurement problem can be stated in exactly this way – if the wave-function is complete and if the wave-function never "collapses" (if one rejects both hidden variables and nonlinear evolution), then it cannot be that making a position measurement on a particle in the state "The particle is at r_1 $\vee$ the particle is at r_2" will certainly either result in a flash at r_1 or a flash at r_2. For if the wave-function never collapses, then the state "The particle is at r_1 $\vee$ the particle is at r_2" will certainly evolve into a state like this: "(The particle is at r_1 $\wedge$ there is a flash at r_1) $\vee$ (The particle is at r_2 $\wedge$ there is a flash at r_2)". But if neither of the "disjuncts" in "The particle is at r_1 $\vee$ the particle is at r_2" is true at the *beginning* of the experiment, then neither of the "disjuncts" of "(The particle is at r_1 $\wedge$ there is a flash at r_1) $\vee$ (The particle is at r_2 $\wedge$ there is a flash at r_2)" will be true at the end, that is, there will neither be a flash at r_1 nor a flash at r_2. More succinctly, if the wave-function is complete and does not collapse, then the experiment *will not have a definite outcome*, contrary to all of our experience.

Notice that our experience in these cases is reported using *classical* connectives. If we do this experiment many times, we find that sometimes we get a flash at r_1 and sometimes we get a flash at r_2, but we always get either one or the other. This is a simple fact of experience – a fact that physics ought to be able to account for. Of course, if the classical connectives were not available in our language, then we would not be able to *report* this fact about our experience, but it would remain a fact nonetheless. One cannot *solve* a problem simply by adopting a language in which the relevant facts cannot be expressed!

How do the extant interpretations explain the truth of the classical disjunction? The explanation goes differently for different theories. In a collapse theory, the interaction of the particle with the screen induces a collapse of the wave-function, such that the final wave-function will either be (very nearly) represented by "The particle is at r_1 $\wedge$ there is a flash at r_1" or by "The particle is at r_2 $\wedge$ there is a flash at r_2". The collapse is typically indeterministic, so that either final state could be the result, but one or the other is certain to obtain. In a "hidden variables" theory, the experiment is handled quite differently. In these theories, the final quantum state of the system is certain to be "(The particle is at r_1 $\wedge$ there is a flash at r_1) $\vee$ (The particle is at r_2 $\wedge$ there is a flash at r_2)", but the wave-function is not complete. The actual flash we see is not represented in the wave-function, it is rather a matter of the values of the additional variables. But the dynamics will be such that, for any initial state of the system, the final state will contain either a flash at r_1 or a flash at r_2. And again, the "or" in the last sentence is a classical "or".

Now that we know what quantum logic is, and how it differs from classical logic, we can finally confront the principle hurdles for Putnam's argument. First, what sorts of problems are produced by the use of classical logic? And second, how could those problems be solved if one were to *reject* classical logic and adopt quantum logic?

There are three places we can look for the needed argumentation. First, as we have seen, Putnam dislikes both "hidden variables" theories and collapse theories. The additional variables and collapses have to be postulated to solve the measurement problem, that is, to permit the theory to predict that experiments like the one described above will eventuate either in a flash at r_1 or a flash at r_2. Can quantum logic alone solve this problem?

Quantum logic alone can certainly not solve the problem in any normal sense. For, as we have seen, there is nothing to prevent someone whose language includes the classical connectives from *also* employing the meet and join – they are, after all, well-defined connectives. So if quantum connectives could solve the problem, then one could just use them – alongside the classical connectives – to solve it. And the result would not be an argument against classical logic, but an argument for using the quantum connectives as well. In any case, as we have seen, the quantum connectives can be used to help *frame* the measurement problem but do not, by themselves, provide a solution.

So the only live option here is the one mentioned above: rejecting classical logic "solves" the problem *by making the problem impossible to state*. But this is no solution at all, and does not answer Putnam's needs. For surely it is true that when we do the experiment we either get a flash in one place or in the other. Nothing in Putnam's argument could serve to convince us that this is not a fact.

The second place to look for an argument in favor of rejecting classical logic is in Putnam's analysis of the probabilistic structure of the two-slit experiment. In that experiment, collections of electrons form inference fringes on the detector screen, even though no fringes form if only one of the slits is open. Putnam claims that classical logic and probability theory imply that no interference bands should form, by means of an argument that can be summarized as follows. (Putnam considers a case using photons rather than electrons, but the principles are the same.) He begins with the probability $P(A_1,R)$ that a photon will hit a region R of the screen given that it passes through slit A_1 *and only slit A_1 is open*, and, similarly, the probability $P(A_2,R)$ that a photon will hit R if it passes through A_2 and only A_2 is open. Putnam says that these probabilities "may be computed from quantum mechanics or classical mechanics (they are the same as long as only one slit is open), and checked experimentally by closing one slit and leaving only A_1 (respectively A_2) open in the case of $P(A_1,R)$ (respectively $P(A_2,R)$)" (1975, p. 180). He then argues that *using classical logic and probability* one can get a prediction for what will happen when *both* slits are open by calculating $P(A_1 \vee A_2,R)$ using standard probability theory. The critical juncture is the following: "Since we count only experiments in which the photon gets through the barrier, and hence when the disjunction $A_1 \vee A_2$ is true, we have . . . (p. 180)". But at this point the argument has already gone off the tracks.

A_1, recall, is the proposition that the photon goes through slit A_1 *when only A_1 is open*, and similarly for A_2. This is critical, since the calculation of $P(A_1,R)$ and its experimental verification depend on only one slit being open, as Putnam states. But then the proposition $A_1 \vee A_2$ is certainly *not* true when we do the two-slit experiment with both slits open, since it is neither the case that the photon goes through A_1 with only A_1 open, nor that it goes through A_2 with only A_2 open. Furthermore, from the fact that the photon gets through the barrier, it does not follow that it either went (entirely) through one slit or the other: if it is "spread out" like a wave, then it could go *partially* through each slit and wholly through neither. But surely classical *logic* has nothing to say about whether the photon is spread out or not! So the remainder of Putnam's derivation, which need not concern us, proves nothing.

But the peculiar failure of the last argument gives us a clue to what Putnam must have had in mind. If the photon gets to the opposite side of the barrier, and the photon *always has a definite, small location*, then it must go through one slit or the other.[6] So Putnam must be assuming that the particle always has a definite, small location. And this fits with his distaste for any theory in which a position measurement disturbs or creates the position. Recall that one virtue of quantum logic is supposed to be that "we do not have to adopt the strange view that *position* measurement 'disturbs' (or 'brings into being', etc.) *position*, or that *momentum* measurement disturbs (or 'brings into being', etc.) *momentum*, or anything of that kind (ibid., p. 186). So Putnam may just be assuming that the photon always has a definite position which is simply *revealed* by a fluorescent screen, since he views any alternative theory as unacceptable.

So let's ask one final question. Suppose that the notion of a position "measurement" helping to create the position found is verboten. It follows that just *before* a mark appears on a fluorescent screen, the photon or electron was *already in the vicinity where the mark appears*. Does the adoption of quantum logic, and the rejection of classical logic, help us to retain *this* view?

It is perhaps here that one can find grounds for the surface appeal of quantum logic. For recall: according to the orthodox interpretation of the wave-function, a position measurement must play a role in creating the position of the observed system because the wave-function before the measurement is typically not in an eigenstate of position, and the wave-function is complete. In the orthodox interpretation, if the wave-function is "spread out" in space, then the particle simply does not *have* a precise position, so a fortiori the "measurement" cannot reveal any such preexistent position. "Hidden variables" theories can postulate that position measurements reveal preexistent positions, but only by adding more to the ontology than is reflected in the wave-function, and Putnam wants no part of that.

But the following line of argument may at first seem attractive. "Hidden variables" theories can maintain that position measurements do not create positions because they maintain that particles always *have* a position. Orthodox interpretations seem not to be able to take this line since, according to them, particles do not always have a position. *But that is only under a classical reading of the phrase "have a position"*. To say that a particle has a position is to use an existential quantifier, and an existential quantifier is really just a sort of infinitary disjunction. So if there is classical disjunction and quantum disjunction, then there must be a classical existential quantifier and a quantum existential quantifier. And *if one uses the quantum existential quantifier, then it is true that the particle always has a position, and a momentum, and indeed always has every measurable quantity.*

Let's see how this works for position. Classically, one can think of "The particle has a position" as asserting the (perhaps unbounded) disjunction "The particle has position p_1 or the particle has position p_2 or the particle has position p_3 or . . . ", with each possible position as a disjunct. And classically, this sentence is true if, and only if, at least one of the disjuncts is true. But the *quantum* "disjunction" "The particle has position p_1 ∨ the particle has position p_2 ∨ the particle has position p_3 ∨ . . . " is just the quantum proposition associated with the entire Hilbert space, since that space is spanned by the position eigenstates. That is, the quantum "disjunction" of all exact location propositions is the quantum tautology: it is always true. And the same goes for momentum. So if one interprets "The particle has a position" and "The particle has a momentum" *quantum logically*, then they are both always true. And it appears that we have overcome the problem of position measurement "creating" positions without postulating hidden variables but rather by adopting a new logic! Isn't this just what we wanted?

But this seeming victory is merely an illusion. For if we want to deny that position measurements create or disturb the position of the particle, we have to assert more than that the particle already had a position – we have to assert that before the measurement was made, the particle *had the very position that corresponds to the location of the mark on the plate.* And *that* claim is simply not true even if one adopts "quantum logic": if the wave-function is complete, there is no particular position such that the particle had it, and a fortiori the particle did not already have the very position that the measurement "revealed". Indeed, one can see that the whole detour through quantum logic here is just a bait-and-switch: we might be making progress if the *classical* sentence "The particle had a position" were true, for then we could inquire exactly *what* position it had, and ask whether it was the same position "revealed" by the measurement. Indeed, if the *classical* sentence were true, then we could understand the probabilities that appear in quantum mechanics: they are probabilities for each particular disjunct being the one that is true. But since the truth of the *quantum* sentence "The particle had a position" does not imply the truth of at least one disjunct, getting it to come out true does no work whatsoever in resolving any of our problems. The "hidden variables" theorist gets the classical disjunction to come out true by adding to the theory the addition variables that make one disjunct true. The quantum logician tries to obtain by theft what the additional variables achieve by honest toil: quantum logic only gets a *similar sounding* sentence to come out true by changing the semantics of the sentence, and the truth of the new sentence brings us no nearer to our goal.

Ironically, the adoption of quantum logic without "hidden variables" makes it *impossible* to retain the view that a position measurement always reveals a preexistent position. For consider the following simple experiment. Create an electron in a momentum eigenstate, so that, on any view, it has momentum p_1. Send the electron toward a fluorescent screen, where a flash appears at, say, location r_2. Now if the "position measurement" *did not* create or disturb the position, then just before the flash, the electron was at, or near to, r_2. Furthermore, just before the flash, the electron was still in the momentum eigenstate, and so had momentum p_1. But according to quantum logic, the proposition "The electron has momentum p_1 $\wedge$ the electron had position r_2" is a *logical falsehood: no* state vector can make it true! So adopting quantum logic makes it *impossible* to maintain that the position measurement neither creates nor disturbs the position!

Notice that the above argument does not hinge on the meaning of connectives like "and" and "or": it hinges instead on the meaning of the terms "create" and "disturb". If the measurement neither creates nor disturbs the position, then the particle had the position before the measurement. But this claim is *untenable* from a standard quantum-logical point of view.

So Putnam's first argument for quantum logic, the argument of "The Logic of Quantum Mechanics", not only fails to reach its conclusion, it undermines itself. The theoretical virtues that Putnam seeks cannot be achieved by rejecting classical logic and adopting solely quantum logic – they are, in fact, incompatible with the usual understanding of quantum logic. The Reichenbachian bargain completely fails: in rejecting the classical connectives we give up much to acquire nothing. That is presumably why Putnam produced an entirely different account of the quantum picture of reality some thirteen years later.

PUTNAM'S SECOND THEORY

In "Quantum Mechanics and the Observer",[7] Putnam returned to the topic of quantum logic, but the general setting and the technical details appear to have changed completely. Let's review some of the differences.

Standard quantum logic is essentially the structure of subspaces of Hilbert space under the operations of intersection and span: these get translated into the meet-and-join operations on the lattice of quantum propositions. As we have seen, under the usual semantics, the meet of two quantum propositions is semantically like their classical conjunction: true if and only if each of the propositions is true. The join, on the other hand, is not like classical disjunction: it can be true even if neither of the joined propositions is. So anyone focusing on the divergence of "quantum logic" from classical logic would naturally focus on disjunctions rather than conjunctions. Furthermore, in standard quantum logic every pair of propositions has both a meet and a join: the operation always yields an element of the lattice of propositions, even though it may be the "logically false" 0-dimensional subspace. As we have seen, the lattice of quantum propositions is nondistributive with respect to meet and join, so this feature has often been used to draw a contrast with classical conjunction and disjunction.

But in the critical section of "Quantum Mechanics and the Observer", the focus is almost exclusively on *conjunction*. According to Putnam, in quantum logic one is not *allowed* to conjoin certain propositions. Indeed, according to him, in quantum logic one is sometimes not allowed to conjoin two propositions *both of which one knows to be true!* Whatever this means, we have wandered very far from standard quantum logic.

Another striking contrast with "The Logic of Quantum Mechanics" is that the project of *rejecting* or *displacing* or *amending* classical logic seems to have disappeared. "Quantum conjunction" is obviously different from classical conjunction, but there is no pretense that we forego use of the latter in favor of the former:

> In effect, not allowing ourselves to conjoin all the statements we know to be true means that we have what amount to two different kinds of conjunction: one amounts to asserting statements in two different 'frames', as I shall call them (different Boolean sub-logics); and the other, for which we reserve the *and*-sign, is conjunction of statements which lie in a common frame. (1983, p. 265)

That is, one kind of conjunction is classical conjunction, the other, a form of conjunction only permitted for particular pairs of statements. Oddly, Putnam decides to reserve the "*and*-sign" for the *non*classical connective. This seems a bit ungrateful: classical conjunction has earned its right to be the meaning of "and" through centuries of hard linguistic service, while the quantum upstart is an untested newcomer. Furthermore, I do not think that Putnam himself adheres to this new convention in the remainder of the paper. But perhaps we cannot deny Putnam Humpty-Dumpty's privilege to make his words mean what he wants them to mean. In any case, as the passage cited above makes clear, the Putnam of "Quantum Mechanics and the Observer" has no intention of foregoing the use of the classical conjunction: indeed, he needs it to make the paper's most astonishing claim. That claim is the "discovery" that there are pairs of statements whose conjunction in old-style quantum logic is logically false, and whose conjunction in new-style quantum logic is not allowed, and that together violate the Heisenberg Uncertainty relation, but that can, both at the same time, be *determined by experiment to be true*.[8] So the old-style quantum logic, which codified the uncertainty principle by making conjunctions of statements that violate it logically false, must certainly be revisited.

Indeed, the obvious motivation for this radical switch from the old-style quantum logic to the new style is exactly the problem that we remarked at the end of the last section. Putnam does not want wave collapses ("quantum jumps") that are induced by interaction with the "measuring" apparatus. This means that whatever values are found by measurement are values that the system already had before the measurement took place. As we have seen, this leads to immediate trouble with the uncertainty relations: if we prepare a particle in a momentum eigenstate and then "measure" its position, and we maintain that the "measurement" did not *create* the position, then we have to hold that, before the measurement, the particle had both a definite momentum and a (at least somewhat) definite position, in violation of the uncertainty relations.

And it is clear that, for all the changes between "The Logic of Quantum Mechanics" and "Quantum Mechanics and the Observer", one thing that remains constant is Putnam's rejection of "quantum jumps". Here is his discussion of the Schrödinger cat example:

What made it seem as if there was a *physical* 'jump' was the idea that we could not *retrodict* and say that the cat was alive before our looking. And it looked as if we could not say this because this would *conflict* with the assumption that before our looking the satellite [with the cat in it] was in the condition we prepared, which was (by hypothesis) $(1/\sqrt{2}) \Psi_{\text{live cat}} + (1/\sqrt{2}) \Psi_{\text{dead cat}}$. But if a system can have more than one state at a time relative to the same observer (provided only one has predictive value), then the argument collapses, and, indeed, the retrodiction that the cat was alive *before* we looked is just as correct as the retrodiction that a photon [in the two-slit experiment] was emitted at t_0. (1983, pp. 262–263)

So Putnam wants there to be pairs of statements that violate the uncertainty relation both of which are true.[9] And while old-style quantum logic was used to rule out such a possibility as *logically impossible*, new-style quantum logic is supposed to come to the rescue here.

So what is the new-style logic, and how does it help? As we have seen, the lattice of quantum propositions is a nondistributive, and hence non-Boolean, lattice. Meet and join are well defined for all pairs of propositions in the lattice, but they do not have the same formal properties as classical conjunction and disjunction. But one can find Boolean sub-lattices of the non-Boolean quantum lattice: parts of the full lattice in which meet, join and complement have the structure of classical conjunction, disjunction and negation.[10] In new-style quantum logic, "conjunctions" are required to be between pairs of propositions drawn from the same Boolean sub-lattice. Hence there can be pairs of propositions whose conjunction is not well formed.

Given the overall setting of "Quantum Mechanics and the Observer", it is not transparent what work this new "quantum logic" is supposed to do. As we have seen, the *classical* conjunction of every pair of propositions exists, and if each of the propositions is true, then so is the classical conjunction. So what exactly is to be gained by also admitting a "quantum conjunction" with the feature that the conjunction is not allowed? What is the point of disallowing the conjunctions? What does it even mean to say that one is not "allowed" to conjoin two propositions (even if they are both true)? As David Albert once asked in a similar setting: "What will happen if I do conjoin them? Will my brain explode?"

Putnam is sensitive to this question, and as the quotation above indicates, he thinks that the answer has something to do with *predictive value*. If there is no "quantum conjunction" of two propositions, says Putnam, then even if *both* of them are known (by the same person) to be true, only *one* of them can have predictive value for the system: the other "has no future value as far as that system is concerned" (ibid., p. 262). Even more explicitly:

> As mentioned previously, the decision not to conjoin statements which are incompatible is a way of making a distinction *in the logic itself* between cases in which both of the statements we know have predictive value and cases where only one of the measurements has predictive value after the measurement. (Ibid., p. 267)

So the new logic is really a logic of *future predictive value* rather than of *truth*.

There is nothing wrong in principle, I suppose, with inventing a "logic of predictive value". Let's see how it would go in a more elementary setting. Suppose that we have a particle confined to one dimension whose dynamics is irreducibly stochastic. In fact, suppose that the particle is undergoing a classical "random walk": every second it jumps either one inch to the left or one inch to the right, with a fixed probability (say .5) for each. And suppose that this is a classical Markov process: where the particle is likely to go next is determined only by where it is now; the rest of the history of the walk is irrelevant. Formally, if we want to ascribe a probability to the particle being at some location in the future, the location of the particle at the present moment probabilistically screens off information about its location at all earlier moments. The prediction made on the basis of its position at any time cannot be changed, or improved, by conditionalizing on its location at any earlier time.

There is a clear-cut sense, in this example, in which one of any pair of statements about the location of the particle has superior predictive value: the predictions one gets by using the *later* location will be better than the ones derived from the earlier value. So one could, if one wanted, introduce a new kind of "conjunction" and *disallow* the conjunction of two statements about the position of the particle at different times. (If we want statements that *can* be conjoined, we need to modify the example: suppose that the color of the particle also changes randomly, but always to an adjacent color on the color wheel. Then a statement about the color can be conjoined to a statement about the position: they both have predictive value.) One could disallow conjunctions for exactly the reason Putnam gives: to make a distinction *in the logic itself* between conjunctions such that both conjuncts have predictive power and conjunctions (i.e., *classical* conjunctions) where the predictive power of one conjunct is screened off by the other.

There are several things to note about this example.

First, even if one does introduce this new "logic", it seems *very extravagant* to reserve the *and*-sign for the new "conjunction". There is nothing wrong with the classical conjunction, and changing the meaning of "and" is sure to engender much confusion.

Second, the ambitions of this "new" logic are extremely circumscribed. It is true that predictive power is something we care about, but it is hardly the only thing we care about, and in the *ontological* interpretation of quantum theory, it is something we hardly care about at all. What we want to know is what quantum mechanics suggests about how the world is, not about how much we can predict. The old project of showing how the *rejection* of classical logic could buy us something has completely evaporated.

Third, even if we are solely concerned with predictive value, this seems like a very *inefficient* way to register our concern. In our little example, the *logic* tells us that "The particle is at position r_1 at t_1" cannot be conjoined with "The particle is at position r_2 at t_2". This warns me that even if I happen to know they are both true, only one of the sentences has predictive value. But the *logic* does not do me the favor of informing me *which* of the two does have predictive value! We know the answer: if you want to make a prediction about the future position of the particle, use the later time. But if we have to add this piece of advice as a separate rider, what is the point of disallowing the conjunction in the first place? Similarly, in Putnam's examples, only one statement of an incompatible pair is supposed to have predictive value, but quantum logic (the theory now of Boolean sub-lattices in the lattice of quantum propositions) does not tell us which one. So this hardly seems like a useful way of reminding ourselves (by building it into the "logic") of what has predictive value.

But lastly, and decisively, the claims that Putnam makes about "quantum logic" and predictive value *are simply untrue*. Let's work through an example.

In the little random walk example given above, it is the case that the later positions of the particle screen off the earlier positions with respect to predictions about the future. But this does not happen with the sort of incompatible quantum propositions that Putnam takes to both be true. Let's go back to the simplest case: we prepare a single electron in a momentum eigenstate (or near eigenstate), and shoot it at a screen to "measure" its position. Since we are concerned with *further predictions*, though, let's make a slight change in the usual procedure. We are going to cut a gap in the screen of some width at some location. Now if there is a flash on the screen at the appropriate time, then that will count as a position measurement that "found" the particle at the location of the flash. But if there is no flash, then that will count as a position measurement which found the particle *in the gap*. The advantage of having the gap, and the lack of a flash as a possible outcome, is that we can ask clear questions about *what we can predict about a particle which makes it through the gap*, for example, what we can predict about its *future* location.

This technique would be accepted by any standard account as a position measurement, where lack of a flash corresponds to a positive finding of the particle in the gap.

Now if no flash occurs, then the standard quantum formalism would "collapse the wave-function" to an eigenstate of the operator associated with being located in the gap. And that new wave-function (because it does not have unlimited uncertainty in position) will be *quantum mechanically incompatible* with the momentum eigenstate (or near eigenstate) we started with. So let's imagine that no flash occurs. According to Putnam's account, this means that the particle was, at the appropriate time, located in the gap. And since there are no *physical* "quantum jumps", that means that *just before* the relevant time, the particle was fairly localized, just in front of the gap.

But at that *same* time, the particle was *also* in a momentum eigenstate. So its momentum had little or no uncertainty, and position little uncertainty, violating the Uncertainty Relations in just the way that Putnam argues the relations can be known to be violated.

Since the momentum eigenstate and the state localizing the particle near the gap do not belong to the same Boolean sub-lattice, there is no "quantum conjunction" of them. And this, according to Putnam, means that *at most one of them* has predictive value. But which one?

In fact, they *both* have predictive value according to quantum formalism – or better, they are *both* used to derive further predictions about the system. *If the gap is extremely narrow*, then most of the "predictive value" will come from the *position* measurement: the particle will refract through the narrow slit, and its subsequent momentum will likely bear little relation to the original. In the limit as the slit becomes vanishing small, all the predictive value will come from the position of the slit. But if the gap is extremely wide, then *most* of the predictive value will come from the original momentum eigenstate (if the gap is as wide as a church door, for example). In that case, there will be very little refraction, and the future values of the momentum will be likely to be almost exactly the same as the original momentum. And as one varies continuously from a wide to a narrow slit, the "proportions" that the two incompatible propositions contribute to the prediction vary continuously. Neither proposition ever "screens off" the other entirely for predictive purposes: if you want to make a prediction, you have to know *both* what the original momentum was *and* how wide, and where, the slit was.

Here are the technical details. The usual rule is: when one gets a particular measurement outcome, one "collapses" the wave-function to an eigenstate of the observable with the appropriate eigenvalue, and then uses the collapsed wave-function for future predictions. So if an observable *has only one* eigenstate with a particular value, then one knows simply from the outcome of the measurement what the new wave-function must be. But typically, there are *many* eigenstates associated with a particular outcome for a measurement (these are called *degenerate observables*). For example, when I do an *approximate* position measurement (as all real measurements are!), there are lots of distinct quantum states that are certain to give me any particular outcome. If the gap in the screen is as wide as a church door, then I will get the same result from a wave-function that localizes the particle in the right half of the door and one that localizes it in the left half: both will register positive for "being in the doorway". There is no *unique* eigenstate of "being in the doorway", there are *lots* of eigenstates. Our measurement rule tells us that after the measurement we are to use an eigenstate, *but it does not yet tell us which one.* How do we decide?

The relevant mathematical rule is called *Lüder's Rule.* It says, in effect, that one should choose the eigenstate that is *closest in Hilbert space to the original state of the system.* More precisely, the technique is this. When an observable is degenerate, then instead of a single eigenvector associated with an outcome, there is an *eigenspace:* a whole subspace of vectors certain to yield the same result to the measurement. So if my original state vector representing the system is V, and I then measure the degenerate observable and get a certain result, I must collapse *V* by *projecting it onto the eigenspace associated with the outcome.* The result will be a unique "collapsed" vector, but which vector it is depends on both *what the eigenspace is* and on *what vector V I started with.* In our little example, this means that the appropriate state to use for future predictions about our particle depends on *both* what momentum eigenstate it was prepared in *and* on the exact location and width of the gap it went through, even though the quantum propositions "The particle has momentum *p*" and "The particle is located in the gap" are quantum-logically incompatible. So on top of all of its other shortcomings, Putnam's new version of quantum logic as the logic of predictive power is simply incorrect.

At this point, the horse of quantum logic has been so thrashed, whipped and pummeled, and is so thoroughly deceased, that I won't bother to promise not to beat it further. The question is not whether the horse will rise again, it is: how in the world did this horse get here in the first place? The tale of quantum logic is not the tale of a promising idea gone bad, it is rather the tale of the unrelenting pursuit of a bad idea. And this pursuit is by no means Putnam's alone: many, many philosophers and physicists have become convinced that a *change of logic* (and most dramatically, the *rejection* of classical logic) will somehow *help* in understanding quantum theory, or is somehow *suggested* or *forced* on us by quantum theory. But quantum logic, even through its many incarnations and variations, both in technical form and in interpretation, has never yielded the goods. Yes, quantum mechanics uses a Hilbert space to represent the wave-function of a system. Yes, various sorts of experiments, and their possible outcomes, can be associated with subspaces of the Hilbert space. Yes, there are intersection and span operations defined on those subspaces, and a corresponding meet-and-join operation on the lattice of "quantum propositions". And yes, to some extent, these operations are like classical logical connectives.

But they are not those connectives, and they are not replacements for those connectives, and the whole mathematical apparatus is perfectly well described and explained and understood using classical logic. And while there are interpretive problems with quantum mechanics that need to be faced, none of those problems can be solved, or even ameliorated, by rejecting classical logic. So why would a philosopher of Putnam's eminence spend so much effort on quantum logic? As we noted at the outset, Putnam finally abandoned quantum logic in the early 1990s, but only after decades of consideration.

To repeat, this is a tale of temptation. The temptation must have been powerful; it must have come from an impeccable source. We know where the trap was set – by none other than Quine, in none other than "Two Dogmas of Empiricism". And, as with all tales of temptation, the moral is just the same: no matter how glimmering and seductive, some temptations ought to be resisted.

Notes

1. It is important to keep in mind that by "experience" Kant means, not *sensation* or *perception*, but rather a species of *knowledge*. In our common parlance, the disorienting effect of being hit on the head with a hammer is an experience, since it is a distinct sort of sensation, but for Kant it would not be, since it is not, per se, knowledge of an objective world.

2. I say "in the vulgar tongue" because the fundamental feature of the General Theory is not the curvature of *space* but the curvature of *space-time*. As non-Euclidean space is to Euclidean space, so is the "curved" space-time of the General Theory to the "flat" space-time of the Special Theory. There is some difficulty about interpreting the question of the geometrical structure of *space* in the General Theory, although on most reasonable approaches to that question, space will, indeed, turn out to be non-Euclidean.

3. For the use of universal forces, see Reichenbach 1958, pp. 12ff. For causal anomalies, see pp. 62ff.

4. Putnam's strategy for advocating quantum logic is consistent with his remarks about statements that are "necessary [or *quasi*-necessary] relative to a body of knowledge [or a conceptual scheme]" (see "It Ain't Necessarily So", chapter 15 of Putnam (1975) and "Rethinking Mathematical Necessity", chapter 12 of Putnam (1994a)). A statement is necessary relative to a body knowledge if one cannot describe from *within* that body of knowledge how the statement could come out to be false. Still, such a statement could ultimately be abandoned after accepting a *different* "conceptual scheme", from which the possibility of the falsehood of the statement is comprehensible. No matter how problematic classical logic may seem, one could not abandon it until one had a new conceptual scheme in which the falsehood of classical theorems becomes comprehensible, and quantum logic can be seen as just such an alternative. Even as late as "Rethinking Mathematical Necessity" (authored in 1990), Putnam acknowledges his "sympathy" for quantum logic (see p. 262, n. 11), although he does not *endorse* quantum logic in that paper.

5. Given this difficulty in accounting for individual marks, we were perhaps too glib to say that the standard interpretations have little trouble accounting for the interference bands: after all, the bands are composed of collections of such individual marks. But the mathematical structure of the bands is easily recoverable from the fundamental theoretical apparatus of these theories.

6. Note that even if this is the case, Putnam's derivation does not go through. Bohmian particles always have definite locations, and always go through exactly one slit, but still exhibit interference bands. That is because the trajectory of a particle when one slit is open is not the same as the trajectory of a similarly located particle when both slits are open. And that is because the wave-function when one slit is open is not the same as the wave-function when both are open. As we have seen the proposition symbolized by A_1 must specify that only one slit is open if it is to provide enough information to calculate $P(A_1, R)$, but in this case $A_1 \vee A_2$ is *not* true when we do the experiment with both slits open, even if the particle is always localized.

7. First published in *Erkenntniss*, 16:193–219. Citations here are to the reprinted version, chapter 14 of *Realism and Reason* (1983).

8. The Putnam of "Quantum Mechanics and the Observer", having renounced "metaphysical realism", is leery of using the term "true", although he does do so at times. He sometimes prefers the term "correct", so that quantum logic is concerned with which statements are correct. I am tempted then to call the field *quantum etiquette*. But the simplest course at this point is just to ignore the terminological innovation, since it does not really matter.

9. One can violate the uncertainty principle in one way by admitting "hidden variables", as in Bohmian mechanics. Bohmian mechanics, of course, agrees with quantum logic that no quantum state is both an eigenstate of position and of momentum: that is just a mathematical fact. But the Bohmian can assert that a particle has a determinate position even when the quantum state is not an eigenstate, since particles always have determinate positions in that theory. Putnam never accepts "hidden variables".

10. To be precise, there are sub-lattices of the lattice of quantum propositions that are Boolean in the mathematical sense. It does not follow that the logic of the quantum connectives on these sub-lattices is classical. For even if one chooses a Boolean sub-lattice, according to the usual interpretation there can be joins of propositions that are true even though neither of the joined propositions is true.

References

Albert, D. Z. (1992). *Quantum Mechanics and Experience*. Cambridge, MA: Harvard University Press.

Bell, J. S. (1990). "Against 'Measurement'". In A. I. Miller (ed.), *Sixty-Two Years of Uncertainty*. New York: Plenum, pp. 17–31.

Clark, P., and Hale, B. (eds.) (1994). *Reading Putnam*. Oxford: Blackwell.

Dürr, D.; Goldstein, S.; and Zanghì, N. (1996). "Bohmian Mechanics as the Foundation of Quantum Mechanics". In *Bohmian Mechanics and Quantum Theory: An Appraisal*, ed. J. T. Cushing, A. Fine, and S. Goldstein. Dordrecht: Kluwer Academic Publishers.

Ghirardi, G. C.; Rimini, A.; and Weber, T. (1986). "Unified Dynamics for Microscopic and Macroscopic Physics". *Physical Review* **D** 34:470–491.

Maudlin, T. (1995). "Three Measurement Problems". *Topoi* 14:7–15.

Perle, P. (1990). "Toward a Relativistic Theory of Statevector Reduction". In *Sixty-Two Years of Uncertainty*, ed. A. I. Miller. New York: Plenum, pp. 193–214.

Putnam, H. (1965). "A Philosopher Looks at Quantum Mechanics". In *Beyond the Edge of Certainty*, ed. R. Colodny. Englewood Cliffs, NJ: Prentice-Hall, pp. 75–101. Reprinted in Putnam 1975, pp. 130–158.

(1968). "Is Logic Empirical?". In *Boston Studies in the Philosophy of Science*, vol. 5, ed. R. Cohen and M. Wartofsky, Dordrecht: D. Reidel. Reprinted as "The Logic of Quantum Mechanics". In Putnam 1975, pp. 174–187.

(1975). *Mathematics Matter and Method: Philosophical Papers, Volume 1*. Cambridge: Cambridge University Press.

(1981). "Quantum Mechanics and the Observer". *Erkenntnis* 16:193–219. Reprinted in Putnam 1983, pp. 248–270.

(1983). *Realism and Reason: Philosophical Papers, Volume 3*. Cambridge: Cambridge University Press.

(1994a). *Words and Life*. Ed. J. Connant. Cambridge, MA: Harvard University Press.

(1994b). "Comments and Replies". In Clark and Hale 1994, pp. 242–295.

Quine, W. (1951). "Two Dogmas of Empiricism". *Philosophical Review* 60:20–43. Reprinted in Quine [1953], pp. 20–46.

(1953). *From a Logical Point of View*. New York: Harper Torchbooks.

Reichenbach, H. (1958). *The Philosophy of Space and Time*. New York: Dover.

7 | Another Philosopher Looks at Quantum Mechanics, or What Quantum Theory Is Not

NANCY CARTWRIGHT

1. INTRODUCTION

In 1965 Hilary Putnam published the standard work on the interpretation of quantum mechanics, a piece that all philosophers of quantum mechanics of the time had to come to terms with. He laid out one-by-one in a clear non-technical way each of the available approaches to the problem and explained, again non-technically but very exactly, what is wrong with them. In his own final words Putnam took 'the modest but essential step of becoming clear on the nature and magnitude of the difficulties' (1965, 158).

In the almost forty years since there have been a variety of advances, technical developments and new points of view. But none of these is un-controversial. In fact each suffers from some one or another of the very difficulties that Putnam summarised. Many of the newer approaches ex-plain why the problem is not a problem after all; a few bury the problems in technical detail; and some make heroic assumptions, often metaphys-ical, that cause the problems to disappear. My conclusion surveying the contemporary literature is the same as Putnam's in 1965: 'no satisfactory interpretation of quantum mechanics exists today' (1965, 157).

The time scale is amazing. Putnam's important piece was written forty years after the first formulations and successes of quantum mechanics. I am writing forty years later, and about a theory that has transformed our technology and our way of thinking about the world. Why does this theory still have 'no satisfactory interpretation'? Because, I shall argue, it does not need one; and that, I shall argue, is exactly the view that Putnam should have taken in 1965. For it is from Putnam himself writing just three years earlier in another context – in his 'What Theories Are Not' – that we learn: *successful theories do not need interpretation.*

Why, then, when it comes to quantum mechanics did Putnam join other philosophers in their hunt for an interpretation? I think that these philosophers were attempting to substitute an interpretive principle – in particular a single interpretive principle – for a very great deal of detailed physics that needs doing; and the attempt was unnecessary, since the physics was being done then, and continues to be done now, very successfully. Theory needs to be attached to the world; and it gets this attachment through experiment, technology, explanation and prediction. It also needs to be rich and detailed with multiple connections among its own concepts and also with concepts from other branches of knowledge. All of this, Putnam argued, is what gives theoretical terms their meanings. Meaning depends, then, on doing more good physics, not on a principle of interpretation. The hunt for interpretation principles was fuelled, I suspect, by the idea that the proper axiomatic formulation of a theory should contain all the principles necessary to fix all the attachments the theory makes to the world. Putnam taught us that this demand is both ill-conceived and impossible to fulfil.

The problem that probably drove Putnam to treat quantum mechanics differently from all other sciences was one long recognised. Much of the successful physics I referred to links quantum mechanics to the world via other more established branches of physics, such as classical mechanics, classical electromagnetic theory, fluid dynamics and classical statistical mechanics. This remains true even as we develop theories like quantum electrodynamics that cover aspects of the same domains that the classical theories treat. This may have seemed unacceptable to Putnam because he expected quantum physics to *replace* classical physics; and he expected replacement, I suppose, because he could see that quantum mechanics offered good treatments in a great many cases in which classical physics failed. Just think about the very first successes of the quantum ideas. Classical electromagnetic theory predicted that orbiting electrons would cycle down into the nucleus and thus the atom would be unstable. Bohr's quantum treatment forbade this. Putnam could have no doubt that Bohr's theory is *better*.

I too acknowledge that the quantum theory tells us far more accurately how an atom is held together than does classical electromagnetic theory. It tells us a great many other things as well, including – to mention an example to which I shall return – the change in time of the quantum state of an atomic dipole oscillator acted on by a classic electromagnetic field. But there are also myriads of things it is silent about, where the knowledge provided by classical theories continues to be highly reliable, such as the effects of the macroscopic polarisation induced in the field by the dipole oscillator.

Two things stand in the way of allowing our body of knowledge to include both quantum and classical theories. One is the presupposition that there must be one single theory that covers everything in the domain of physics. I shall not comment here on this presupposition, which I have attacked at length in *The Dappled World* (Cartwright 1999). We know that

Putnam has been inclined towards it, but I think it is a presupposition best avoided. The empirical evidence available at this time is too scanty to push us very far towards either unity or disunity; and a commitment to unity stands in the way of taking seriously our current heterogeneous body of knowledge, with all the successes it has provided us. Second is the assumption that quantum mechanics itself must tell us with one single interpretive formula how quantum concepts relate to classical concepts, or to the concepts with which we test and apply the quantum theory. Putnam's own teachings about theory, observation and meaning show that this is not so.

I should make explicit at the start one clear implication of my claims here. Contrary to standard accounts, the famous 'Born interpretation' of quantum mechanics can not serve as an *interpretation* of the quantum wave function, for all the same reasons that Putman gives against 'interpretations' of theoretical concepts in general. But this is not problematic, for two reasons. The first is Putman's own: if a theory is working correctly, its terms do not need special principles to interpret them.

The other reason is more peculiar to the case in hand. If we look at how quantum theory is tested and how it is applied, we find that the Born rule does not play the ubiquitous and irreplacable role attributed to it. The Born rule tells us, for every quantity Q represented by a quantum operator, what the probability is in a given quantum state for various values of Q to result if Q is measured.

This way of linking quantum theory to other concepts is sometimes of use, but often it is not. As we look through examples where quantum theory gets out of itself and connects with other matters, we see a great variety of different kinds of connections. There are myriad ways to link quantum and classical concepts as well as to connect quantum concepts directly with concepts that describe the materials out of which we build our instruments. Nor do these connections derive from any one central principle like the Born rule. They are part of the network of knowledge that we build up as we expand and fill in the details of quantum mechanics.

2. THE FAILURE OF QUANTUM INTERPRETATIONS

Putnam's concern in asking for an interpretation of quantum mechanics was specifically with the quantum state function, or 'Ψ-function':

> the state of a physical system can be represented by a set of waves ... what is the significance of the 'waves'? Answers to this question are usually known as 'interpretations' of quantum mechanics. . . . (1965, 133)

He catalogued four standard answers: (1) the De Broglie interpretation: 'physical systems are sets of waves' (ibid.); (2) the original Born interpretation: quantum systems '*are* particles in the classical sense – point masses having at each instant both a definite position and a definite velocity.... The wave corresponding to a system of particles does *not* represent the state of the system (simultaneous position and velocity of each particle), but rather our *knowledge* of the state, which is always incomplete' (1965, 135); (3) hidden variable theories (like the Bohm theory) that assign 'a definite position and momentum to each system but avoid the difficulties of the original Born interpretation by adding "strange laws"' (1965, 139) to account for the strange phenomena connected with quantum interference; (4) the Copenhagen interpretation: '"observables" such as position, *exist* only when a suitable measurement is actually being made' (1965, 140). The Ψ-function describes the probability distribution of the results that occur when an observable is measured.

As I said in the introduction, Putnam then lays out what came to be the canonical catalogue of difficulties that undermine these interpretations. In the course of examining each in turn Putnam came to impose 'three *conditions of adequacy* upon proposed interpretations of quantum mechanics':

A. The principle ND [that a measurement does not disturb the observable measured] should not be assumed even for position measurement.

B. The symmetry of quantum mechanics, represented by the fact that one 'interpretation' [i.e., a representation in terms of one particular observable, such as position, rather than some other observable, such as momentum] has no more physical significance than any other, should not be broken. In particular, we should not treat the waves employed in one representation (the position representation in the case of the [Bohm-type] hidden variable theorists) as descriptions of physically real waves in ordinary space.

C. The phenomena of superposition of states...must be explained in a unitary way. (1965, 146–147)

I present these three conditions explicitly because they can still bear on newer accounts developed since Putnam first wrote. It is, for instance, open to question whether Arthur Fine's prism models account (1982), in which some kinds of particles systematically get undercounted at measurement, involves an unacceptable violation of condition A or not. Or consider condition B. Does it rule out theories like the Ghirardi-Rimini-Weber account in which the Ψ-function makes spontaneous reductions into states highly localised in *position?* If we demand, as Putnam does, that we do not privilege representations in terms of one observable over others, it seems we may have to settle for a much more open-ended account of spontaneous reduction of the kind outlined in *How the Laws of Physics Lie* (Cartwright 1983).

Putnam showed then that at the time his paper was published in 1965, there were no unproblematic interpretations of the Ψ-function available. Many believe that his conclusion is still true today. But why is that a problem? For only three years before, in his famous paper 'What Theories Are Not', Putnam himself had shown that theoretical terms do not need interpretation.

At the time of writing this paper Putnam was well known for arguing that the meaning of a scientific concept is often given by all the laws that are taken to be true of it (cf. the section on law-cluster concepts in his 1962b). Quantum mechanics is a rich theory with much to say involving the quantum state, both about its relations to other theoretical quantities inside and outside of quantum theory and about how this state relates to the world in a vast variety of concrete situations. The theory itself, the entire theory with all its diverse uses and implications, gives meaning to the quantum state. A concept from a theory like this comes already interpreted. This doctrine about meaning begins in 'What Theories Are Not', where Putnam attacks the idea that scientific concepts should ever be in need of interpretation.

3. PUTNAM AGAINST INTERPRETATION

I begin with a short pre-history to Putman's 'What Theories Are Not'. Logical positivists were keen to ensure that genuine science should talk sense, unlike the Freudians, some Marxists and most Hegelians. The surest way to guarantee that theoretical claims have a clear and settled signification, it seems, is to demand that the theory itself provide for each theoretical term an operational procedure for ascertaining whether it applies or not. But this requirement for one-to-one operationalization proved too demanding.

In the first place, operational procedures will not do the job. Many different procedures are equally appropriate for measuring the same theoretical quantity and different procedures are required in different circumstances. Moreover, the operational procedures associated with a theoretical term do not seem to contribute much to what that term signifies. In the second place, it seems that for a good many perfectly acceptable theoretical terms direct measurements are not available. The canonical example here was the *velocity* of an individual gas molecule in the kinetic theory of gases. We do not know how to measure that. But we can measure various quantities that depend on it, such as the mean kinetic energy, $<\frac{1}{2}mv^2>$, which kinetic theory teaches is equal to the temperature of the gas.

In the face of these difficulties, two concessions were made. First, the rules of interpretation need not be (indeed perhaps should not be) measurement procedures. New terms, rather, should be mapped onto ones 'antecedently understood'. Second, it is sufficient to map only some theoretical terms onto features that are observable or can be directly measured. This resulted in the view of theory that Putnam attacks in 'What Theories Are Not': 'the view that theories are to be thought of as "partially interpreted calculi" in which only "the observation terms" are "directly interpreted" (the theoretical terms being only "partially interpreted", or, some people even say, "partially understood")' (1962a, 215).

Putnam had three objections to this view of theory.

1. 'The *problem* for which this dichotomy was invented ("how is it possible to interpret theoretical terms?") does not exist'. (1962a, 216)

2. 'A basic reason . . . for introducing the dichotomy is false: namely, justification in science does not proceed "down" in the direction of observation terms' (1962a, 216). In fact justification in science proceeds in any direction that may be handy – more observational assertions sometimes being justified with the aid of more theoretical ones and vice versa!

3. 'The distinction between theoretical and observational terms is "completely broken backed."' (1962a, 216)

Claims (2) and (3) are by now well assimilated into the philosophy of science literature, in good part due to the arguments of Putnam in "What Theory Is Not" and elsewhere. Claim (2) denies the so-called "foundationalist" account of scientific knowledge, which supposes that there is some observational basis about which we can form relatively secure knowledge claims and that all of science is justified by its ties to this base. The fall from dominance of the foundationalist pictures and the catalogue of its vices and virtues is so well known that I do not need to rehearse it here; moreover, it is not immediately relevant to my main points here about quantum mechanics and the need for interpretation.

Claim (3) is part of the attack, new at the time, on the so-called theory-observation distinction: that is, on the claim that scientific concepts can be divided into observational concepts, about which (following

the foundationalist account) it was usually supposed we could have secure knowledge, and the theoretical, whose meanings and whose claims to
knowledge must both derive from the observational base. Putnam argued –
and many took up the battle in support – that such a distinction could not
be drawn. The attack on the theory-observation distinction, and the more
recent defences of it are well known.

There is, however, one feature of Putnam's discussion that I should like
to underline. Often the attacks on the theory-observation distinction are
summarized in the slogan 'All observation terms are theory laden'. That
is only half of the story. We must also remember that theoretical terms
themselves play a direct role in observation in science, especially in those
observations that test theory or help put it to use. Putnam argues 'That
observation statements may contain theoretical terms is easy to establish.
For example, it is easy to imagine a situation in which the following sentence
might occur: "We also *observed* the creation of two electron-positron pairs."'
(1962a, 219; italics in original).

This point is closely connected with Putnam's assumption that we ought
to accept new theories like quantum mechanics because they provide adequate treatments of phenomena that the older theories get wrong. Putnam's
claim echoes that of Wilfrid Sellars, who stresses that the chief reason for
introducing new theories with new concepts is that the concepts of the older
theories are not adequate for describing the world on their own. In Sellars's
picture, where getting it right matters, we should learn to respond to the
world directly with our newer, more accurate theoretical concepts (Sellars
1963).

My own conclusion from studying a large number of cases where theory
is brought to bear on real phenomena is that neither quantum nor classical theories are sufficient on their own for providing accurate descriptions
of the phenomena in their domain. Some situations require quantum descriptions, some classical and some a mix of both. But the practices in physics
that support this eclectic view go no way towards supporting the claim that
the application of quantum concepts is always via classical ones. On the
contrary, there are many situations that can only be correctly described by
quantum concepts: we cannot patch together classical descriptions that will
serve instead. Following Sellars, our best strategy is to learn to describe
these situations directly in quantum terms. And we can learn to do so.

Putnam mentions the observation of the creation of an electron-
positron pair. For a strict quantum mechanical example we can consider
superconductivity. The superconducting state in a metal is by now a well-
known quantum mechanical state and there is no classical surrogate for it.

In the experimental group in which I participated at Stanford University it was not unusual for the senior physicists to come into the laboratory with its familiar apparatuses (dewars for supercooling, complicated electrical circuitry, and so forth), note the characteristic intensity-voltage curve on the screen and remark, 'I see you've finally got a superconducting state.' When the situation is set up correctly, physicists can tell by looking that a system is in this particular quantum state. Of course they do not do so infallibly and not without a very great deal of background knowledge. But that, we have learned from the attacks of Putman and others on the theory-observation distinction, is true of all observation.

Putman's argument for (1) begins with an attack on the whole idea of a partial interpretation. He reviews at some length two things that might have been meant by 'partial interpretation' by Rudolf Carnap, who championed the idea, and argues that they are both inadequate. The third meaning Putman considers is the one I gave at the beginning of this section, which by the time of his article was the standard reading: 'to partially interpret a formal *language* is to *interpret part* of the language' (1962a, 221; italics in original). This he dismisses with a single sentence: 'Finally, the third sense of 'partial interpretation' leads to the view that theoretical terms have *no meaning at all*, that they are mere computing devices, and is thus unacceptable' (1962a, 224; italics in original). Partial interpretation turns theories into instruments; so it is no view for a realist to hold.

How then do we give meaning to theoretical terms? Putman turns the question on its head: 'Why should one not be able to give the meaning of a theoretical term?' (1962a, 225). In a few sentences he undermines a whole philosophical tradition that had created a pseudoproblem.

> Something like this may be said: suppose we make a 'dictionary' of theoretical terms. If we allow theoretical terms to appear both as 'entries' and in the *definitions*, then there will be 'circles' in our dictionary. But there are circles in every dictionary! (1962a, 226)

To finish off, Putman considers two other possible versions of the problem: how theoretical terms are learned and how they are first introduced. In both cases the answer is the same as before. Theoretical terms are learned and they are introduced in exactly the same way as any other terms. There is no special problem with theoretical terms:

> We perhaps come closer to the problem if we observe that, if dictionaries are useful, they are useful only to speakers who already know a good deal of the language. One cannot learn one's native language to begin with from

a dictionary. This suggests that the problem is really to give an account of how the use of theoretical terms is learned (in the life-history of an individual speaker); or perhaps, of how theoretical terms are 'introduced' (in the history of the language).

To take the first form of the problem (the language-learning of the in-dividual speaker): it appears that theoretical terms are learned in essentially the way most words are learned. Sometimes we are given lexical definitions (e.g. 'a *tigon* is a cross between a tiger and a lion'); more often, we simply imitate other speakers; many times we combine these (e.g. we are given a lexical definition, from which we obtain a rough idea of the use, and then we bring our linguistic behaviour more closely into line with that of other speakers via imitation).

The story in connection with the introduction of a new technical term into the *language* is roughly similar. Usually, the scientist introduces the term via some kind of paraphrase. For example, one might explain 'mass' as 'that physical magnitude which determines how strongly a body resists being accelerated, e.g. if a body has twice the mass it will be twice as hard to accelerate'. (Instead of 'physical magnitude' one might say, in ordinary lan-guage, 'that property of the body', of 'that *in* the body which . . .' such 'broad spectrum' notions occur in every natural language; and our present notion of a 'physical magnitude' is already an extreme refinement.) Frequently, as in the case of 'force' and 'mass', the term will be a common language term whose new technical use is in some respects quite continuous with the or-dinary use. In such cases, a lexical definition is frequently omitted, and in its place one has merely a statement of some of the differences between the usual use and the technical use being introduced. Usually one gains only a rough idea of the use of a technical term from these explicit metalinguistic statements, and this rough idea is then refined by reading the theory or text in which the term is employed. (1962a, 226)

We know that Putman's views about meaning have changed over the years and also that he no longer defends 'realism' without putting any qualifi-cations in but instead insists on 'internal realism'. At some times he has argued that the world itself plays a role in fixing the reference of our terms (cf. Putnam 1975). At other times he has argued exactly the opposite. Our access to the world is always mediated by our experiences of it and our beliefs about it. So if we are ever to know what we are talking about, it must be the world as presented in our beliefs and experiences that fixes the reference of our terms, not the world as it is in itself. This leads naturally to 'internal realism' (cf. his 1981). We can reasonably be realists about a good many things, but these must always be things in the world as presented in our beliefs and experiences, since these are the only things that we can ever talk about; we cannot succeed in referring to anything else. The view that knowledge accumulates, which I believe Putnam supposed in his work on quantum mechanics, makes equal sense whether one is an internalist or not. One can suppose both that theory provides knowledge and that its terms are meaningful whether one thinks it describes the world "in itself" or thinks that it describes a world internal to our beliefs and experiences.

None of these changes in Putnam's views have any effect on the point here: there is nothing peculiar about meanings of theoretical terms. Their meanings are fixed in the same way as all other terms in the language. They do not need some special kind of interpretation. With respect to the particular project of interpreting them in observation terms, I repeat Putman's own question 'Why should we suppose that this is or ought to be possible?' (1962a, 225). My claim here is that there is nothing peculiar about the quantum-state function. It is just like any other theoretical term, and Putman's own conclusions apply to it. It does not need an interpretation, much less an interpretation in observational/classical terms; nor is such an interpretation likely to be possible.

4. RETURN TO THE QUANTUM STATE

There may seem to be one advantage that attempts to interpret the quantum state have in the face of Putman's criticism of such enterprises in general. These attempts try to provide a direct observational or classical correlate for the quantum state. They thus avoid Putman's objection to *partial* interpretation: they aim to ensure that the quantum state does not have, as Putman describes, 'no meaning at all', that it does not function as a 'mere computing device', both results which, as we have seen, Putman regards as unacceptable to a realist. But the question remains: can any of these attempts, should they prove problem free, serve as an *interpretation* at all? These attempts look like the same crude one-to-one operationalism that we long ago discarded. Just as with any other theoretical concept, the meaning of the quantum state cannot be given by one operational procedure, or one thing the quantum state does, or one set of consequences it implies. To understand what the quantum state means, we must know a great deal about how the quantum state behaves and what kinds of consequences it has in a vast variety of different situations.

Of course we must face questions not just of meaning but of verification and of use. Putman himself, in defending the need for an interpretation of the quantum state argues, 'Any formalization of quantum mechanics must either leave the question of interpretation open – in which case no testable predictions whatsoever will be derivable within the formalization, and we will have formalized only the *mathematics* of quantum mechanics, and not the physical theory – or we must include in the formalization at least the minimal statistical interpretation, in which case the term "measurement" [and thereby the usual "measurement problem"] automatically enters' (1965, 147). But I think Putman has made a mistake in this, as we can see by looking at the great variety of ways in which we do in fact test the quantum theory. I do not wish to say that the statistical interpretation never plays a role. It does, for instance, in cases like the ones for which Max Born originally introduced it – for scattering. But a detailed survey of tests and applications shows that it plays little role in other kinds of cases and certainly is not central to testing as Putman here maintains.

The story with testing in quantum mechanics is exactly the same as with any other theory. We verify the thousands of different claims in quantum theory by thousands of different connections in thousands of different circumstances. And as Putman himself argues (and Sellars's arguments support), there is no reason to think that the vocabulary in which we describe the test procedures or their outcomes can or should be stripped of quantum concepts.

In my own view, what we see in looking at how quantum mechanics is tested and how we use it in modern technology – SQIDS, transistors or lasers, for example – is that there are a great many situations, usually requiring a mix of quantum and classical concepts to pick out, in which quantum theory does have consequences appropriately described in purely classical terms. Perhaps it is this kind of fact that encouraged Putman to look for a classical interpretation of quantum mechanics, despite his own arguments against both the need for and the possibility of interpretation in general. But when we look at these cases, we see that there is no single formula that covers all the various connections we find. Discovering them is the stuff from which ongoing physics is made.

For example, at the heart of the first quantum theory of the laser is the claim that a quantum dipole oscillator (i.e., a quantum state that changes shape in a certain way in time) produces a polarization in the electromagnetic field in which it is embedded. Here *polarization* is a purely classical concept that can then be used in all the usual ways to make calculations via classical electromagnetic theory. This is a link central to how we use quantum theory to construct and understand lasers. But it is not a link built into quantum theory from the start, in one magic formula. It is something we learned as quantum theory expanded to cover new situations. Moreover, it is facts like this that we keep learning as we keep doing quantum physics. What is important to the question of issue here is that we *discover* them: we do not deduce them from some single pre-given interpretation of the quantum state. Putman's own views about interpretation, it seems, apply just as much to quantum mechanics as to other theories. With respect to providing an interpretation of the quantum state, 'Why should we suppose that this is or ought to be possible?' (1962a, 225).

5. SCHROEDINGER'S CAT

What then, on this view, of Schroedinger's famous cat, whom Putman describes in his look at quantum mechanics? We may think of Schroedinger's cat in two ways, either as an exemplar of a micro-macro interaction or as a picturesque example of a measurement, in that odd abstract sense of 'measurement' that is special to the statistical 'interpretation' of quantum mechanics. In either case the story of Schroedinger's cat is a fantasy. In the fantasy we couple the life of a cat to the location of a single photon vis-à-vis a half-silvered mirror: reflected, the cat lives; transmitted it dies. But we have never yet succeeded in actualising this fantasy. It is, rather, a story invented to match an abstract piece of formalism and an abstract concept of measurement. It does not match any real physical process – and it is only real physical processes that our theories need to treat.

Viewed as a micro-macro interaction Schroendinger's cat can be treated either with or without the assumption of reduction of the wave packet. Consider first the story as it is supposed to proceed without reduction. By a series of quantum interactions a familiar quantum state in the photon is supposed to lead to a very unfamiliar quantum state in the cat: a superposition of a 'cat-alive' quantum state with a 'cat-dead' quantum state. But these are not real quantum interactions that we study in any branch of quantum physics; they are part of a 'just-so' story that has no physics to back it up. And of course there are no such quantum states as 'cat alive' and 'cat dead'. There are no such states described in any physics at all, let alone in quantum physics. The idea that there should be is sometimes defended by the slogan 'Every observable is represented by a quantum operator'. But this slogan is absurd. There is no such thing as the 'cat-alive/cat-dead' operator.

Even if we restrict the slogan less fancifully to what many seem to believe – that every classical dynamical quantity is represented by a quantum operator – it still won't do. First, it flies in the face of Putman's and Sellars's lesson that the most accurate terms with which we can respond to the world will be infected through and through with our best theories. Second, the empirical support for this as a universal principle is strongly insufficient. There are applications in which such associations are made, but these are generally highly context dependent; they do not presuppose a once-and-for-all association between the given operator and the corresponding classical quantity to which it is matched. Moreover, they comprise only a small portion of the links between quantum and classical descriptions in successful application.

In rejecting the claim that the interaction with the photon casts the cat into an objectionable state, I do not mean to suggest that in reality quantum states in microsystems never interact with macrosystems. To the contrary, it happens all the time, both between micro-quantum states and macro-quantum states and between quantum descriptions and classical descriptions. Understanding exactly how it happens is central to the many technologies we build today with the help of quantum theory. Consider my earlier example. Superconductors are macroscopic objects and, so far as our best theories can tell, the superconducting state is an irredeemably quantum state, with no classical surrogates. The same is true of causally important states in lasers and transistors as well. Real quantum physics and real quantum engineering teach us regularly about quantum states in macrosystems. But these states are not problematic. The quantum superconducting state is just the state we want in order to treat the behaviour of a superconductor.

Look next at the case of reduction: the photon and cat interact and the cat ends up genuinely alive or dead. As Putnam described, a conundrum is supposedly created by assigning to the cat either the putative quantum 'cat-alive' state or the putative 'cat-dead' state – we then 'back-read' that in this case the photon could no longer be in a state with significant components on both sides of the mirror, which is in contradiction with the original hypothesis.

I have already argued that the mapping between quantum states and the states of the cat is a mistake. I also said that 'cat-alive' and 'cat-dead' are not physics states at all, not even in classical physics. But by this I did not mean to imply that there are no irreducibly classical states nor that quantum and classical states never interact. To the contrary, I have explained that in my view much of the physics of testing and application studies just such interactions. But then, from this perspective, the whole idea that we could back-read anything about the interaction itself or about the state of the photon from the just-so story of Schroedinger's cat is absurd.

If we look at the physics where our successes suggest that we really know about quantum-classical interactions, we see, as I said before, that accounts of different processes work in different ways, and – what is important for the present discussion – *none of these quantum-classical interactions are subject to any special paradoxes*,[1] unlike the caricature of Schroedinger's cat. The second way to view Schroedinger's cat is as a picturesque exhibition of the problems that beset the attempt to interpret the state function in terms of measurement. The cat is a measuring instrument for whether the photon is transmitted or reflected. We then argue, 'Ah, but the cat must be either alive or dead: the pointer must point to either "reflected" or "transmitted". But the photon itself, quantum theory teaches us, is neither reflected nor transmitted; it is in a superposition of both'. The obvious answer to this is that in this case we have got ourselves a very poorly designed measurement. Nothing about the apparatus we are trying to use can tell us the facts we wish to learn. If we want better information, we need a better measurement design, where effects are produced from which we can infer what the state of the photon really is. The second remark is the central theme of this essay. The apparition of measurement employed in the statistical 'interpretation' connects with real measurement in only a few special kinds of cases.[2] That's okay, because the quantum state, deeply imbedded in a rich texture of real physics treating real problems, does not need the concept of measurement in its interpretation. And that is because –

6. CONCLUSION

– quantum mechanics is no exception to Putman's general views on theories and interpretation. An abstract calculus may require an interpretation. But a live working theory does not.

Notes

Research was conducted in conjunction with the Physics and Economics Project at the London School of Economics. I would like to thank Roman Frigg for his help.
1. I say "special" because of course *all* physics is messy, all theories are inaccurate and no treatments are ever final or entirely problem free.
2. For more about real measurements, quantum and classical, see Chang 1997.

References

Cartwright, Nancy (1983). *How the Laws of Physics Lie*. Oxford: Clarendon.
    (1999). *The Dappled World. A Study in the Boundaries of Science*. Cambridge: Cambridge University Press.

Chang, Hasok (1997). 'On the Applicability of the Quantum Measurement Formalism'. *Erkenntnis* 46, 143–163.

Fine, Arthur (1982). 'Some Local Models for Correlation Experiments'. *Synthese* 50, 279–294.

Putnam, Hilary (1962a). 'What Theories Are Not'. In Ernest Nagel, Patrick Suppes, and Alfred Tarski (eds.) (1975) *Logic, Methodology, and Science*. Stanford, CA: Standford University Press. Reprinted in Hilary Putnam, *Mathematics, Matter, and Method. Philosophical Papers, Vol. I*. Cambridge: Cambridge University Press, 1975, 215–227.

(1962b). 'The Analytic and the Synthetic'. In Herbert Feigl and Grover Maxwell, *Minnesota Studies in the Philosophy of Science, Vol. III*. Reprinted in Hilary Putnam, *Mind, Language, and Reality. Philosophical Papers, Vol. II*. Cambridge: Cambridge University Press, 1975, 33–69.

(1965). 'A Philosopher Looks at Quantum Mechanics'. In Robert G, Colodny (ed.), *Beyond the Edge of Certainty: Essays in Contemporary Science and Philosophy*. Englewood Cliffs, NJ: Prentice-Hall. Reprinted in Hilary Putnam, *Mathematics, Matter, and Method. Philosophical Papers, Vol. I*. Cambridge: Cambridge University Press, 1975, 130–158.

(1975). 'The Meaning of "Meaning"'. In K.Gunderson (ed.), *Language, Mind, and Knowledge. Minnesota Studies in the Philosophy of Science, Vol. VII*. Reprinted in *Mind, Language, and Reality. Philosophical Papers, Vol. II*. Cambridge: Cambridge University Press, 1975, 215–271.

(1981). *Reason, Truth, and History*. Cambridge: Cambridge University Press.

Sellars, Wilfrid (1963). 'Philosophy and the Scientific Image of Man'. In *Science, Perception, and Reality*. London: Routledge and Kegan Paul, 1–41.

8 | Structural Realism and Contextual Individuality

JOHN STACHEL

ANOTHER PROBLEM OF REFERENCE

Hilary Putnam's "A Problem of Reference" poses the question: "how representations can enable us to refer to what is outside the mind" (Putnam 1981, p. 27). His approach is based upon "giv[ing] up the idea that . . . words stand in some sort of one-one relation to (discourse-independent) things and sets of things," and facing the fact that "nature does not single out any one correspondence between our terms and external things" (ibid., p. 41).

Hallett (1994, p. 69) points out that "Putnam has used essentially two different arguments" to prove this, which Hallett calls "the *Löwenheim-Skolem argument* . . . and . . . the *permutation argument*."[1] Putnam 1981 focuses on the permutation argument, stating and proving the following theorem:

> Let *L* be a language with predicates *F1, F2, . . . , Fk* (not necessarily monadic). Let *I* be an interpretation, in the sense of an assignment of an intension to every predicate of *L*. Then if *I* is non-trivial in the sense that at least one predicate has an extension which is neither empty or universal in at least one possible world, there exists a second interpretation *J* which disagrees with *I*, but which makes the same sentences true in every possible world as *I* does. (Putnam 1981, pp. 216–217)

His proof is based on the existence of permutations of the individuals and the relations[2] between them in all such possible worlds that preserve all truth values.[3]

Putnam 1983 presents the Löwenheim-Skolem argument, based on the noncategorical nature of the axioms for any formal system sufficiently strong to include arithmetic: the Löwenheim-Skolem theorem shows that there are then always unintended interpretations of such a system. In particular, the downward Löwenheim-Skolem theorem "shows that even a *formalization of total science* (if one could construct such a thing), or even a *formalization of all our beliefs* (whether they count as 'science' or not) could not rule out denumerable interpretations, and, *a fortiori*, such a formalization could not rule out *unintended* interpretations of this notion [of set]" (p. 3). What both of Putnam's arguments have in common, and that (to my knowledge) he takes for granted, is the individual identity of the members of his sets. For example, "the word 'cat' in the sentence I think or say refers to a set of entities of which [our cat] Mitty is a member" (Putnam 1981, p. 43); and he never considers the possibility of a set of entities, the members of which cannot be uniquely referred to by a name such as "Mitty," not because of either of the aforementioned problems of reference, but because such entities lack the feature of intrinsic individuality. In particular, numerous references to "rational space-time points" in Putnam 1983[4] indicate that he thinks it meaningful to individuate space-time points by the values of their coordinates in an appropriately chosen coordinate system.

Yet contemporary physics provides us with a plethora of examples of entities that are not intrinsically individuated: each of the many species of elementary particles and the points of general-relativistic space-times being the two cases that I shall discuss in some detail. We can see the problem using the two examples of individuation in Putnam cited above: if we substitute "electron" for "cat" in the first example, there is no way to single out a "Mitty" from the set of electrons. And if we consider that, in the words of Eugene Wigner: "The basic premise of this theory [general relativity] is that coordinates are only auxiliary quantities which can be given arbitrary values for every event . . . the coordinates can be given any value one wants" (Wigner 1957, p. 255), we see that, in general relativity, "rational space-time points" is a meaningless expression.

QUIDDITY AND HAECCEITY

I have suggested (Stachel 2002b) the revival of an old philosophical distinction to help describe this situation:[5] I shall say that entities may have intrinsic *quiddity* without intrinsic *haecceity*. Electrons possess such a quiddity – an electron is not a proton, or a logarithm or anything else – but there is no way intrinsic to electrons to single one out from all others; so it lacks haecceity. The situation is analogous to that of the points of space-time in general relativity. How are we able to treat such entities in our physical theories? For the elementary particles, two ways are in general use, one in nonrelativistic quantum mechanics (QM) and the other in special-relativistic quantum field theory (QFT).

In QM, we label the particles as if they were individually distinguishable, and then demand that all physically meaningful results be independent of all possible permutations of these labels. One might call this a "dialectical method": we first posit the distinct individuality of the particles by labeling them; then we negate this positing by denying it any physical significance. Is there any way to avoid this dialectical detour? There is, although it is not often used. Suppose there are N particles in the system in question. Their QM treatment will then require an N-particle configuration space, which is the Cartesian product of N one-particle configuration spaces, one for each particle (see Stachel 1997, pp. 250–251). This is fine if the N particles are all of distinct types; but if they are all of the same type (i.e., have the same quiddity), we can reduce this configuration space by identifying all points in it that differ only in being permutations of each other[6] – we permute the points and identify them, rather than permuting the particles (see ibid., pp. 252–253). The use of such a reduced configuration space for identical particles removes the need for labeling and permuting them: we need merely specify their total number. Then, at any moment of time, we may ask whether a point of the reduced configuration space is occupied or not, without any need to ascribe individuality to the particles.[7]

This second method in QM is closer than is the first to the one used in QFT. In QFT, the analog of the QM particle concept is that of field quantum. While a quantum field need not be in a state in which it has a definite number of field quanta, it is always possible to build up an arbitrary state out of superpositions of states, for which the number of field quanta is sharply defined (see my Appendix). A Fock space can be constructed for each field, and it provides a complete basis for all field states: any such state can be constructed out of superpositions of Fock space states. A state in Fock space is characterized by a list of the substates of that state (e.g., a definite momentum might be associated with each substate), together with a specification of the number of quanta in each such substate.[8]

There is another important way of characterizing fermionic particles in QM, when they form part of a more or less stable structure, such as an atom or a nucleus. Such particles obey the so-called Pauli exclusion principle, according to which no more than one such particle can be in a state characterized by a given set of quantum numbers. So in atomic spectroscopy, for example, in a stationary state of an atom, an electron in it may be characterized by a set of quantum numbers describing which atomic shell it is in and the component of its spin with respect to some fixed axis. Similar considerations apply to nucleons in a nucleus. What these cases have in common is that the particle acquires a certain measure of individuality (haecceity) from its position within a structure. I have referred (Stachel 2002a, p. 241) to entities that acquire a certain degree of individuality in this way, as the "bearers" of these relations. As will be discussed further, there seems to be a range of possibilities between the complete absence of haecceity and its complete presence.

In both Galilei-invariant QM and special-relativistic QFT, we take advantage of the fact that the underlying space-times (Galilei-Newtonian space-time and Minkowski space-time, respectively) are characterized by fixed, nondynamical structures; so its points can be individuated and specified by the construction of a fixed space-time framework.[9] For example, in some inertial frame of reference, a framework of rigidly moving (ideal) rods and clocks can be set up – the rods and clocks at rest in the inertial frame, the clocks having been synchronized by the Poincaré-Einstein convention. Then, after choice of an origin and three mutually perpendicular directions, and of units of length and (proper) time, any point in space-time can be specified by giving its spatial and temporal coordinates with respect to this framework. This is presumably the situation Putnam had in mind when he spoke of "rational space-time points."

But this is not the situation that we confront in general relativity, or indeed in any theory involving a generally covariant set of field equations, in which all the space-time structures are among the dynamical fields. In such a theory, points of space-time cannot be specified or individuated before specifying a solution to the field equations that they obey. Any attempt to do so falls foul of the famous "hole argument":[10] It was this argument that, in late 1913, convinced Einstein that he would have to abandon the search for generally covariant field equations, and thus contributed to delaying the development of general relativity for two years. Only after he was forced to return to general covariance for other reasons late in November 1915 did Einstein find the way to "pull out of"the hole argument discussed below in modern mathematical language.

Consider an open region H (the hole) of the manifold M, on which the field equations are being solved. Consider any solution to the field equations on M. Because the field equations are generally covariant, any diffeomorphism will carry the original solution of the field equations into another solution, often called the carry-along of the original solution, or carried-along solution for short. Now consider any diffeomorphism that reduces to the identity on M-H, the complement of the hole, but is not the identity inside of H. Then the carried-along solution will be identical to the original solution outside the hole, but differ from it inside the hole. Suppose we assume that the space-time points could be "kinematically" individuated, that is, individuated independently of the specification of the dynamical fields. Then, the carried-along solution would be not only mathematically distinct from the original one, but physically distinct as well. For the original solution and the carried-along solution would assign the *same* field values to *different* points of the hole. Since there are actually a four-function-fold infinity of diffeomorphisms meeting our requirements, this means that there would be a corresponding number of *different* solutions inside the hole corresponding to the *same* solution outside of it. This means that no amount of specification of initial data and/or boundary conditions for the field equations could specify a unique solution. Since the hole can be arbitrarily small, to pick out a unique solution to the field equations, we would have to specify it everywhere on M, and the field equations would be useless.

The way to pull ourselves out of this "hole" argument is clear. We must assert that the points of space-time cannot be kinematically individuated, but are only individuated (to the extent that they are) by the values of the dynamical fields at each space-time point. Then the entire class of diffeomorphically related but mathematically distinct solutions to the field equations corresponds to only one physically distinct solution. Again, we may say that, in a generally covariant theory, the points of space-time only acquire (a certain degree of) individuality from their role as the "bearers" of certain dynamical fields.

There is more similarity between the two cases – elementary particles and space-time points in generally covariant theories – than might appear at first glance: diffeomorphisms are nothing but *permutations* of the points of space-time, subject to conditions of continuity and differentiability appropriate to their role in a differentiable manifold. So in both cases we are dealing with a lack of haecceity that manifests itself as invariance of a theory under all (admissible) permutations of the underlying entities. In Stachel 2002b and 2003, I have proposed that this idea be generalized to the principle of *general permutability* of all fundamental entities and adopted as a criterion for any future (more) fundamental theory, such as the elusive theory of quantum gravity.

STRUCTURAL REALISM

Before turning to some of the problems raised by the role of individuality in various physical structures, it seems proper to say what I mean by "structural realism." As discussed in Stachel 2002b, this term has been given various interpretations. For short (and with no claim of historical accuracy), I group these interpretations under three headings: Pythagorean, Platonic and Aristotelian. For the Pythagorean, mathematical structures are the only reality. For the Platonist, structures impose themselves on inherently (formless) matter. For the Aristotelian, matter is inherently structured.

I would describe myself as a "genetic Aristotelian." That is, I take processes rather than things as fundamental. But these processes have a material basis. At any stage of its development, matter is inherently structured in many complex ways. This is the synchronic aspect of structure. But there is also a diachronic aspect. Any given structures are the result of preceding processes of structuration: they have a history of their formation, a limited duration, and their dissolution results in the formation of other structures.

THE CHAIN OF PHYSICAL STRUCTURES

In his history of science, J. D. Bernal, the renowned British crystallographer, sums up one of its major lessons:

> [The] general picture [of the world] has already revealed a characteristic structure ... applying all the way through nature. We find everywhere a system of box within box of units, aggregating at a certain stage to form larger units which can then aggregate in turn. For example, gas and dust form stars, stars form clusters, clusters form galaxies, galaxies form galactic clusters and meta-galaxies. In an analogous way, organisms are composed of organs composed of tissues, composed of cells with organelles built from characteristic macromolecules such as nucleic acids. All these are arrangements that exist not only in space but also in time. Each complex appears at a specific stage in its own evolution, but not everywhere at the same rate, for new stars are being formed today and organisms existed two or three thousand million years ago. (Bernal 1969, p. 12)

In short, a characteristic feature of the universe is that it is highly and complexly structured. These structures come into being and pass away, but remain relatively stable during some period of time, characteristic for each type of structure. This structural stability may involve the persistence of the underlying elements, units or complexes, out of which a structure is built (often, but not always, the case for inanimate structures), or just the persistence of the structure itself, within which the constituent elements, units or complexes constantly change (usually the case for living structures, which undergo metabolic processes).

Bernal's account requires supplementation. It applies well to ponderable matter, but the world is composed of both matter and radiation, and the latter is not organized into such structured hierarchies. Even for ponderable matter, Bernal's image of boxes within boxes might suggest that such structures must form a linear sequence, an ordered set. A more appropriate metaphor would be an interlinking network, a partially ordered set. However, his examples do suggest that, for some purposes, it is advantageous to focus attention on some linear chain within this network.

One possible chain of such material "boxes," important in physics, runs from quantum fields, with their field quanta, the lowest level so far reached, through atoms and molecules at the microscopic level, to macroscopic solid, liquid and gaseous bodies, and up to stars, galaxies, clusters and super-clusters of galaxies at the megascopic level.

THE PUZZLE OF INDIVIDUALITY

Reading this chain from the top down, one is struck by the *loss* of individuality as we proceed downward. In Bernal's biological examples, one organism is certainly distinct from another, even if both are of the same species; and this feature of distinctive individuality persists all the way down to the macromolecules containing an organism's genetic code. But in our physical chain, while one star is certainly distinct from another, by the point at which we get down to the atoms – let alone the nuclei and electrons of which an atom is composed – this feature of distinctive individuality (haecceity) has been lost.

Conversely, if we read the physical chain from the bottom up, the striking thing is the *emergence*, first of indistinguishable units – field quanta – from the quantum fields; then the organization of these units into still indistinguishable complexes, but all possessing quiddity; and, only further up the chain, the emergence of complex units with a distinctive individuality. A quantum field has an aspect of global wholeness that manifests itself under certain circumstances, and only under certain other conditions does such a field manifest itself as an ensemble of units, the field quanta. While quantum field theory successfully describes the deepest level of matter and radiation as yet successfully probed by physics, it seems quite probable that further probing at higher energies – to say nothing of a solution to the problem of quantum gravity – will lead to the uncovering of deeper layers, the structure of which need bear no resemblance to those revealed by quantum field theory. To quote Steven Weinberg:

> We have learned in recent years to think of our successful quantum field theories... as 'effective field theories,' low energy approximations to a deeper theory that may not even be a field theory, but something different like a string theory.... [T]he reason that quantum field theories describe physics at accessible energies is that *any* relativistic quantum theory will look at sufficiently low energies like a quantum field theory. (1995, p. xxi)

So we have every reason to expect that new links will appear as we proceed further downward on the chain (or inward in space, or upward in energy, to change metaphors). Some have held out hopes – or dreams – of a final theory; but we have no need to commit ourselves to such an ideal in order to suggest that the solution to a number of problems raised within the framework of existing theories – above all, the need to find a framework big enough to encompass both existing Poincaré-invariant quantum field theories and generally covariant classical theories such as a general relativity – will take us to deeper levels than heretofore reached. So I suggest that the chain metaphor may extend downward indefinitely.

The level of the elementary particles provide an interesting vantage point from which to look both upward and downward on the chain. Looking downward from the perspective of nonrelativistic theory, and starting from the classical particle concept with the individuality inherent in the use of Boltzmann statistics to treat ensembles of these particles (a classical gas, for example), one is struck by the loss of this individuality in the transition to quantum mechanics and the associated need to use Bose-Einstein or Fermi-Dirac statistics for ensembles of quantum-mechanical particles. Looking upward from the perspective of relativistic field theory, classically there is no particle concept associated with a field. In relativistic quantum field theory, the closest analog to the particle concept is that of "field quantum," and one is struck by the limited range of applicability of this concept: only certain states of a quantum field diagonalize the occupation number operator for the field; and, even if the system is in such a state, one cannot attribute individuality to units that are truly field quanta. They come in different kinds; but within a kind they manifest no inherent individuality. As noted above, they possess *quiddity* but not *haecceity*.

THE PUZZLE OF STRUCTURAL HIERARCHY

The most striking fact about the chain is that, from this point upward, the entire chain of ponderable matter is organized around primary structures built up from the fermionic quanta (e.g., nucleons from quarks), secondary structures built up from the primary structures (e.g., nuclei from nucleons), and so on. There is something deeply puzzling about this fact. While the field concept appears to be primary in quantum field theory,[11] the (composite) particle concept seems essential to an understanding of the hierarchical organization of ponderable matter that dominates the entire upward chain.

Although I do not have the answer to this puzzle, it appears to be closely related to two important distinctions: between fermions and bosons, and between massive and massless field quanta. So far we have not discussed the radiation side of the matter-radiation dichotomy mentioned above. The "forces" that bind together the fermions are all represented by bosonic quantum fields that, again under certain circumstances only, manifest a field-quanta aspect.

A surprising amount of structure is possible for massless bosonic fields, as exemplified, for example, by coherent states of laser light (see Glauber 1963, and, for a more general discussion of coherence, Sewell 2002, chap. 3). But no hierarchy of structures built out of such bosonic units is manifest. What is different here is the possibility of unlimited occupation numbers for states in the Fock space of a bosonic field, contrasted with the simple dichotomy occupied-unoccupied for states of a fermionic field. This leads, at least in the case of massless fields like the electromagnetic field, to the possibility of states that behave like classical fields. Massive bosonic fields, such as the pi-meson field, could in principle manifest themselves classically; but in practice no such classical fields are observed, perhaps because of the small range of the field (on a macroscopic scale) associated with even the lightest massive bosons (Yukawa-type potential as opposed to Coulomb-type).

Returning to fermions, massless ones do not appear to organize themselves into complex structures: there appears to be no neutrino–anti-neutrino "atom," analogous to positronium – the "atom" composed of an electron-positron pair.[12] So it is for massive fermions that the problem arises of the transition from indistinguishable primary units to complex entities with individuality. Again it is noteworthy and puzzling that such individuality only manifests itself against a background of uniformity or similarity, so we must look for it among the units at a given level, which manifest such similarities, or, as I shall say, among units of the same *kind*. That is, it is a question of a transition from pure *quiddity* to *quiddity*-plus-*haecceity*.

Within this framework, it seems that individual uniqueness and complete uniformity of kind are but the two extreme ends of a spectrum, with many intermediate stages. To revert to an earlier example, within an atom, the set of quantum numbers that characterize each orbital electron seems to establish a certain distinction between these electrons without fully individualizing them. Their *haecceity* is not inherent but is inherited from the atomic structures in which they are embedded (see note 14).

More generally, there are distinctions conferred on otherwise indistinguishable elements of the same kind by virtue of their positions in a certain structure. But there is also a type of individuality that is inherent in the unit itself, apart from its structural relations. This type of individuality arises at a more advanced level of complexity; the transition to this type of inherent individuality seems to be connected with questions of complexity and irreversibility. At the level of crystals, for example, the possibility arises of distinguishing between crystals of the same kind, size and shape by the pattern of *defects* in an individual crystal. More generally, the possibility – or perhaps inevitability – of such inherent individuality arises when a unit has a structure that is sufficiently complex and stable over time to carry a distinguishing "mark" that also remains stable over time. To sum up, inherent individuality seems to be a property that is found, if we consider only the synchronic aspect of the chain – or that emerges, if we take into account its diachronic aspect – once one moves upward on the chain to a point at which a certain level of complexity is reached that can sustain "irreversible" processes, and persists thereafter as we move upward.

BIOLOGICAL INDIVIDUALITY AND SOCIAL RELATIONS

We have looked at several possible relations between structure and individuality. The following possibilities regarding the individuation of the entities in a structured set of relations may be distinguished:

1. The entities are individuated independently of their position in the relational structure under consideration,[13] and either (*a*) this independent individuation determines their role in the relations constituting that structure; or (*b*) in addition to this independent individuation, there is a further individuation, either partial or complete, that depends on their position in the relational structure.
2. The entities are individuated only by their position in the relational structure; this individuation being either (*a*) partial or (*b*) complete.

Category 1*a* constitutes the case usually considered: we have well-individuated things with determinate relations between them. As mentioned in the first section, this case of "the relations between things" is the only one that Putnam appears to have considered. Category 2, with its subdivisions (*a*) and (*b*), includes the cases of elementary particles and space-time points in generally covariant theories, with which most of this chapter has been concerned. In Stachel 2002a, I called these cases of "the things between relations."

So far I have neglected category 1*b*, so I shall conclude by briefly discussing the most important example of it that I know: the social relations between biologically individuated human beings.

As discussed in Stachel 2002a (pp. 239–244), it was Karl Marx who drew attention to this category by sharply distinguishing between biological and social individuation. Neglect of this distinction is the basis of his concept of *fetichism*, the attribution of a natural – or supernatural – origin to human social relations. As early as 1843, Marx discussed this problem in connection with his critique of Hegel's *Philosophy of Law:*

> Birth only provides a man with his *individual* existence and constitutes him in the first instance only as a *natural* individual, while political determinations (*Bestimmungen*) . . . are *social* products, born of society and not of the natural individual. Hence what is striking [in Hegel] and even *miraculous* is to conceive of an immediate identity, an immediate coincidence, between *the birth of an individual* and the individual conceived as the *individual embodiment of a particular social position or function*. In this system nature *creates* kings and peers directly just as it creates eyes and noses. . . . I am a man simply by my birth without the agreement of society; a particular birth can become the birth of a peer or a king only by virtue of general agreement. Only this agreement can convert the birth of a man into the birth of a king. . . . (Marx [1843] 1975, p. 174)

Elsewhere in the same text, he criticizes Hegel for forgetting

> that the essence of the 'particular person' is not his beard and blood and abstract *Physis* [i.e., physical corporeality] but his social quality. . . . It is self-evident, therefore, that in so far as individuals are to be regarded as the bearers (*Träger*) of the functions and powers of the state, it is their social and not their private capacity that should be taken into account. (Marx [1843] 1975, pp. 77–7; translation of "*Träger*" changed)

The dangers of attributing a natural origin to social relations are far-reaching, especially for those living under capitalist social systems, since capitalism (by its nature and through its propagandists) tries to "naturalize" all important social relations, starting with capital itself.

> Capital consists of raw materials, instruments of labor and means of subsistence of all kinds that are applied to the generation of new raw materials,

instruments of labor and means of subsistence.... Embodied labor that serves as the means of new production is capital.

So say the economists.

What is a Negro slave? A human being of the black race. The one explanation is worth as much as the other. A Negro is a Negro. Only in certain definite [social] relations is he transformed into a *slave*. A cotton-spinning machine is a machine for spinning cotton. Only in certain relations is it transformed into *capital*. Sundered from these relations, it is as little capital as gold in and for itself is *money*, or sugar is the *price* of sugar. (Marx [1849] 1977, p. 211; translation modified)

I shall not go further into the important complex of social questions this issue raises, but close with a citation from Shakespeare, showing that he was well aware of the perils of the naturalization of social relations:

Dogberry: Come hither, neighbor Seacoal: God hath blessed you with a good name: to be a well-favored man is the gift of fortune; but to write and read comes by nature. (*Much Ado about Nothing*, act 3, scene 3)

APPENDIX: PUTNAM ON PARTICLE NUMBER

I am grateful to Yemima Ben-Menahem for pointing out to me that Putnam has recognized that quantum mechanics allows for states in which particle number is indefinite:

[I]n quantum mechanics, any two states of a system can be in a 'superposition'; that is to say, any particular state of a system, involving having a particular number of particles or a particular energy or a particular momentum, can be represented by a kind of 'vector' in an abstract space, and the superposition of any two such states can be represented by forming a vector sum. These vector sums are sometimes classically very difficult to interpret: what do we make of a state in which the answer to the question 'How many electrons are there in this box?' is 'Well, there is a superposition of there being three electrons in the box and there being seventeen'? (Putnam 1992, pp. 120–121)

This passage calls for several comments. First of all, it is not the case that "in quantum mechanics, *any* [my emphasis] two states of a system can be in a 'superposition.'" For if Ψ_A and Ψ_B are two states in which a system can be prepared, "it may not be possible to prepare the system in a state represented by [their superposition] $\Psi_A + \Psi_B$" (Weinberg 1995, p. 53]. Such situations are usually handled by introducing what are called "superselection rules" that forbid certain superpositions of states "which do not correspond to any physically realizable state" (Schweber 1961, p. 5). For example, two or more states corresponding to distinct charges cannot be superposed (see, e.g., Schweber 1961, p. 6), nor can states corresponding to integral (bosonic) and half-integral (fermionic) total angular momentum (see, e.g., Weinberg 1995, p. 53).

Second, one must distinguish between the situation in, for example, nonrelativistic quantum mechanics and special-relativistic quantum field theory. In nonrelativistic quantum mechanics of many-particle systems, we always deal with a given system, which is characterized by a fixed number of particles of each type (to take Putnam's example, a box with a number of electrons in it), and all states of this system are characterized by the same fixed number of particles (for a discussion of superselection rules in non-relativistic quantum mechanics, see, e.g., Cisneros et al. 1998). So, in nonrelativistic quantum mechanics, it makes no sense to speak of a state in which "there is a superposition of there being three electrons in the box and there being seventeen."

Now, when we go over to special-relativistic quantum field theory, it must be emphasized that the field concept is primary, and that one should properly speak (as I do in the text) of "field quanta" rather than of "particles" insofar as the word "particle" carries inappropriate classical implications of individuality and uniqueness. One may perhaps make this clearer by reference to a nonrelativistic analogy.

The fact that, in quantum mechanics, we are forced to introduce "by hand" the symmetrization and antisymmetrization rules for the wave functions of systems of bosonic or fermionic particles of the same species (quiddity), respectively, is the nonrelativistic "residue," so to speak, of their special-relativistic nature as field quanta – of the need, even at this level, to deprive them of many of the attributes that the concept of "particle" classically carries with it.

Returning to relativistic quantum theory, there are, then, indeed states that are superpositions of two or more states with differing numbers of field quanta (see discussion of Fock space in the main text). But even here, a "superposition of there being three electrons in the box and there being seventeen" is not possible, since it would violate the charge conservation superselection rule, which still holds in the relativistic theory. One would have to introduce sufficient positrons into the story to balance out the total charges. For example, "a superposition of there being three electrons in the box and there being seventeen electrons and fourteen positrons in the box" is possible.

But an even more fundamental problem with Putnam's account is that it is too wedded to the traditional particle concept. As noted above, in quantum field theory, the field concept is primary. There are states of the field that correspond to a fixed number of field quanta; and there are states (such as superpositions of the states with fixed numbers of field quanta) that do not. In particular, those states of a quantum field that correspond to states of a classical field (and these can only exist for bosonic fields) in having a definite phase and amplitude cannot be associated with a definite number of field quanta, since these are complementary properties (like position and momentum in nonrelativistic quantum mechanics).

The main point of relevance here is that nowhere in his discussion does Putnam single out the feature of nonindividuality that makes a quantum particle (or better, a field quantum) so different from a classical particle – nowhere does he mention the need to attribute a bosonic or femionic nature to these quanta.

Finally, one must emphasize, with Bohr, that quantum mechanics is not designed to allow the interpretation of a "quantum state" in isolation. Rather, we must consider an entire "phenomenon," involving an initial preparation and a final registration ("measurement"). That is, we can only use quantum theory to formulate and answer questions of the form: if we prepare a system in a certain way, resulting in a given quantum state, what is the probability that a certain measurement on the system in that state will yield a certain result?[14] So the fact that "the system may be thought of as consisting of either fields or of particles" (Putnam 1992, p. 121) should be interpreted as meaning: if we take a bosonic quantum field (note that this stipulation excludes electrons) that has been prepared in a certain way, *either* we may ask a question about that field involving certain properties (such as relative phases and amplitudes) that would be identified with a classical wave, *or* we may ask a question about it that involves certain properties (such as numbers of field quanta with given momenta) that would be associated with a classical particle. We can calculate the probabilities of any of the various appropriate answers to either type of question, and check the accuracy of these probability predictions by registering the result of an appropriate experiment, that is, by producing one or the other type of phenomenon. But, if quantum field theory is correct, we can never devise an experiment, that is, produce some phenomenon, that would enable us to pose and answer both kinds of questions together.

Notes

I am very grateful to Yemima Ben-Menahem for her encouraging me to write this essay, and for her help in learning about and understanding Putnam's work.

Parts of this essay are based on a talk given at the Workshop on Canonical and Quantum Gravity III, June 7–19, 2001, Banach Center, Polish Academy of Sciences, Warsaw.

1. Hallett notes (1944, p. 67) that both arguments are based on the assumption that "our beliefs about the world, including our scientific theories, can be framed reasonably accurately as a theory Σ cast in a regimented language $\mathcal{L}(\Sigma)$ of the kind mathematical logic normally deals with." This assumption (as well as several further ones that depend on it) is needed so that these beliefs and theories become "amenable to model-theoretic treatment." In his "Conclusion" (p. 92), he points out that the upshot of Putnam's arguments may well be to cast doubt on this assumption.

2. Putnam prefers the term "predicates," stipulating that they are "not necessarily monadic"(1981, p. 217). I have employed the term "relations," stipulating that this concept includes one-place relations or properties (Stachel 2002a, p. 257, n. [41]), and shall continue to do so in this essay.

3. "Let me emphasize that possible worlds, sets, functions are to be thought of as abstract extra-mental entities in this theory, and not to be confused with representations or descriptions of these entities" (Putnam 1981, p. 27).

4. E.g.: "the values of countably many magnitudes at all rational space-time points" (Putnam 1983, p. 3); "the assignment which assigns to each member of the MAG [countable set of physical magnitudes] the value that that magnitude actually has at each rational space-time point" (p. 6); and "we can find a model *for the entire language of science* which satisfies '*everything is constructible*' and which assigns the correct values to all the physical magnitudes in MAG at all rational space-time points" (p. 7). I assume that "rational space-time points" is shorthand for "space-time points identified by the rational values of their coordinates in an appropriately-chosen, physically identifiable coordinate system."

5. "Haeccity:...A term employed by Duns Scotus to express that, by which a quiddity, or general essence, becomes an individual, particular nature, or being" (Runes 1974, p. 121).

6. Stated more fully: any points in the product configuration space that differ only by having coordinates that are permutations of the coordinates of two or more of the N one-particle configuration space coordinates are to be identified as the same point of the reduced configuration space.

7. I am omitting discussion of some technical points, such as the distinction between bosons and fermions, and the problem of collision points, at which the coordinates of two or more of the N points have the same values, which do not affect the point I am making.

8. Again, I omit here such important technical details as the difference between fermions, for which only one quantum can occupy each substate, and bosons, for which any finite number of quanta can occupy the substate. Later, we shall return to this important distinction.

9. See, e.g., Stachel 2003.

10. For an account of the hole argument, with numerous references to the original literature, see Stachel 1993.

11. See, e.g., Wald 1994.

12. Of course, if it exists, such an "atom" would have to be held together by weak forces or gravitation since neutrinos are electrically chargeless.

13. I add this qualification to take care of cases in which entities may be relationally individuated at one level and preserve this individuality when entering into relations at another level.

14. The astute reader will realize that, in my discussion of the distinction between electrons in stationary states of an atom based on the differences in their quantum numbers (see pp. 205 and 212), I have violated this stricture against the physical interpretation of states of an isolated quantum mechanical system. My discussion in the text is oversimplified in two respects.

First of all: For any atom, the states in which all of its electrons have fixed, distinct quantum numbers do indeed form a complete set. But a stationary state of the atom is specified by just *one* of these states only if the interactions between its electrons are neglected; otherwise, a stationary state is specified by a *superposition* of such states.

Now to the second, more relevant point: In making predictions about its behavior, an atom cannot be considered as an isolated quantum system. It must be considered in the context of some macroscopic preparation of its initial state and some macroscopic registration of the results of a measurement made on its final state. We can prepare a state characterized by a set of quantum numbers for all the electrons in the atom; this state, in general, will not be a stationary one. If left alone, after some time the system will settle into a final stationary state (generally after emission of some radiation), and we can then measure the set of quantum numbers for all the electrons in the atom. Given the initial state, and a description of the entire phenomenon, quantum mechanics enables us to predict the probability for finding each set of such final quantum numbers.

Thus, the situation for particles in quantum mechanics is rather more complicated than that for space-time points in general relativity. Both require a relational context for their (partial or total) individuation. But space-time points can be individuated more-or-less locally by physical events in their neighborhood in classical general relativity, while the individuation of particles requires a more global, macroscopic context in quantum mechanics.

References

Bernal, J. D. (1969). "Preface to the Third Edition." In *Science in History, Illustrated Edition*, vol. 1: *The Emergence of Science*. London: C. A. Watts & Co., pp. 9–14.

Cisneros, C.; Martinez-y-Romero, R. P.; Nunez-Lopez, H. N.; and Salas-Brito, A. L. (1998). "Limitations on the Superposition Principle: Superselection Rules in Non-relativistic Quantum Mechanics." *European Journal of Physics* 19:237–243.

Glauber, R. J. (1963). "The Quantum Theory of Optical Coherence." *Physical Review* 130:2529–2539.

Hallett, M. (1994). "Putnam and the Skolem Paradox." In P. Clark and B. Hale, eds., *Reading Putnam*. Oxford and Cambridge, MA: Blackwell, pp. 66–97.

Marx, K. [1843] (1975) "Critique of Hegel's Doctrine of the State." In R. Livingston and Q. Hoare, eds., G. Benton, trans., *Early Writings*. New York: Vintage Books, pp. 57–198.

[1849] (1977). "Wage Labour and Capital." In Karl Marx and Frederick Engels, *Collected Works*, vol. 9: *Marx and Engels 1849*. New York: International Publishers, pp. 197–228.

Putnam, H. (1981). "A Problem of Reference." In *Reason, Truth and History*. Cambridge: Cambridge University Press, pp. 22–48; and "Appendix" in ibid., pp. 217–218.

(1983). "Models and Reality." In *Realism and Reason/Philosophical Papers, Volume 3*. Cambridge: Cambridge University Press, pp. 1–25.

(1992). *Renewing Philosophy*. Cambridge, MA: Harvard University Press.

Runes, D., ed. (1974). *Dictionary of Philosophy*. Totowa, NJ: Littlefield, Adams.

Schweber, S. S. (1961). *An Introduction to Relativistic Quantum Field Theory*. Evanston, IL/Elmsford, NY: Row, Peterson and Company.

Sewell, G. (2002). *Quantum Mechanics and Its Emergent Macrophysics*. Princeton, NJ: Princeton University Press.

Stachel, J. (1993). "The Meaning of General Covariance/The Hole Story." In J. Earman, A. I. Janis, G. J. Massey and N. Rescher, eds., *Philosophical Problems of the Internal and External Worlds: Essays on the Philosophy of Adolf Grünbaum*. Pittsburgh: University of Pittsburgh Press/Universitätsverlag Konstanz, pp. 129–160.

(1997). "Feynman Paths and Quantum Entanglement." In R. S. Cohen, M. Horne and J. Stachel, eds., *Potentiality, Entanglement and Passion-at-a-Distance*. Dordrecht: Kluwer Academic Press, pp. 245–256.

(2002a). "'The Relations between Things' versus 'The Things between Relations': The Deeper Meaning of the Hole Argument." In D. Malament, ed., *Reading Natural Philosophy: Essays in the History and Philosophy of Science and Mathematics*. Chicago and LaSalle, IL: Open Court, pp. 231–266.

(2002b). "Structural Realism and Quantum Gravity." Paper presented at the Annual Meeting of the Philosophy of Science Association. Revised version to appear in Steven French, ed., *Structural Foundation of Quantum Gravity*. Oxford: Oxford University Press.

(2003). "A Brief History of Space-Time." In I. Ciufolini, D. Dominici and L. Lusanna, eds., *2001: A Relativistic Spacetime Odyssey*. Singapore: World Scientific, pp. 15–34.

Wald, R. M. (1994). *Quantum Field Theory in Curved Spacetime and Black Hole Thermodynamics*. Chicago and London: University of Chicago Press.

Weinberg, S. (1995). *The Quantum Theory of Fields*, vol. 1: *Foundations*. Cambridge: Cambridge University Press.

Wigner, E. (1957). "Relativistic Invariance and Quantum Phenomena." *Reviews of Modern Physics* 29:255–268.

9 The Rise and Fall of Computational Functionalism

ORON SHAGRIR

1. INTRODUCTION

Hilary Putnam is the father of computational functionalism, a doctrine he developed in a series of papers beginning with "Minds and Machines" (1960) and culminating in "The Nature of Mental States" (1967b). Enormously influential ever since, it became the received view of the nature of mental states. In recent years, however, there has been growing dissatisfaction with computational functionalism. Putnam himself, having advanced powerful arguments against the very doctrine he had previously championed, is largely responsible for its demise. Today, he has little patience for either computational functionalism or its underlying philosophical agenda. Echoing despair of naturalism, he dismisses computational functionalism as a utopian enterprise.

My aim in this essay is to present both Putnam's arguments for computational functionalism and his later critique of the position.[1] In section 2, I examine the rise of computational functionalism. In section 3, I offer an account of its demise, arguing that it can be attributed to recognition of the gap between the computational-functional aspects of mentality and its intentional character. This recognition can be traced to two of Putnam's results: the familiar Twin-Earth argument, and the less familiar theorem that every ordinary physical system implements every finite automaton. I close with implications for cognitive science.

2. THE RISE OF COMPUTATIONAL FUNCTIONALISM

Computational functionalism is the view that mental states and events – pains, beliefs, desires, thoughts and so forth – are computational states of the brain, and so are defined in terms of "computational parameters plus relations to biologically characterized inputs and outputs" (1988:7). The nature of the mind is independent of the physical making of the brain: "we could be made of Swiss cheese and it wouldn't matter" (1975b:291).[2] What matters is our functional organization: the way in which mental states are causally related to each other, to sensory inputs and to motor outputs. Stones, trees, carburetors and kidneys do not have minds, not because they are not made out of the right materials, but because they do not have the right kind of functional organization; their functional organization does not appear to be sufficiently complex to render them minds. Yet there could be other thinking creatures, perhaps even made of Swiss cheese, with the appropriate functional organization.

Computational functionalism was an immediate success, though several key elements of it were not worked out until much later. For one thing, computational functionalism presented an attractive alternative to the two dominant theories of the time: classical materialism and behaviorism. Classical materialism – the hypothesis that mental states are brain states – was revived in the 1950s by Place (1956), Smart (1959) and Feigl (1958). Behaviorism – the hypothesis that mental states are behavior dispositions – was advanced, in different forms, by Carnap (1932/33), Hempel (1949) and Ryle (1949), and was inspired by the dominance of the behaviorist approach in psychology at the time. Both doctrines, however, were plagued by difficulties that did not, or so it seemed, beset computational functionalism. Indeed, Putnam's main argument for functionalism is that it is a more reasonable hypothesis than classical materialism and behaviorism.

The rise of computational functionalism can be also explained by the "cognitive revolution" of the mid-1950s. Noam Chomsky's devastating review of B. F. Skinner's *Verbal Behavior*, and the development of experimental instruments in psychological research, led to the replacement of the behaviorist approach in psychology by the cognitivist. In addition, Chomsky's novel mentalistic theory of language (Chomsky 1957), which revolutionized the field of linguistics, and the emerging research in the area of artificial intelligence, together produced a new science of the mind, now known as cognitive science. The working hypothesis in this science has been that the mechanisms underlying our cognitive capacities are species of information processing, namely, computations that operate on mental representations. Computational functionalism was inspired by these dramatic developments. Putnam, and even more so Jerry Fodor (1968, 1975) thought of mental states in terms of the computational theories of cognitive science. Many even see computational functionalism as furnishing the requisite conceptual foundations for cognitive science. Given its close relationship with the new science of the mental, it is not surprising that computational functionalism was so eagerly embraced.

Putnam develops computational functionalism in two phases. In the earlier papers (1960, 1964) he does not put forward a theory about the nature of mental states. Rather, he uses an analogy between minds and machines to show that "the various issues and puzzles that make up the traditional mind-body problem are wholly linguistic and logical in character... all of the issues arise in connection with any computing system capable of answering questions about its own structure" (1960:362). Only in 1967 does Putnam make the additional move of identifying mental states with functional states, suggesting that "to know for certain that a human being has a particular belief, or preference, or whatever, involves knowing something about the functional organization of the human being" (1967a:424). In "The nature of mental states", Putnam explicitly proposes "the hypothesis that pain, or the state of being in pain, is a functional state of a whole organism" (1967b:433).

2.1. The Analogy between Minds and Machines

Putnam advances the analogy between minds and machines because he thinks that the case of machines and robots "will carry with it clarity with respect to the 'central area' of talk about feelings, thoughts, consciousness, life, etc." (1964:387). This does not mean that the issues associated with the mind-body problem arise for machines; at this stage Putnam does not propose a theory of the mind. His claim is just that it is possible to clarify issues pertaining to the mind in terms of a machine analogue, "and that all of the question of 'mind-body identity' can be mirrored in terms of the analogue" (1960:362). The type of machine used for the analogy is the Turing machine, still the paradigm example of a computing machine.

A Turing machine is an abstract device consisting of a finite program, a read-write head, and a memory tape (Figure 1). The memory tape is finite, though indefinitely extendable, and divided into cells, each of which contains exactly one (token) symbol from a finite alphabet (an empty cell is represented by the symbol B). The tape's initial configuration is described as the 'input'; the final configuration as the 'output'. The read-write mechanism is always located above one of the cells. It can scan the symbol printed in the cell, erase it, or replace it with another. The program consists of a finite number of states, for example, A, B, C, D, in Figure 1. It can be presented as a machine table, quadruples, or, as in our case, a flow chart.

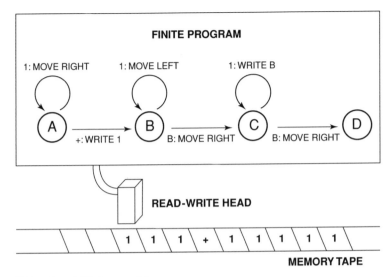

Figure 1. A Turing machine

The computation, which mediates an input and an output, proceeds stepwise. At each step, the read-write mechanism scans the symbol from the cell above which it is located, and the machine then performs one or more of the following simple operations: (1) erasing the scanned symbol, replacing it with another symbol, or moving the read-write mechanism to the cell immediately to the right or left of the cell just scanned; (2) changing the state of the machine program; (3) halting. The operations the machine performs at each step are uniquely determined by the scanned symbols and the program's instructions. If, in our example, the scanned symbol is '1' and the machine is in state A, then it will follow the instruction specified for state A, for instance, 1:MOVE RIGHT, meaning that it will move the read-write mechanism to the cell immediately to the right, and will stay in state A.

Overall, any Turing machine is completely described by a flow chart. The machine described by the flow chart in Figure 1 is intended to compute the function of addition, for example, '111 + 11', where the numbers are represented in unary notation. The machine starts in state A, with the read-write mechanism above the leftmost '1' of the input. The machine scans the first '1' and then proceeds to arrive at the sum by replacing the '+' symbol by '1' and erasing the leftmost '1' of the input, replacing it with the symbol B (blank space). Thus if the input is '111 + 11', the printed output is '11111'.

The notion of a Turing machine immediately calls into question some of the classic arguments for the superiority of minds over machines. Take for example Descartes's claim that no machine, even one whose parts are identical to those of human body, can produce the variety of human behavior: "even though such machines might do some things as well as we do them, or perhaps even better, they would inevitably fail in others" (1637/1985:140). It is true that our Turing machine is only capable of computing addition. But as Turing proved in 1936, there is also a universal Turing machine capable of computing any function that can be computed by a Turing machine. In fact, almost all the computing machines used today are such universal machines. Assuming that human behavior is governed by some finite rule, it is hard to see why a machine cannot manifest the same behavior.[3]

As Putnam shows, however, minds and Turing machines are analogous not just in the behavior they are capable of generating, but also in their internal composition. Take our Turing machine. One characterization of it is given in terms of the program it runs, that is, the flow chart, which determines the order in which the states succeed each other and what symbols are printed when. Putnam refers to these states as the "logical states" of the machine, states that are described in logical or formal terms, not physical ones (1960:371). But "as soon as a Turing machine is physically realized" (ibid.) the machine, as a physical object, can also be characterized in physical terms referring to its physical states – for example, the electronic components. Today, we call these logical states 'software' and the physical states that realize them 'hardware'. We say that we can describe the internal makeup of a machine and its behavior both in terms of the software it runs (e.g., WORD), and in terms of the physical hardware that realizes the software.

Just as there are two possible descriptions of a Turing machine, so there are two possible descriptions of a human being. One refers to its physical and chemical structure; this corresponds to the description that refers to the computing machine's hardware. But "it would also be possible to seek a more abstract description of human mental processes, in terms of 'mental states' . . . a description which would specify the laws controlling the order in which the states succeeded one another" (1960:373). This description would be analogous to the machine's software: the flow chart that specifies laws governing the succession of the machine's logical states. The mental and logical descriptions are not similar only in differing from physical descriptions. They are also similar in that both thought and 'program' are "open to rational criticism" (1960:373). We could even design a Turing machine that behaves according to rational preference functions (i.e., rules of inductive logic and economics theory), which, arguably, are the very rules that govern the psychology of human beings; such a Turing machine could be seen as a rational agent (1967a:409–410).

There is thus a striking analogy between humans and machines. The internal makeup and behavior of both can be described, on the one hand, in terms of physical states governed by physical laws, and on the other, more abstractly, in terms of logical states (machines) or mental states (humans) governed by laws of reasoning. Putnam contends that this analogy should help us clarify the notion of a mental state, arguing that we can avoid a variety of mistakes and obscurities if we discuss questions about the mental – the nature of mental states, the mind-body problem and the problem of other minds – in the context of their machine analogue. Take, for example, the claim that if I observe an afterimage, and at the same time observe that some of my neurons are activated, I observe two things, not one. This claim supposedly shows that my afterimage cannot be a property of the brain, that is, a certain neural activity. But, Putnam (1960:374) observes, this claim is clearly mistaken. We can have a clever Turing machine that can print 'I am in state A', and at the same time (if equipped with the appropriate instrumentation) 'observes' that flip-flop 36 is on. This, however, does not show that two different events are taking place in a machine. One who nonetheless draws the conclusion from the afterimage argument that souls exist, "will have to be prepared to hug the souls of Turing machines to his philosophical bosom!" (1960:376).

2.2. The Functional Nature of Mental States

In 1967a and 1967b, Putnam takes the analogy between minds and machines a step further, arguing that pain, or any other mental state, is neither a brain state nor a behavior disposition, but a functional state. Before looking at the notion of a functional state (section 2.2.2) and at Putnam's specific arguments for functionalism (section 2.2.3), let us elucidate the context in which these claims are made.

2.2.1. Is Pain a Brain State? In 1967b, Putnam raises the question: what is pain? In particular, is it a brain state? On the face of it, the question seems odd. After all, it is quite obvious, even if hard to define, what pain is. Pain is a kind of subjective conscious experience associated with a certain 'feel' ('quale' in philosophical parlance). Even Putnam agrees that pain is associated with a certain unpleasant conscious experience: "must an organism have a *brain* to feel pain?" (1967b:439). Why, then, does Putnam question what pain is, and what could be his motivation for wondering if pain could be something else, for instance, a brain state?

To inquire into the definition of pain is to try and identify that which is common to all pains, or that which is such as to render a certain phenomenon pain. At a more general level, philosophers seek the ultimate mark of the mental: the feature that distinguishes mental from nonmental phenomena. Conscious experience is often deemed that which is characteristic of the mental. Other serious contenders are intentionality (Brentano), rationality (Aristotle), and disposition (Ryle). And even if no single such mark exists, it is nonetheless edifying to explore the relations between the different aspects of mentality.

Functionalism is, roughly, the view that the mark of the mental has to do with the role it plays in the life of the organism. To help us grasp the functionalist account of the mental, it may be useful to consider functionalist definitions of other entities. A carburetor is an object defined by its role in the functioning of an engine (namely, mixing fuel and air). A heart is defined by the role it plays in the human body (namely, pumping blood). The role each object plays is understood in the context of the larger organ of which it is a part, and is explicated in terms of its relations to the other parts of that organ. The material from which the object is made is of little significance, provided it allows the object to function properly. Similarly, the functionalist argues, mental states are defined by their causal relations to *other mental states*, sensory inputs and motor outputs. An early version of functionalism is sometimes attributed to Aristotle. Some versions of functionalism are popular in contemporary philosophical thinking. Computational functionalism is distinguished from other versions of functionalism in that it explicates the pertinent causal relations in terms of computational parameters.[4]

Some philosophers require that the distinguishing mark of pain be described in 'nonmental' terms, for example, physically, neurologically, behaviorally, or even formally. These philosophers ask what pain is, not because they deny that pain is associated with a subjective conscious experience, but because they maintain that if pain is a real phenomenon, it must really be something else – for example, C-fiber stimulation. The task of the philosopher, they argue, is to uncover the hidden nature of pain, which, they all agree, is indeed, among other things, an unpleasant conscious experience. Such accounts of mental states are called naturalistic or *reductive*. Whereas Aristotle's version of functionalism is not reductive, computational functionalism has always been conceived as a reductive account. Indeed, in advancing computational functionalism, Putnam sought to provide a reductive alternative to the reigning reductive hypotheses of the time: classical materialism and behaviorism.

Having considered why a philosopher would ask whether pain is a brain state, let us now consider what would constitute an admissible answer: under what conditions would we affirm that pain *is* a brain state (or a behavior disposition, or a functional state)? It is customary in contemporary philosophy of mind to distinguish two senses of the claim that 'pain is a brain state', one at the level of events (token-identity), another at the level of properties (type-identity). At the level of events, 'pain is a brain state' means that any token of pain – any event that is painful – is also a token of some brain activity. At the level of properties, 'pain is a brain state' means that the property of being painful is identical with some property of the brain, for example, C-fiber stimulation. Token-identity does not entail type-identity. It might be the case that *any* pain token is *some* brain state in the sense that it has neurological properties, though there is no single neurological property that applies to all pain tokens. My pain could be realized in C-fiber stimulation, whereas that of other organisms is realized in very different brain states. It is important to see that Putnam's question about pain and brain states is framed at the level of *properties*, not events. The question he is asking is whether the property of being in pain is identical with some property of the brain.[5]

We still have to say something about the identity of properties. On what basis would we affirm or deny that pain is a property of the brain (or a type of behavior disposition or a functional property)? Putnam is undecided on the issue in his earlier papers (1960, 1964, 1967a), but in 1967b settles on the view that the truth of identity claims such as 'pain is C-fiber stimulation' is to be understood in the context of *theoretical identification*. The inspiration comes from true identity claims such as 'water *is* H_2O', 'light *is* electromagnetic radiation' and 'temperature *is* mean molecular kinetic energy'. In saying that 'water is H_2O', we assert that: (1) The properties of being water and being H_2O molecules are the same in the sense that they apply to exactly the same objects and events; or, at the linguistic level, that the terms 'water' and 'H_2O' (which 'express' the properties) are coextensive. (2) The terms have the same extension (or the properties apply to the same objects/events), not only in our world, but in every possible physical world; they are, roughly speaking, necessarily coextensive and their coextensiveness is a matter of the laws of science. (3) Affirming that they are coextensive is likely to be a matter, not of conceptual analysis (one could think about water yet know nothing about molecules of H_2O), but of empirical-theoretical inquiry: the inquiry is empirical in the sense that it was *discovered*, by way of scientific research, that the extension of 'water', namely, the stuff that fills our lakes, runs in our faucets, and so on, is H_2O; and it is theoretical in the sense that familiar explanatory practices enjoin us to deem the empirical coextensiveness identity.

Similarly, to say that 'pain is C-fiber stimulation' is to assert that the two properties apply to the same class of physically possible events and states. Or in other words, that the terms 'pain' and 'C-fiber stimulation' refer, necessarily, to exactly the same states and events. Yet this assertion is not likely to be determined by a conceptual analysis (one could think about pain yet know nothing about C-fiber stimulation). 'Pain is C-fiber stimulation' is a hypothesis whose truth-value is likely to be ascertained through empirical-theoretical research, possibly conducted by cognitive scientists.

In sum, then, pain *is* a brain state (or a behavior disposition, etc.) just in case there is a brain property (or a kind of behavior disposition, etc.) Q, such that the following two conditions hold:

Unique Realization (UR_Q): any physically possible pain-event is also a Q-event (event of type Q).

Supervenience (SUP_Q): any physically possible Q-event is also a pain-event.

The first condition, UR_Q, asserts that all pains, actual and possible, are realized in events of type Q. I call this condition Unique Realization to signify that there cannot be two organisms both of which feel pain, but one of which has Q and the other not. Pain is always realized in Q-events. The second condition, SUP_Q, complements the first. It asserts that all Q-events are realizations of pain. I call this condition Supervenience to signify that there cannot be two organisms both of which have exactly the same property Q, only one of which feels pain. Being in pain is determined by, that is, dependent on, having Q.

2.2.2. What Is Computational Functionalism?

2.2.2. What Is Computational Functionalism? Putnam set out the concepts and ideas underlying computational functionalism as far back as 1960. In a discussion of computing machines, he mentions that the term 'functional organization' is used to describe a computing machine in terms of sequences of logical states (1960:373). He also mentions that logical states are characterized in terms of their "*relations* to each other and to what appears on the tape" (1960:367). And he emphasizes that this characterization is expressed in logical-mathematical language, for example, a flow-chart description, that makes reference *neither* to the 'physical realization' of the logical states, in copper, platinum, and so on (1960:367,

373), *nor* to the interpretation given to the symbols. For example, being in state C of our Turing machine is represented by the following 'maximal' description:

> Being in C: being in the third of four states S_1, S_2, S_3, S_4 that are related to one another and to inputs and outputs as follows. If being in S_1, then getting '1' as an input results in moving one cell to the right; and getting '+' as an input results in writing '1' as an output and going to S_2. If being in S_2, then getting '1' as an input results in moving one cell to the left; and getting B as an input results in moving one cell to the right, and going to state S_3. If being in S_3, then getting '1' as an input results in writing B as an output; and getting B as an input results in moving one cell to the right. If being in S_4, then halting.

In 1967, Putnam takes the additional step of identifying the mind with the functional organization of thinking organisms, and mental states with functional states: "being capable of feeling pain *is* possessing an appropriate kind of Functional Organization" (1967b:434). This move encompasses two claims: *computationalism* and (computational) *functionalism* (henceforth, I will use 'functionalism' to denote computational functionalism). Computationalism is the claim that organisms with minds have functional organization, that is, there is a true 'flow-chart' description of the organism in terms of states and their relations to each other and to inputs and outputs. Functionalism is the claim that having a mind is having the right sort of functional organization, and any mental property is a certain *kind* of this functional organization. This means that being in pain is having some property that is characteristic of this functional organization. More generally, for any mental property M there is a functional property F such that the following two conditions hold:

UR_F: any M-event is also an F-event.

SUP_F: any F-event is also an M-event.

Given what we know about the functional organizations of machines, functionalism has two important consequences. One consequence is that pain, as a state of the functional organization, is defined by its causal relations to other states (e.g., the belief that I am in pain), inputs (e.g., being punched), and outputs (e.g., the vocalization 'ouch'). The other is that the specification of pain is *reductive* in the sense that it is formulated in nonmental terms. That is, the specification of a mental state in terms of other mental states is eliminated in favor of a formula that contains logical terms (e.g., 'there is', 'and'), variables (i.e., x, $S_1, \ldots, S_n$), and biological/physical terms (for the inputs and outputs), but no mental terms.

To see how the elimination works, assume that FO $(S_1, \ldots, S_n, i_1, \ldots, i_k, o_1, \ldots o_l)$ is my functional organization, namely, a full description of the relations between my internal states $S_1, \ldots, S_n$, sensory inputs $i_1, \ldots, i_k$, and motor outputs $o_1, \ldots o_l$. The functionalist claim is that my being in pain is a state, say S_5, of this functional organization, and that any other organism is in pain just in the case this organism has this (or an isomorphic) FO, and is in S_5. Thus being in pain can be specified as follows:

> Being in pain = being the fifth of n states, $S_1, \ldots, S_n$, whose relations to one another and to inputs and outputs are specified by $FO(S_1, \ldots, S_n, i_1, \ldots, i_k, o_1, \ldots o_l)$.[6]

Thinking about next summer's vacation is defined by the same formula, except that 'being in state S_5' is replaced with 'being in state S_{87}', and so forth.

While the characterization of mental states is analogous in some respects to the characterization of the logical states of a Turing machine, there are also important respects in which the characterizations differ. One such respect is the mode of specification of inputs and outputs. The inputs and outputs of Turing machines are specified in syntactic terms (e.g., '1'). But this specification is much too liberal to be used for the purposes of characterizing mental states, both because it does not fix the semantics of mental states, and because it may also be true of other complex organizations, such as the economics of Liberia, that lack any mentality whatsoever (Block 1978). To remedy this situation, Putnam is careful to specify sensory inputs and motor outputs in physical or biological terms.

In "Philosophy and Our Mental Life", Putnam (1975b) also modifies his earlier claim that mental states are, literally, states of a complex Turing machine. One reason for the modification is that a Turing machine model cannot perspicuously represent learning and memory (1975b:298–299; see also 1992a:8–14, and 1997:34). Another is that when one is in a state of pain one is also in many other mental states (e.g., the state of believing that one is in pain), but a Turing machine instantiates only a single state at any given time (see also Block and Fodor 1972). These modifications do not undermine functionalism. Functionalism is committed to the claim that mental states are computational states, not to the Turing machine model. It might well be that the functional organization of cognizing organisms is best represented in terms of neural networks, and not in terms of Turing machines (see, e.g., Churchland and Sejnowski 1992).

Computationalism is often associated with the maxim that the brain is a sort of computer and, as such, runs a program ('software'). Functionalism is commonly associated with the maxim that the mind is the software of the brain. But why should we believe either of these claims? Putnam does not provide a detailed argument for computationalism. He feels little need to do so, as he takes computationalism to be "obviously, redundant, and only introduced for expository reasons . . . since everything is a Probabilistic Automaton under *some* description" (1967b:435).[7] And even if it is not the case that everything can be seen as some kind of probabilistic automaton, cognitive science nonetheless insists that cognizing organisms are species of computing machines.[8] As for functionalism, the argument here is that it does a better job than the other reductive accounts, namely, classical materialism and behaviorism (1967a, 1967b). In fact, functionalism can be seen as correcting the deficiencies of classical materialism and behaviorism. Let us see why.

2.2.3. *Functional States, Brain States, and Behavioral Dispositions.* Classical materialism, recall, is the claim that any mental property is a property of the brain. Take pain. Pain is a brain property P (e.g., C-fiber stimulation) just in case the following two conditions are met: (1) UR_P: any organism that is in pain has P; and (2) SUP_P: any organism that has P is in pain. Putnam challenges UR_P on the grounds that there may be an organism that feels pain, but in which pain is realized very differently than it is in humans – if, say, human pain is realized in C-fiber stimulation but the other organism has no C-fibers at all. And after all, it is very likely that the brains of mammals, reptiles and mollusks are in very different physical-chemical states when these organisms are in pain (1967b:436). All this is still consistent with the materialist's claim that any pain token is also a physical-chemical event. What is being denied is the further claim that the property of being in pain is a physical-chemical property. It is much more reasonable to assume that different tokens of pain are realized in events with different physical-chemical properties.

Functionalism, on the other hand, is consistent with the multiple realizability of the mental. For what we learn from the case of machines is that "any Turing machine that can be physically realized at all can be realized in a host of totally different ways" (1967a:418). In fact, if functionalism is true, and mental states are computational states, then it *must* be physically possible for them to be multiply realizable: "our mental states, e.g., *thinking about next summer's vacation*, cannot be *identical* with any physical or chemical states. For it is clear from what we already know about computers etc., that whatever the program of the brain may be, it must be physically possible, though not necessarily feasible, to produce something with the same program but quite a different physical and chemical constitution" (1975b:293). So, with respect to the multiple realization of mental properties, functionalism is much further ahead than classical materialism. It is consistent with the materialist's claim that any pain token is likewise a token of a physical state, but *also* consistent with the claim that being in pain is not a brain property.

Putnam elaborates his argument against behaviorism in his "Brains and Behavior" (1963). On the behaviorist account, pain is a kind of behavioral disposition: the disposition to emit certain responses (e.g., 'ouch') under certain stimuli (e.g., being punched in the face). In a sense, behaviorism welcomes the idea that pain is defined by its functional role, defined, that is, by the responses the organism produces under certain stimuli. As Putnam argues, however, behavioral dispositions do not successfully explicate the concept of pain. Pain is a kind of behavioral-disposition B just in case (1) UR_B: any organism that is in pain is disposed to behave in the B-way, e.g., to emit the sound 'ouch' when punched in the face; and (2) SUP_B: any organism that is disposed to behave in the B-way is in pain. But behaviorism fails on both counts. UR_B fails because there might be a community of super-Spartans who, though they feel pain, are trained never to utter the word 'ouch' when punched in the face. SUP_B fails because there could well be perfect actors who can display the same behavioral dispositions we do when we are injured even if their pain fibers have been surgically removed.

What these and other examples demonstrate is that my pain behavior is not just a result of my being in pain, but also of my being in *other* mental states – for example, that of believing that uttering 'ouch' is not outrageous behavior. We can, indeed, address this deficiency of the behavioristic account by admitting that pain is not just the disposition to utter 'ouch' when punched in the face, but the disposition to utter 'ouch' when punched in the face and when in *other mental states*. But this correction is tantamount to endorsing functionalism: pain is not identified just by the relations between stimuli and responses, but by the relations between stimuli, responses and mental states. Functionalism does away with the aforementioned counterexamples to behaviorism easily. The super-Spartan is also in other mental states, hence he or she may react in a manner unlike ordinary humans. And the 'pain behavior' of the perfect actor results from mental states other than pain. Compared to classical materialism and behaviorism, functionalism seems to win hands down.

3. TROUBLES WITH FUNCTIONALISM

Upon emerging as the received view of the mental, functionalism became the focus of increasing scholarly attention. Many philosophers advanced arguments *against* it. I will not survey all the arguments here; for an exhaustive survey, see Block 1996. My aim is to present Putnam's line of argument against functionalism, which, I believe, goes a long way toward explaining its demise. The argument consists of two steps. It is first argued that there is a gap between mental states' functional-computational properties, on the one hand, and their intentional aspects, on the other, meaning that either UR_F or SUP_F is false. For example, Putnam (1988, 1992b) argues against UR_F by pointing out that the same thought can be realized in different computational structures. The argument is simple: functionalism is a holistic theory on which a mental state is defined by its causal relations to other mental states. But it is quite possible that two individuals, John and Mary, though somewhat different in functional organization (for Mary believes some proposition John does not), both believe that water is wet. Thus either we cannot attribute to John and Mary, or any other pair of individuals, the same belief – which is patently absurd – or we must admit that the same belief can be realized in different functional states. But if the latter is the case, then UR_F appears to be false: the same mental property can indeed be realized in different functional organizations (1988:80–84; 1992b:448–453).

Later, I discuss in some detail two further arguments Putnam makes against SUP_F. Both seek to show that the functional-computational properties of a mental state do not fix its intentional character. One is the well-known Twin-Earth argument (3.1); the other, the realization problem (3.2), which has received more attention of late. The upshot of all three arguments is that the functionalists must revise their initial characterization of mental states. They have to find an equivalence relation among the different types of functional organization, something they all have in common. Here, however, the second step in the argumentation kicks in. The second step is to argue that there is no hope the functionalist can specify such an equivalence relation yet preserve key elements of the theory. In particular, there is no hope of specifying the equivalence relation in nonintentional terms, something that is essential if the reductive character of the theory is to be preserved.

For example, to avoid the above-mentioned argument against UR_F, the functionalists have no choice but to adopt a less fine-grained individuation scheme. There are two routes the functionalists can take. One is to fix some of the beliefs, for example, that water is wet, as analytic. This would make these beliefs' individuation invulnerable to realizations in different functional organizations, and affect the individuation of the other beliefs as well. But this move is not only undesirable, but will not help anyway (1988:81–82; 1992b:450–451; see also Fodor and Lepore 1992). The other is to appeal to physical facts, a move that would blur the differences between functionalism and classical materialism, and turn functionalism into a utopian enterprise (1988, chaps. 5 and 6; 1992b). I shall expand on this line of argumentation, pointing to the difficulties that would beset any attempt to rehabilitate functionalism (3.3).

3.1. Content, Computation and Twin-Earth

That there might be a gap between the functional and the intentional – that the former may not determine the latter – should have been clear from the outset. After all, it is obvious that any computer program can be interpreted in different ways. One user may construe the program as playing chess, and another, as calculating the next month's payroll. What reason is there, then, to think that the program our brains run definitively determines the content of our thoughts, beliefs and other intentional states?

Let us be clearer about this multiple interpretation problem. A computer program is a formal-mathematical description containing only logical and mathematical operations that are defined over a finite set of symbols (e.g., '1', '+'). The symbols do, however, also have a semantic dimension. We take the machine in Figure 1 to compute addition because we interpret the numeral '1' as representing the number ONE, and '+' as representing the function PLUS. When talking semantics, there are two elements that have to be taken into account. One is the symbol's extension, which is just the object or set of objects to which the symbol refers. Thus the extension of the numeral '1' is the number ONE, and the extension of 'water' is the set of things that consist of H_2O molecules. The other dimension is the symbol's content, which is what makes the symbol into the representation it is. It is the content of the symbol '1' that makes it represent ONE and not ZERO. Content is often associated with 'meaning', 'sense' and 'intension', and its nature is highly disputable. It is much less disputable, however, that (*a*) two symbols, i.e., 'water' and 'H_2O', can differ in their contents yet have the same extension, and (*b*) if two symbols have the same content, they also have the same extension. In a nutshell, content determines extension, but not vice versa.

The problem is now evident: there is a tension between the claim that mental content is computational-functional and the claim that mental content determines extension. On the one hand, if functionalism is correct, then the mental is, in its entirety, functional. In particular, the content of our thoughts, beliefs and so forth, is exhaustively specified by their computational-functional properties. These are the functional properties of my thought that water is wet, for instance, which determine that I'm thinking about water and not cats. In other words, if functionalism is correct, then the content of our thoughts must supervene on their functional properties. If two organisms have exactly the same functional organization, then the content of their thoughts, beliefs, desires and so forth must be the same. And a fortiori, their thoughts must be about the same things. If the two organisms say that water is wet, both are thinking about water and not about cats: the extension of their concept WATER is the set of molecules of H_2O, not the set of cats.

But, on the other hand, we know from the case of machines that the program – as a formal-syntactic entity – does not determine the extension of the symbols over which the operations are defined. In our toy example, we could take the '1' to stand for TWO, in which case the function computed would be quite different. We could also take the '1' to represent kinds of animals and not numbers at all. Functional organization constrains the set of possible interpretations, but does not determine a unique interpretation. It is always possible for two machines to have the same functional organization though their users interpret the symbols over which their operations are defined quite differently. Similarly, it appears, two thinking organisms can be alike in functional organization though the extensions of what they say and think differ. If so, then computational functionalism is false: the contents of our thoughts do not supervene on functional properties.

It might be suggested that a sufficiently complex functional organization has a single interpretation. I think about water and not cats because the complexity of the program my brain runs rules out any nonhydrous content. But this suggestion won't work. Assuming that the program is complex enough (and formulated in a first-order language), it is guaranteed (by the Löwenheim-Skolem results) that the organization will have several nonisomorphic interpretations (see, e.g., Putnam 1980). This would explain why Putnam insists on biologically specified inputs and outputs (I/O). The hope is that if the specification of I/O is biological/physical and not merely formal-syntactic, this will rule out nonstandard interpretations. I think about water and not cats because the physical perceptual inputs associated with this thought fix the hydrous content and rule out the feline content. Functional organization, then, consists of an implemented program (abstract automation) plus physically specified I/O.

In "The Meaning of 'Meaning'", however, Putnam (1975c) advances an argument whose upshot is that the appeal to physical I/O will not help either. Two individuals, Oscar and Toscar, can have exactly the same functional organization, including the same physically specified sensory and motor I/O, yet their concepts, thoughts, beliefs, desires and so forth have different contents. To see this, imagine that Toscar lives on Twin-Earth, which is exactly like Earth, except that the term 'water' refers to a liquid with the chemical structure XYZ, a liquid that is thus very different from H_2O. Oscar and Toscar, however, cannot tell XYZ from H_2O, as the two liquids look, taste, smell and sound exactly the same. On Twin-Earth they have XYZ in those places where we have H_2O: rivers, clouds, faucets and so on. It is thus possible for Oscar and Toscar to have exactly the same functional organization although their thoughts differ considerably in content. When Oscar says 'water is wet', he is referring to the liquid that is H_2O; whereas Toscar, when saying 'water is wet', refers to the liquid that is XYZ. Let us assume that Oscar and Toscar know nothing about H_2O or XYZ, as they live prior to 1750, when no one knew the chemical structure of the liquids. What Oscar and Toscar know is that 'water' refers to a liquid that is familiar to them in their respective environments. Yet the liquids to which Oscar's and Toscar's thoughts refer are in fact very different. But given that content determines extension, and that the extensions are different, Oscar's and Toscar's thoughts must differ in content. Hence, mental contents do not supervene on functional properties.

The Twin-Earth argument created a storm in the philosophical community, reviving the view known as psychological externalism, according to which some determinants of mental content are located in the speaker's environment. Some functionalists have argued in response that the argument only shows that content comprises two factors. (Indeed, Putnam [1975c] himself suggested something along these lines, though he has since repudiated that view [1992b].) One factor determines extension and is associated with "meaning". This factor is "wide", in the sense that some of its identity conditions make an essential reference to the individual's environment. The other factor is associated with features having to do with psychological/phenomenal properties. This factor is "narrow", in the sense that it is not wide. This factor can still be identified functionally. The two-factor account is no longer popular, perhaps because it has proved difficult to explain how the factors are related, or due to the convincing arguments that have been advanced for the thesis that theories in cognitive science utilize "wide" individuation (e.g., Burge 1986).

Other functionalists have suggested that I/O should be understood as extending all the way to the distal environment; this view is known as wide or global functionalism (e.g., Harman 1988). The thoughts of Oscar and Toscar differ in content because they are causally related to different I/O. Oscar's thoughts are related to water, Toscar's, to "twater". As it turns out, however, the troubles for functionalism do not stop here.

3.2. The Realization Problem

In the appendix to *Representation and Reality* (1988:121–125), Putnam proves that every ordinary open system is a realization of every abstract finite automaton. This result clearly threatens SUP_F. A corollary of the theorem is that there can be two objects, a human and a rock, with the same functional organization (save the physical I/O), only one of which is deemed to have mentality. Differently put, if a functional organization of a certain complexity is sufficient for having a mind, as the functionalist claims, then the rock, too, should be deemed to have a mind. In fact, almost everything, given that it realizes this automaton, has a mind. Moreover, if Putnam's theorem is true, then my brain simultaneously implements infinitely many different functional organizations, each constituting a different mind. It thus seems that I should simultaneously be endowed with an infinite number of minds!

Putnam's theorem therefore seems to undermine SUP_F in two ways: (*a*) a rock implements the same functional organization I do, but the rock is deemed lacking in mentality; (*b*) my brain implements many functional organizations, each of which normally constitutes an independent mind, yet I have but a single mind. I will call these results the realization problem.

The realization problem cuts deeper than the Twin-Earth problem. Even if, adopting a less fine-grained scheme of individuation, we take the thoughts of Oscar and Toscar to be the same, this would do little to alleviate the realization problem. It would still be the case that the rock implements the functional organization of Oscar (and Toscar), and so should be deemed endowed with their minds. And it would still be the case that my brain implements all the functional organizations that constitute other minds. One reason the realization problem is so interesting is that it highlights the computationalism thesis. Initially, computationalism seemed innocuous, in that it seemed highly plausible that a cognizing organism would be functionally organized – that it would realize a probabilistic automaton of some sort. It turns out, however, that not only does such an organism have one functional organization, it has infinitely many: it realizes every finite automaton, and perhaps even many other kinds of automata, something that leads directly to the realization problem.

3.2.1. An Outline of Putnam's Proof.

Putnam's theorem pertains to abstract finite-state automata (FSA) without inputs/outputs. Take the FSA that runs through the state-sequence ABABABA in the time interval we want to simulate. Here A and B are the states of the FSA. Assume that a rock can realize this run in a six-minute interval, say from 12:00 to 12:06. Assume that the rock is in a maximal physical state S_0 at 12:00, S_1 at 12:01, and so forth (a maximal physical state being its total physical makeup specified in complete detail). Also assume that the states differ from each other (this is Putnam's Principle of Noncyclical Behavior). Now let us define a physical state a as S_0 v S_2 v S_4 v S_6, and state b as S_1 v S_3 v S_5. The rock implements the FSA in the sense that the causal structure of the rock "mirrors" the formal structure of the FSA. The physical state a corresponds to the logical state A, the physical b corresponds to the logical B, and the causal transitions from a to b correspond to the computational transitions from A to B. A complete proof would require further elaboration, as well as a Principle of Physical Continuity. But the idea is wonderfully simple, and can be extended to any I/O-less FSA.

Putnam notes (1988:124) that the proof cannot be immediately extended to FSA with I/O. If the I/O are functionally individuated, then the I/O can be treated much like abstract internal states, and the extension is more natural. But if the I/O are specific kinds of physical organs, as the functionalist requires, then the rock, which lacks motor or sensory organs of the required sort, cannot realize the automaton. The rock cannot implement a mind because it lacks the motor and sensory organs of thinking organisms.

The functionalist is in real trouble, I would argue, if the difference between rocks and humans is exhausted by the I/O issue. After all, the whole point of functionalism is that the difference between thinking organisms and rocks is rooted in the complexity of functional organization. But if Putnam's argument is correct, the difference between humans and rocks does not lie in the complexity of their respective internal computational arrangements (which turn out to be the same for humans and rocks), but in the kinds of I/O they can handle. Is this not behaviorism in a new guise?

Indeed, Putnam points out (1988:124–125) that reliance on physical I/O causes functionalism to collapse into behaviorism. Functionalism improves on behaviorism by taking into account not only I/O but also the mediating algorithm. Behaviorism is false because there are beings that have the same I/O dependencies as humans but different mentalities, for example, perfect actors; or are altogether lacking in mentality (Block 1981). Functionalism holds that the reason they differ is that the 'internal' relations among the logical states differ, that is, the implemented algorithm differs. But consider a physical object with the right kind of I/O (e.g., a perfect actor). What is true of this entity, on Putnam's theorem, is that it realizes all the possible algorithms that mediate the I/O. There can be no difference between the algorithms implemented by this entity and the algorithms implemented by humans: "In short, 'functionalism', if it were correct, would imply behaviorism! If it is true that to possess given mental states is simply to possess a certain 'functional organization', then it is also true that to possess given mental states is simply to possess certain behavior dispositions!" (1988:124–125).

3.2.2. Chalmers's Reply. Many attempted to downplay Putnam's result, arguing that it takes more than he allows to implement the functional organizations that are minds. David Chalmers (1996) provides a detailed counterargument along these lines. His contention is that there are constraints on the notion of implementation that are not taken into account by Putnam, constraints not satisfied by rocks. For one thing, the state transitions of the implementing machine must be reliable and counterfactual supporting. For another, the causal structure of the physical object should mirror all the possible formal state transitions of the implemented FSA. In Putnam's proof, the rock implements only a *single run* (the transition from A and B and back), but not other runs that might exist. If the FSA has other state transitions, for example, C→D and D→C, these transitions should also be mirrored by the rock's dynamics.

It thus follows, according to Chalmers, that Putnam's proof applies to relatively simple kinds of automata, but not to the combinatorial state automata (CSA) that are more likely to be the minds implemented by brains. Roughly, a CSA is much like a FSA, except that it has a more complex, combinatorial internal structure. Each state is a combination of substates, and any state transition is sensitive to the combinatorial structure of the previous combined state. "CSAs are much less vulnerable to Putnam-style objections than FSAs. Unlike FSA implementations, CSA implementations are required to have complex internal structure and complex dependencies among their parts. For a complex CSA, the right sort of complex structure will be found in very few physical systems" (1996:325). Chalmers concludes that brains, but not rocks, implement the complex CSA that is more likely to constitute a mind.

While his points about implementation are well taken, Chalmers's conclusion that "for a complex CSA, the right sort of complex structure will be found in very few physical systems" does not follow. What does follow is that the proof that the rock implements the functional organization of a thinking organism has to be fixed, but nothing that Chalmers says proves that this cannot be done. As long as no constraints are imposed on the groupings of physical properties that form the implementing states, it is not clear that Putnam's theorem cannot be rehabilitated. As Matthias Scheutz observes, "if no restrictions are imposed on groupings of physical states, then simple, finite, deterministic physical systems . . . can possibly be seen to implement complex, infinite, and non-deterministic computations" (2001:551). Indeed, Moore (1990) shows that even a universal Turing machine can be embedded in the motion of a single particle moving in space, bouncing between parabolic and linear mirrors like an ideal billiard ball. The infinite tape and table of instructions can be embedded in the binary development of the coordinates of the particle's position. It might even turn out that if the groupings are defined over the quantum makeup of a rock, the rock implements a complex CSA that is, arguably, constitutive of mind. In light of these results, it is up to the functionalist to demonstrate that there are CSAs implemented by thinking organisms, but by no objects that lack minds.[9]

Furthermore, even if Chalmers is right, and the rock does not implement the functional organization deemed a mind, the other problem – that of my brain's simultaneously implementing a wide variety of independent CSAs – remains. It is still possible that the same system – for example, my brain – simultaneously implements many complex independent CSAs, each of which is sufficient to embody an independent mind. Indeed, elsewhere I have demonstrated that even a slight change in the grouping of a single neural property can completely alter the *logical operators* we take the brain to implement. Under a grouping of 0–50mv neural activity into groups of 0–25mv and 25–50mv, the resulting logical operation is AND, but under a grouping into 0–15mv and 15–50mv groups, it is OR. Moreover, it can be shown that even if the proximal sensory-motor I/O organs are given, we can *group* their physical properties in different ways, each matching an implemented abstract CSA (see Shagrir 2001). Thus the fact that "simple" physical objects such as rocks cannot implement complex

CSA does not itself entail that "complex" physical objects such as brains implement a single complex CSA. Indeed, if my brain simultaneously implements different independent CSAs, and if each such implemented CSA is associated with a certain belief-desire scheme (as the functionalist claims), then I must *simultaneously* have all these belief-desire schemes, which I cannot do.[10]

3.3. Why Functionalism Didn't Work

I don't think any of the above arguments deal functionalism a knockdown blow. But they force functionalists to try and escape the conclusions of these arguments by appealing to physical facts, among them, facts pertaining to the distal environment and the implementing hardware. The appeal to facts in the physical environment is motivated by the need to explain why the thoughts of Oscar and Toscar differ. The appeal to certain conditionals and/or the physics of the implementing hardware is motivated by the need to explain why only humans, but not rocks, implement the automaton that constitutes a mind. Now why is it that this is problematic?

One problem is that the appeal to physical facts blurs the differences between functionalism and classical materialism. The initial attraction of functionalism was the idea that the matter from which we are made is not all that important. What counts is the complexity of the automaton that the organism implements. There could be other organisms, made of very different materials, that implement it as well. It is true that from the beginning, Putnam specified proximal I/O in biological terms. But virtually all the internal causal relations – the whole internal causal network – were specified in some formal-syntactic language. As it now turns out, however, we must also take into account many more physical facts: those pertaining to the distal environment, and those pertaining to the proper implementation of the automaton. We must include many more physical or biological terms in the functionalist specification of mental states.

Worse still, multiple realizability, once the principal argument *for* functionalism, now becomes a threat. Jaegwon Kim, who objected to the multiple realization argument early on (Kim 1972), pointed out, among other things, that there are seemingly high-order properties, such as the temperature of a gas, that are realized in very different physical substrates yet are identical with a physical property (mean kinetic energy). Similarly, the fact that a mental property can be realized in both neural tissue and silicon chips does not entail that this property cannot be identical with one particular physical property. Functionalists have responded that "it is difficult to see how there *could be* a non-trivial first-order physical property in common to all and only the possible physical realizations of a given Turing-machine state" (Block 1978:270–271). It is indeed difficult to see how there could be such a physical property on the weak notion of realization Block has in mind. But, as we just saw, the functionalists cannot use this notion of realization if they are to avoid the disastrous results of Putnam's theorem. They must use a much stronger notion of realization that will most likely exclude many of the "possible" realizations the weaker notion allows. So there might, after all, be a physical property common to all the realizers of a mental property. This is the physical property to which the functionalists must appeal if they are to avoid the conclusions of the arguments *against* functionalism. It is this result, among others, that inclines many to regard functionalism as no better a hypothesis than classical materialism.[11]

The appeal to physical facts has another drawback, first pointed out by Block with respect to the biological/physical specification of I/O (Block 1978). The problem is that such specification seems to exclude intelligent beings that lack our biological sensory and motor I/O organs. Such specification is thus unjustly chauvinistic. Why should we assume that there are no possible intelligent beings whose I/O organs differ from ours? If functionalism is correct, then there must be a *nonintentional* equivalence relation over all the biological/physical I/O. But it now turns out that this equivalence relation is to be defined, not just over biological/physical proximal I/O, but also over the physical environment, the implementing hardware, and even different abstract automata that realize the same belief. The functionalist has to take all these issues into account when arguing that two thoughts are of the same type, that is, have something in common. To accomplish this task, the functionalist must survey of all the beliefs and reasoning – scientific, religious and so forth – of all humans, individuals and societies, actual and possible. In addition, to satisfy the reductive aspirations of the theory, "this 'something in common' must itself be describable at a physical, or at worst a computational, level" (1988:100). But it is hard to see how one can succeed in this task. This enterprise, Putnam suggests, is nothing less than utopian (1994:510–512).[12]

4. COGNITIVE SCIENCE

What can we conclude about the scientific study of the mind from the arguments against functionalism? What is the outlook for the tenets and aspirations of cognitive science, given that functionalism provides its philosophical underpinning? John Searle (1992) contends that cognitive science lacks a firm foundation. Putnam goes further than that, implying that cognitive science is no less than science fiction (1997;1999:118–119). My conclusions are quite different. While I am persuaded that Putnam's arguments against functionalism are by and large correct, I do not think they pose a threat to cognitive science. Given that cognitive science has generated an impressive body of empirical and theoretical knowledge, I am inclined to reject the other premise – namely, that functionalism provides the conceptual framework for cognitive science. What Putnam's arguments really indicate, in my view, is that computational functionalism is not helpful for assessing the outlook of cognitive science, and that it rests on a misinterpretation of the scientific and explanatory practices of cognitive science. What follows is a brief diagnosis of the nature of this misinterpretation.

Functionalism did not become so influential only because it provides an attractive theory of mind. Its impact is also due to its linkage with cognitive science. Putnam (1967b:434–435) even presents functionalism and cognitive science as complementary. Functionalism is a project undertaken by philosophers who seek to formulate a comprehensive account of the mind, preferably in nonsemantic and nonintentional terms. Inspired by the computational models of cognition, functionalists put forward the theory that cognitive capacities, thoughts, beliefs and so on, are computational states, specified in terms that are formal-syntactic. Functionalism, however, provides neither a detailed specification of the functional organization of the thinking organism nor a computational description of its thoughts and beliefs. That is, functionalism asserts that the thought (type) that water is wet is a certain computational type, but does not specify *what* computational type it is. This specification is to be arrived at by scientists. The aim of the scientific project is to specify what type of computational state each cognitive capacity, thought and so on actually is. And, on this picture, cognitive science does exactly that. By specifying the computational structure of cognitive systems, thoughts, beliefs and so forth, cognitive science spells out the computational type identical with each mental type. Thus functionalism, if correct, not only provides a theory of the mental, but also inspires a comprehensive picture of the goals and practices of cognitive science. The aim of cognitive science, on this picture, is to *discover* the functional organization of cognizing organisms, and to specify the computational type identified with each mental type.

Putnam's arguments against functionalism directly challenge this alleged scientific project. If Putnam's arguments are correct, there are no identity relations of the said type in the first place. The same computational type can yield different thoughts: for example, Oscar's thought that water is wet, and Toscar's thought that twater is wet. We could try to enrich the program, and individuate mental content by appealing to communities and environments. But "how useful is it to speak of 'computational-cum-physical states' of such vast systems?" (Putnam 1997:37). Moreover, even if there were such computational-mental types, it would be impossible to discover them, for the characterization of the content of a thought would make it necessary to "describe the content of every belief of every possible kind, or at least every human belief of every possible kind, even of kinds that are not yet invented, or that go with institutions that have not yet come into existence. That is why I say that the idea of such a theory is pure 'science fiction'" (1997:38).

But there is another option: perhaps the picture inspired by functionalism fails to capture the goals and program of cognitive science. Perhaps cognitive science and functionalism are not complementary projects at all. The aim of cognitive science is not to provide an exhaustive specification of mind, let alone a full-fledged theory of mental content. Thus Putnam's arguments against functionalism have little impact on the success of cognitive science. In "Computational Psychology and Interpretation Theory," Putnam (1983b) endorses this option. Arguing that "functionalist psychology" cannot account for mental content, he concludes that "the theory of interpretation and cognitive psychology deal with quite different projects" and that "to a large extent success in one of these projects is independent of success in the other" (1983b:150). Cognitive science seeks to provide a description of how the system of mental representations works, to ascertain what rules of computation drive the system of representations. Its business is to reveal the interaction between different patterns of representations, to describe, for example, how the visual system extracts information about shape from information about shading, or how it constructs a three-dimensional representation from the disparity between two retinal images. But it does not provide a comprehensive account of the specific content of mental representations, misrepresentation and so forth. Such an account is the concern of interpretation theory, or what we now call theory of content. It is the interpretative theory, and not the scientific theory, that seeks to provide the pertinent interpretation for the system of mental representations.[13]

I favor the latter proposal, which, I think, offers a much better description of the objectives and practices of cognitive science. Cognitive science is here to stay for the foreseeable future, and for good reason. But the question is, why has Putnam become so critical of cognitive science in recent years? Why is he presently "convinced that the dream of Psychological Physics that seems to be thinly disguised under many of the programs currently announced for 'cognitive science' will sooner or later be realized to be as illusory as Comte's dream of the Social Physics" (1997:41)? My impression is that the answer has little to do with the arguments against functionalism, none of which presents any immediate danger to the programs of cognitive science. Rather, to better understand the shift in Putnam's views about cognitive science, we would have to look into his current Wittgensteinian aversion to the notion of mental representation. But this will have to wait for another occasion.

Notes

1. For a short survey of Putnam's views written by Putnam himself, see Putnam (1994b). For a useful survey of functionalism in general, emphasizing the computational version of the thesis, see Block (1995, 1996). For a critical overview of the origins of computational functionalism, and Fodor's contribution to it, see Piccinini (forthcoming).
2. The page numbers here and throughout the essay refer to the reprinted versions.
3. Here I assume the truth of the Church-Turing thesis, which states that any input-output function that can be computed by finite means (i.e., by a finite effective procedure) can also be computed by a universal Turing machine. This result motivated Turing (1950), even before Putnam, to associate computing machinery and intelligence.
4. For a survey of other versions of functionalism, see Block (1978, 1996).
5. This idea that any token of a mental event is identical with a token of some physical event, but that mental types (properties) are not identical with physical types, is known as nonreductive monism. Putnam advances the view in its most explicit form in 1973 and 1975b. Well-known versions of this view are also advanced by Davidson (1970) and by Fodor (1974). Putnam, however, also notes that "the functional-state hypothesis is *not* incompatible with dualism!" (1967b:436). Since the hypothesis is simply that mental types are functional types, which are abstract, it is still compatible with the dualistic view that tokens of mental/functional events are not tokens of physical events.
6. See Block (1996), also for a second-order quantification over the states $S_1, \ldots S_n$.
7. A probabilistic automaton is a device similar to a Turing machine. The two differ in that: (*a*) the automaton has a fixed finite memory, whereas the Turing machine has unbounded memory; (*b*) the state transitions of the automaton might be probabilistic rather than deterministic (though there are also nondeterministic Turing machines). All these devices do not have more computational power than a universal Turing machine.

   In "The Project of Artificial Intelligence", the first chapter of his *Renewing Philosophy*, Putnam (1992a) qualifies this claim. He explains (pp. 4–7) that he once believed that everything can be seen as some kind of a Turing machine, because he assumed that a Turing machine can, in principle, simulate and predict the behavior of any finite system (and a human being is finite in space and time). It was meanwhile proved (Pour-El and Richards 1981), however, that there are possible physical systems whose time evolution is not describable by a Turing machine computable function, even when the initial condition of the system is so describable.

This result does not defy computationalism, however. First, Pour-El and Richards constructed examples for the wave equation in which the initial data is real recursive (can be sufficiently approximated by a Turing machine), but the solution is not. There is no *empirical* evidence that there are *brain processes* whose evolution is not real recursive (Roger Penrose [1989, 1994] advances a *philosophical* argument that there might be such processes, but Putnam [1995] rightly dismisses it). Second, computationalism is not committed to the Turing machine model. It is true that a universal Turing machine can compute every function that any 'conventional' automaton computes, as well as every function that is 'effectively' computable (assuming the truth of the Church-Turing thesis). But this does not rule out the possibility of devices that compute (non-effectively) functions which are not Turing-machine computable. For a detailed relevant discussion, see Copeland (2000).

8. Putnam himself tends to accept that *"the mind uses a formalized language . . . both as medium of computation and medium of representation"* (1983b:141), even while expressing serious reservations about functionalism.

9. Scheutz (2001) offers an alternative theory of implementation that is relative to a fixed canonical physical theory (e.g., circuit theory), a theory on which the grouping into physical types is already given. In this context, there is a characteristic automaton, which is the most complex implemented automaton. I find the theory interesting and highly useful for the purposes of computer science. But the theory is of little help to the functionalist. As Putnam repeatedly notes, the functionalist has to pick out one physical grouping and not another without appealing to any semantic or intentional traits. Given that functionalism is a reductive theory, it would be unfair to describe humans but not rocks in terms of the pertinent characteristic automaton only because humans are deemed to have minds and rocks are not. To do so would be totally circular. The computer scientist is in a very different position. To fix the canonical grouping, the computer scientist can and does appeal to traits like goals, purposes and desiderata such as easy-to-build and user-friendly interfaces. The job of the computer scientist is not, and has never been, akin to that of the functionalist, namely, to provide a reductive theory of content.

10. Chalmers addresses this possibility, saying that "a given physical hunk of matter can be associated with more than one mind" (1996:332), yet he does not find it too troubling. But it is troubling. For functionalists have to sort out the 'canonical' from the 'noncanonical' implementations. They have to account in nonintentional terms for the alleged fact that my mind is constituted by one implemented automaton as opposed to others.

11. For recent critical discussions of the multiple realization argument, see, e.g., Shagrir (1998), Bechtel and Mundale (1999), Shapiro (2000), and Perebum

(2002). It should be noted that there are functionalists who are *also* functional-to-physical reductionists, e.g., Churchland (1984).

12. Putnam, however, did not abandon all his views about functionalism. He seems to embrace the Aristotelian version even today, and the seeds of his more recent criticisms can be found in his early papers. The chief change in Putnam's views is the total rejection of the reductive assumption taken for granted in the early papers.

13. There still remains the issue of accounting for the exact relationship between computation and content. This topic has drawn the attention of many philosophers in recent years. For various accounts see Burge (1986), Fodor (1994), Egan (1995), and Shagrir (2001).

References

Bechtel, W., and J. Mundale (1999). "Multiple Realizability Revisited: Linking Cognitive and Neural States". *Philosophy of Science* 66:175–207.

Block, N. (1978). "Troubles with Functionalism". In W. Savage (ed.), *Issues in the Foundations of Psychology*. Minnesota Studies in the Philosophy of Science, Vol. 9. Minneapolis: University of Minnesota Press, pp. 261–325. Reprinted in Block 1980:268–305.

(1980). *Readings in Philosophy of Psychology, Volume 1*. Cambridge, MA: Harvard University Press.

(1981). "Psychologism and Behaviorism". *Philosophical Review* 90:5–43.

(1990). "Can the Mind Change the World?". In G. Boolos (ed.), *Meaning and Method: Essays in Honor of Hilary Putnam*. Cambridge: Cambridge University Press, pp. 137–170.

(1995). "The Mind as the Software of the Brain". In D. Osherson, L. Gleitman, S. Kosslyn, E. Smith and S. Sternberg (eds.), *An Invitation to Cognitive Science, Volume 3: Thinking*. 2 ed. Cambridge, MA: MIT Press, pp. 377–425.

(1996). "Functionalism". *The Encyclopedia of Philosophy Supplement*. New York: Macmillan.

Block, N., and J. A. Fodor (1972). "What Psychological States Are Not". *Philosophical Review* 81:159–181.

Burge, T. (1986). "Individualism and Psychology". *Philosophical Review* 95:3–45.

Carnap, R. (1932/33). "Psychology in Physical Language". *Erkenntnis* 3:107–142. English version (trans. by George Schick) in A. J. Ayer (ed.), *Logical Positivism*. New York: The Free Press, pp. 165–198.

Chalmers, J. D. (1996). "Does a Rock Implement Every Finite-State Automaton?" *Synthese* 108:309–333.

Chomsky, N. (1957). *Syntactic Structures*. The Hague: Mouton.

(1959). Review of Skinner's *Verbal Behavior*. *Language* 35:26–58.

Churchland, P. (1984). *Matter and Consciousness*. Cambridge, MA.: MIT Press.

Churchland, P. S., and T. Sejnowski (1992). *The Computational Brain*. Cambridge, MA.: MIT Press.

Copeland, B. J. (2000). "Narrow versus Wide Mechanism". *Journal of Philosophy* 97:1–32.

Davidson, D. (1970). "Mental Events". In L. Foster and J. W. Swanson (eds.), *Experience and Theory*. Amherst: University of Massachusetts Press, pp. 79–101.

Descartes, R. (1637). *Discourse on the Method*. In J. Cottingham, R. Stoothoff and D. Murdoch (trans.), *The Philosophical Writings of Descartes: Volume 1* (1985). Cambridge: Cambridge University Press.

Egan, F. (1995). "Computation and Content". *Philosophical Review* 104:181–204.

Feigl, H. (1958). "The 'Mental' and the 'Physical'". In H. Feigl, M. Scriven and G. Maxwell (eds.), *Concepts, Theories and the Mind-Body Problem*. Minnesota Studies in the Philosophy of Science, Vol. 2. Minneapolis: University of Minnesota Press, pp. 370–497. Reissued in 1967 with a postscript by University of Minnesota Press.

Fodor, J. A. (1968). *Psychological Explanation*. New York: Random House.

  (1974). "Special Sciences, or the Disunity of Science as a Working Hypothesis". *Synthese* 28:97–115.

  (1975). *The Language of Thought*. New York: Thomas Y. Crowell.

  (1994). *The Elm and the Expert, Mentalese and Its Semantics*. Cambridge, MA: MIT Press.

Fodor, J. A., and E. Lepore (1992). *Holism: A Shopper's Guide*. Oxford: Blackwell.

Harman, G. (1988). "Wide Functionalism". In S. Schiffer and S. Steele (eds.), *Cognition and Representation*. Boulder: Westview, pp. 11–20.

Hempel, C. G. (1949). "The Logical Analysis of Psychology". In H. Feigl and W. Sellars (eds.), *Readings in Philosophical Analysis*. New York: Appleton-Century-Crofts, pp. 373–384.

Kim, J. (1972). "Phenomenal Properties, Psychophysical Laws, and the Identity Theory". *The Monist* 56:177–192.

Lewis, D. K. (1972). "Psychophysical and Theoretical Identifications". *Australasian Journal of Philosophy* 50: 249–258.

Lycan, W. (1987). *Consciousness*. Cambridge, MA: MIT Press.

Moore, C. (1990). "Unpredictability and Undecidability in Dynamical Systems". *Physical Review Letters* 64:2354–2357.

Penrose, R. (1989). *The Emperor's New Mind*. Oxford: Oxford University Press.

  (1994). *Shadows of the Mind*. New York and Oxford: Oxford University Press.

Pereboom, D. (2002). "Robust Nonreductive Materialism". *Journal of Philosophy* 99:499–531.

Piccinini, G. (forthcoming). "Functionalism, Computationalism, and Mental States". *Studies in the History and Philosophy of Science*.

Place, U. T. (1956). "Is Consciousness a Brain Process?" *British Journal of Psychology* 47:44–50.

Pour-El, M. B., and I. Richards (1981). "The Wave Equation with Computable Initial Data Such That Its Unique Solution Is Not Computable". *Advances in Mathematics* 39:215–239.

Putnam, H. (1960). "Minds and Machines". In S. Hook (ed.), *Dimensions of Mind.* New York: University of New York Press, pp. 148–180. Reprinted in Putnam 1975a:362–385.

(1963). "Brains and Behavior". In R. Butler (ed.), *Analytical Philosophy. Second Series.* Oxford: Basil Blackwell & Mott, pp. 1–19. Reprinted in Putnam 1975a:325–341.

(1964). "Robots: Machines or Artificially Created Life?" *Journal of Philosophy* 61:668–691. Reprinted in Putnam 1975a:386–407.

(1967a). "The Mental Life of Some Machines". In Hector-Neri Castañeda (ed.), *Intentionality, Minds and Perception.* Detroit: Wayne State University Press, pp. 177–200. Reprinted in Putnam 1975a:408–428.

(1967b). "The Nature of Mental States" (originally published as "Psychological Predicates"). In W. H. Captain and D. D. Merrill (eds.), *Art, Mind and Religion.* Pittsburgh: University of Pittsburgh Press, pp. 37–48. Reprinted in Putnam 1975a:429–440.

(1973). "Reductionism and the Nature of Psychology". *Cognition* 2:131–149. Reprinted in Putnam 1994a:428–440.

(1975a). *Mind, Language and Reality, Philosophical Papers, Volume 2.* Cambridge: Cambridge University Press.

(1975b). "Philosophy and Our Mental Life". In Putnam 1975a:291–303.

(1975c). "The Meaning of 'Meaning'". In K. Gunderson (ed.), *Language, Mind and Knowledge.* Minnesota Studies in the Philosophy of Science, Vol. 7. Minneapolis: University of Minnesota Press, pp. 131–193. Reprinted in Putnam 1975a:215–271.

(1980). "Models and Reality". *Journal of Symbolic Logic* 45:464–482. Reprinted in Putnam 1983a:1–25.

(1983a). *Realism and Reason, Philosophical Papers, Volume 3.* Cambridge: Cambridge University Press.

(1983b). "Computational Psychology and Interpretation Theory". In Putnam 1983a:139–154.

(1988). *Representation and Reality.* Cambridge, MA: MIT Press.

(1992a). *Renewing Philosophy.* Cambridge, MA: Harvard University Press.

(1992b). "Why Functionalism Didn't Work". In J. Earman (ed.), *Inference, Explanation and Other Philosophical Frustrations.* Berkeley: University of California Press, pp. 255–270. Reprinted in Putnam 1994a:441–459.

(1994a). *Words and Life.* Edited by J. Conant. Cambridge, MA: Harvard University Press.

(1994b). "Putnam, Hilary". In S. Guttenplan (ed.), *A Companion to the Philosophy of Mind.* Cambridge: Blackwell, pp. 507–513.

(1995). "Review of Roger Penrose, *Shadows of the Mind*". *Bulletin of the American Mathematical Society* 32.3:370–373.

(1997). "Functionalism: Cognitive Science or Science Fiction?" In D. M. Johnson and C. E. Erneling (eds.), *The Future of the Cognitive Revolution.* Oxford: Oxford University Press, pp. 32–44.

(1999). *The Threefold Cord: Mind, Body, and World*. New York: Columbia University Press.

Ryle, G. (1949). *The Concept of Mind*. London: Hutchinson.

Scheutz, M. (2001). "Causal vs. Computational Complexity?" *Minds and Machines* 11:534–566.

Searle, J. (1992). *The Rediscovery of the Mind*. Cambridge, MA: MIT Press.

Shagrir, O. (1998). "Multiple Realization, Computation and the Taxonomy of Psychological States". *Synthese* 114:445–461.

(2001). "Content, Computation and Externalism". *Mind* 110:369–400.

Shapiro, L. (2000). "Multiple Realizations". *Journal of Philosophy* 97:635–654.

Smart, J. J. C. (1959). "Sensations and Brain Processes". *Philosophical Review* 68:141–156.

Turing, A. M. (1936). "On Computable Numbers, with an Application to the Entscheidungsproblem". *Proceedings of the London Mathematical Society* (2), 42:230–265; a correction in 43 (1937):544–546.

(1950). "Computing Machines and Intelligence". *Mind* 59:433–460.

10 | The Pragmatic Turn: The Entanglement of Fact and Value

RICHARD J. BERNSTEIN

If one wanted to write a history of the most important and exciting philosophic debates of the past half-century, there is no better place to begin than with the writings of Hilary Putnam. His philosophic range is enormous and deep. In the philosophy of science, logic, mathematics, language, mind, perception, epistemology, and metaphysics, Putnam's challenging and controversial claims have been at the very center of discussion. He has critically engaged virtually every major contemporary Anglo-American and Continental philosopher. He frequently brings to his philosophical encounters a subtle knowledge of the history of philosophy that reaches back to Classical Greek philosophy. The variety of theses that he has defended, revised, and sometimes abandoned can strike one as bewildering. But a careful reading of his works reveals an underlying coherence to the philosophic vision he has been articulating – one that is genuinely dialectical in the sense that we can see why he advocated certain theses and his reasons for revising, correcting, and even abandoning them. We can also detect what he seeks to preserve and integrate in his ongoing philosophical journey. "Philosophers," he tells us "have a double task: to integrate our various views of our world and ourselves . . . , and to help us find a meaningful orientation in life. Finding a meaningful orientation in life is not, I think, a matter of finding a set of doctrines to live by, although it certainly includes having views; it is much more a matter of developing a *sensibility*" (Putnam 1997, p. 52).[1]

In this essay, I want to probe a theme (or more accurately a cluster of themes) that have become increasingly dominant for Putnam, especially during the past few decades when he has reflectively sought to take pragmatism seriously. Putnam finds in American pragmatism "a certain group of theses which can and indeed were argued differently by different philosophers with different concerns, and which became the basis of the philosophies of Peirce, and above all James and Dewey."

Cursorily summarized, those theses are (1) antiskepticism: pragmatists hold that doubt requires justification just as much as belief (recall Peirce's famous

252 Richard J. Bernstein

distinction between "real" and "philosophical" doubt); (2) *fallibilism:* pragmatists hold that there is never a metaphysical guarantee to be had that such-and-such a belief will never need revision (that one can be both fallibilistic *and* antiskeptical is perhaps *the* unique insight of American pragmatism); (3) the thesis that there is no *fundamental* dichotomy between "facts" and values"; and (4) the thesis that, in a certain sense, practice is primary in philosophy. (Putnam 1994, p. 152)

Putnam defends each of these theses in his *own* distinctive manner. In the preface to *Realism with a Human Face*, he tells us, "All of these ideas – that fact/value dichotomy is untenable, and that the fact/convention dichotomy is also untenable, that truth and justification of ideas are closely connected, that the alternative to metaphysical realism is not any form of skepticism, that philosophy is an attempt to achieve the good – are ideas that have been long associated with the American pragmatic tradition" (Putnam 1990, p. xi).

I will be focusing on the thesis that the fact/value dichotomy is untenable. Or to put the point positively – that there is an *entanglement* of fact and value. We will see that this thesis has ramifications for a wide range of philosophical issues. To set the context for my discussion, I want to situate Putnam's thinking – both philosophically and existentially. One cannot underestimate the influence of his early mentors, Hans Reichenbach and Rudolf Carnap. Putnam was never a slavish disciple of either of them. Indeed, he began his philosophic career criticizing specific claims they advanced, but he took the philosophic challenge they presented with the utmost seriousness – especially their claims about the fact/value and the fact/convention dichotomies. In the opening chapter of his recent book, *The Collapse of the Fact/Value Dichotomy*, he presents one of the clearest and most succinct statements of how these dichotomies were understood by the logical positivists.

> The logical positivists famously introduced a tripartite classification of all putative judgments into those that are "synthetic" (and hence – according to the logical positivists – empirically verifiable or falsifiable), those that are "analytic" (and hence – according to the logical positivists, "true [or false] on the basis of the [logical] rules alone"), and those – and this, notoriously included all our ethical, metaphysical, and aesthetic judgments – that are "cognitively meaningless." ... (Putnam 2002, p. 10)

He also declares:

> But the confidence of the logical positivists that they could expel ethics from the domain of the rationally discussable was in part derived from the

way in which the analytic-synthetic and the fact-value dualisms reinforced one another in their hands. According to the positivists, in order to be knowledge, ethical "sentences" would have either to be analytic, which they manifestly are not, or else would have to be "factual." And their confidence that they could not be factual... derived from their confidence that they knew exactly what a *fact* was. (Putnam 2002, pp. 20–21)

Ever since Quine's famous attack on the analytic-synthetic dichotomy in 1951, this dichotomy has been discredited. Putnam introduces an important caveat, for he distinguishes between a *distinction* and a *dichotomy*. Following John Dewey, Putnam insists that making distinctions (even if changing and open-ended) is all-important for *specific* philosophic purposes, but can be disastrous when these functional distinctions are reified into rigid dichotomies (as the logical positivists reified the analytic-synthetic distinction). For specific purposes, and in specific contexts, we may want to draw a distinction between analytic and synthetic sentences, but this is not a fixed dichotomy. Furthermore, it is unwarranted to think that *all* meaningful sentences or propositions neatly divide under these two rubrics. Even though the analytic-synthetic and the fact-convention dichotomies (at least as drawn by the logical positivists) have collapsed, the idea that there really is an unbridgeable gap between fact and value stubbornly persists. This is closely related to an older dichotomy – the allegedly categorical gap between the "is" and the "ought."[2] According to Putnam, and I completely agree with him, the fact-value dichotomy has had a pervasive and pernicious influence on the social sciences, as well as on our everyday understanding of ethical and political judgments.[3] Few philosophers who endorse the fact-value dichotomy subscribe to "emotivism" – the thesis that the primary function of value judgments is to *express* or *evince* emotions. But many would assert that value judgments are noncognitive; they are not the sort of judgments that can be true or false. At best, such judgments are nothing more that the expression of individual (or group) preferences or attitudes. They are "merely subjective." Those who subscribe to the fact-value dichotomy may be open to a variety of ways of characterizing precisely what makes a fact a fact, but they still insist that factual claims must be *sharply* distinguished from value judgments. Facts are facts and values are values; it is a "category mistake" to confuse the two – or so it is claimed. It is just this claim – this dogma – that Putnam calls into question. We might even label this the "fourth dogma" of empiricism, except that it has also been held by many nonempiricists.

I mentioned that there is also an existential context for understanding why Putnam wants to challenge the fact-value dichotomy. In his essay "The Place of Facts in a World of Values" (Putnam 1990), he gives a brief autobiographical sketch of his changing views. He tells us that his training as a philosopher of science came from the logical positivists. Although Putnam himself never advocated the emotive theory of ethical discourse, he did hold a "sophisticated" version of a sharp fact-value dichotomy. Concerning moral values, he thought "something was good in the specifically moral sense if it 'answers to the interests associated with the institution of morality'." By this he meant that "the decision to try to be or do good is just a 'choice of a way of life', namely to subscribe or not to subscribe to an 'institution'." But Putnam tells us – when he held this meta-ethical conviction – "he found himself with a severe moral problem" and agonized over whether what he was doing "was *right – really* right" (Putnam 1990, pp. 144–145).

> And I did not just mean whether it was in accord with the Utilitarian maxim to do what will lead to the greatest happiness of the greatest number..., but whether, if it was, then was that the *right* maxim for such a case? And I do not think I meant would some semantic analysis of the word "good," or some analysis of "the institution of morality," support what I was doing. But the *most* interesting thing is that it never occurred to me that there was any inconsistency between my meta-ethical view that it was all just a choice of a "way of life" and my agonized belief that what I was doing had to be either *right* or *wrong*. (Putnam 1990, p. 145)

But what precisely does Putnam mean by the entanglement of fact and value, and how does he argue for this claim? In a pragmatic spirit, he notes that there are different types of values – and we must be philosophically sensitive to their differences. There is a class of values that Putnam calls "epistemological values," or "cognitive values." Some of his most persuasive arguments concerning the entanglement of fact and value deal with these epistemological values.

"Value and normativity permeate *all* of experience," and "normative judgments are essential to the practice of science itself" (Putnam 2002, 30). "Judgments of 'coherence', 'plausibility', 'reasonableness,' 'simplicity,' and what Dirac famously called the 'beauty' of a hypothesis are all normative judgments in Charles Peirce's sense, judgments of 'what ought to be' in the case of reasoning" (Putnam 2002, p. 31).

It is difficult to imagine *any* philosopher of science – including the most orthodox positivists – denying that such criteria as simplicity, coherence, and plausibility are relevant to the assessment of scientific hypotheses and theories, so one may wonder what is the force of Putnam's claim. Putnam's point is that there is no way of making sense of these concepts unless we understand that they are values and involve normative judgments about what ought to be; they cannot be analyzed or reduced to what is "merely" factual.[4] He supports his claim in a variety of ways, appealing to what he calls "indispensability arguments."[5] Values and norms are indispensable for an analysis and assessment of knowledge claims; they are *epistemologically* indispensable.

> To suppose that "coherence" and "simple" are themselves just emotive words – words that express a "pro attitude" toward a theory, but which do not ascribe any definite properties to the theory – would be to regard *justification* as an entirely subjective matter. On the other hand, to suppose that "coherent" and "simple" name *neutral* properties – properties toward which people may have a "pro attitude" but there is no objective rightness in doing so – runs into difficulties at once. Like the paradigm value terms (such as "courageous," "kind," "honest," or "good"), "coherent" and "simple" are used as terms of praise. Indeed, they are *action guiding* terms: to describe a theory as "coherent, simple, explanatory" is, in the right setting, to say that acceptance of the theory is *justified*; and to say that acceptance of a statement is (completely) justified is to say that one ought to accept the statement or theory. (Putnam 1990, p. 138)

Putnam agrees – indeed he insists – that our views on the nature of coherence and simplicity are themselves historically conditioned, just as our views on the nature of justice or goodness are. But this is not an "argument" for relativism. Rather it indicates that "there is no neutral conception of rationality to which one can appeal when the nature of rationality is itself what is at issue" (Putnam 1990, p. 139). Putnam is right when he claims that all the classical pragmatists sought to support the claim that there is an entanglement of fact and value in *this sense*, that we cannot make sense of science and rationality without appeal to normative considerations. And he can also draw support for his claim from the development of this pragmatic strain in such thinkers as Sellars, McDowell, and Brandom, as well as Apel and Habermas. All would agree with what Sellars says when he declares: "The essential point is that in characterizing an episode or state as that of knowing . . . we are placing it in the logical space of reasons, of justifying and being able to justify what one says" (Sellars 1956, p. 169). This, of course, is just as true of the *facts* that we claim to know. Without the indispensable commitment to values and norms there is no world and no facts.

But suppose we grant Putnam's pragmatic claim about the entanglement of fact and epistemological values and norms; we may still want to know what is the relevance of this claim for understanding ethical and political values.[6] Here we encounter another theme in Putnam's thinking about

values – one that also echoes the classical pragmatists, and has more recently been emphasized by Iris Murdoch, John McDowell, and Bernard
Williams. Murdoch tells us that languages "have two very different sorts of
ethical concepts: abstract ethical concepts (Williams calls them 'thin' ethical concepts), such as 'good' and 'right,' and more descriptive, less abstract
concepts (Williams call them 'thick' ethical concepts) such as, for example, *cruel, pert, inconsiderate, chaste*" (Putnam 1990, p. 166). The point that
Putnam emphasizes is "that there is no way of saying what the 'descriptive
component' of the meaning of a word like cruel or inconsiderate is without using a word of the same kind. . . . The attempt of non-cognitivists to
split such words into a 'descriptive meaning component' and 'a prescriptive meaning component' founders on the impossibility of saying what the
'descriptive meaning' of, say, *cruel* is without using the word *cruel* itself, or
a synonym" (Putnam 1990, p. 166).

Putnam, Murdoch, Williams, and McDowell are right in noting the
extreme artificiality of trying to sort out the "descriptive" and "prescriptive" components of thick ethical concepts. If we already hold the (a priori)
conviction that there *must* be a dichotomy between the "descriptive" and
"prescriptive," then we will feel the compulsion to sort out these components in thick ethical concepts. Here again, we can see how deeply Putnam
is influenced by a pragmatic temper. It is, of course, true that there are
some concepts that we do classify as primarily "descriptive" and others as
primarily "prescriptive," and drawing this distinction in specific contexts
can be helpful and illuminating. But – as Wittgenstein might say – we are
on the very brink of misunderstanding if we think that these are separable
and distinguishable components in *all* ethical concepts. But what does this
establish about ethical values? This observation about the thickness of some
ethical concepts is certainly not *sufficient* to defeat ethical or cultural relativism. On the contrary, it is not only compatible with relativism, the appeal
to thick ethical concepts has been used to support cultural and ethical relativism. Consider such a thick concept as *pert* or *inconsiderate*. One does not
have to appeal to any sophisticated anthropological or historical evidence
to realize that there are many communities in which such concepts do not
seem to have any applicability. Furthermore, what one community considers
inconsiderate may be classified as honest, blunt behavior in another community. There is even a sense in which we can say that such concepts are
"objective." We sometimes do disagree about whether some action *really* is
or is not cruel – and we will offer objective reasons to support our judgment.
We may rationally persuade a conversation partner that she is *mistaken* in
her belief that the action was *really* cruel. There are criteria and standards

in a given community (even if they are fuzzy) for *correctly* judging cruelty. No one in our society is going to judge (correctly) that helping a blind person to cross a dangerous intersection is *cruel*. Consequently such judgments can be *true* or *false*. In short, claiming that thick ethical or political concepts exhibit the entanglement of fact and value does not in any way challenge cultural or ethical relativism.

Putnam is perfectly aware of the point that I have been making about the compatibility of this analysis of thick ethical concepts with relativism – a relativism that *he* wants to defeat. He makes the same point in his critique of Bernard Williams. Williams endorses this distinction between thin and thick ethical concepts, and he uses this very distinction to support a form of ethical relativism. And, according to Putnam, Williams's dichotomy be-tween science and ethics is a "sophisticated" version of an older form of noncognitivism.

> [Bernard] Williams still defends a sharp "science/ethics" dichotomy; and he regards his science/ethics dichotomy as capturing something that was essentially right about the old "fact/value" dichotomy.
>
> Something else has accompanied this change in the way the dichotomy is defended. The old position, in several versions – emotivism, voluntarism, prescriptivism – was usually referred to as "non-cognitivism." . . . Today, philosophers like Williams do not deny that ethical sentences can be true or false; what they deny is that they can be true or false *non-perspectivally*. Thus, the position has been (appropriately) renamed: while the proprietary versions of the new approved drug still have various differences one from the other, they all accept the name relativism. *Non-cognitivism has been rebaptized as relativism.* (Putnam 1990, p. 165)

There is nothing quite so damning for Putnam as the label "relativism," except the twin label "metaphysical realism." One of the many reasons why he is attracted to pragmatism is because he believes that it shows the *right* way to avoid these extremes. Putnam's main strategy in "going after" Williams is to criticize the claim that science is based on a notion of *the world as it really is;* that science depends on a nonperspectival concept of "absoluteness." Putnam argues that the "dichotomy between what the world is like independent of any local perspective [the absolute conception of the world] and what is projected by us" is not just mistaken, it is *incoherent* (Putnam 1990, p. 170). This dichotomy is "utterly indefensible." Putnam brings a whole battery of arguments to show this.[7]

Like John Dewey, one of his heroes, Putnam argues that philosophical dichotomies – whether metaphysical, ontological, or epistemological – are, at best, useful *distinctions* relative to specific human interests and purposes. His master strategy is to show that *alleged* hard-and-fast dichotomies (when closely scrutinized) actually turn out to be differences of degree. Contrary to what Williams claims, there is no absolute conception of the world; the idea of the world as it really is in itself, independent of *any* perspective, is illusory. The world does not have a structure that is independent of any of our conceptual schemes. This is a lesson philosophers should have learned from Kant. All knowing is *perspectival* and involves conceptual choices. That is why knowledge always involves human interests. This is just as true of the "formal" sciences and the "hard" physical sciences as it is of ethics, history, and politics. Putnam tells us, "Mathematics and physics, as well as ethics and history and politics, show our conceptual choices: the world is not going to impose a single language upon us, no matter what we choose to talk about" (Putnam 1990, p. 171). Because he realizes that some of his own claims about how all knowing is perspectival sound "relativistic," Putnam is at pains to stress his own robust pragmatic realism – realism with a human face. There are facts of the matter, even though these facts are relative to the adoption of a conceptual scheme – and even though alternative conceptual schemes may be incompatible with each other.

Putnam's pragmatic strategy is to "soften" rigid dichotomies by showing that they turn out to be flexible differences related to human interests. And this strategy is intimately related to his attack on metaphysical realism, his relentless critique of relativism, his rejection of scientism, his rejection of the God's-eye point of view, his critique of appeal to absolutes, and his defense of pluralism. *Putnam's claims about the entanglement of fact and value stand at the heart of this philosophic vision.*

But how does Putnam's argument that there is no *intrinsic* difference between science and ethics, and his claim that the range of rational argumentation is much broader than science, bear on the issue of *moral objectivity?* I want to begin by clarifying just what Putnam means (and does not mean) by objectivity. Objectivity is not to be confused with metaphysical realism, nor does it presuppose metaphysical realism. There are those who do think that unless one is a metaphysical realist then there is no possibility of giving a proper account of objectivity. But this is precisely the dogma that Putnam has been criticizing ever since he turned against his own flirtation with metaphysical realism. His conceptual, internal, and more recent pragmatic realism can be viewed as successive stages in showing how objectivity is compatible with different conceptual choices. Objectivity is not to be confused or identified with algorithmic reasoning, where we assert that there is a *univocal* solution to a problem. There is a place for *phronesis* and reasonable objective disagreement. This is a feature of objectivity that turns out to be highly relevant for ethical and political disputes, but it also has a place in the "hardest" physical sciences. More generally, objectivity is compatible with pluralism (and pluralism is not to be confused with relativism). We see how flexible Putnam's concept of objectivity is, and how deep his commitment to pluralism, from his recent reply to Habermas.

The following claim is at the heart of my own pluralism:

> *One cannot be a consistent pluralist and accept that at least some people who have other ways of life, religious traditions, sexual orientations, etc., is "light" and the others are all "darkness."* But this claim defines only a "minimal pluralism." A stronger form is defined by the claim, which I also accept, that at least some people who have other ways of life, religious traditions, sexual orientations, etc. than mine have insights that I do not have, or that I have not developed to anything like the same extent, precisely *because* they have those other ways of life, religious traditions, sexual orientations, etc.[8]

But even if we concede all of this, still we may feel some uneasiness with Putnam's claims concerning moral objectivity. After all, even if one claims that there is no difference in *kind* between scientific objectivity and moral objectivity, a good pragmatist is not going to deny that there are *real* differences between scientific reasoning and ethical reasoning, that objectivity in the case of a scientific dispute is not quite the same as objectivity in a moral dispute. Putnam is frequently far more effective and persuasive in criticizing dichotomies than he is in doing justice to important differences. Stated in another way, I do not think that even Putnam would deny that normally there is much more agreement in the formal and natural sciences about the criteria of objectivity (even when there are rational disagreements) than we find when we turn to ethical and political disputes. How, then, are we to account for these apparent differences?

Putnam is *not* claiming that moral and political philosophers have ignored or disregarded the type of moral objectivity that *already* exists as a matter of fact. It is not as if such philosophers were disregarding moral facts that exist "out there," independent of our points of view. He is not advocating a moral metaphysical realism. Putnam is acutely aware of just how deep disagreement can be in ethical and political matters. His case for moral objectivity is not a case for how matters *now* stand. It is rather self-consciously a *normative* argument – an argument about what *ought* to be. We ought to develop those *practices* in which there will be a greater moral objectivity, where there will be a stronger attempt to engage in rational argumentation about what is right and wrong, where there will also be a wider acceptance of the pluralism of different moral orientations.

It may be objected that even if this is not a difference in kind, there is nevertheless a major difference between science and ethics. In science we do not have to argue about standards of objectivity; they exist. But in morality or politics they do not exist, they must be instituted. Yet this objection is misguided. It fails to acknowledge that even in the hard sciences there is an ongoing discussion and debate about what constitutes objectivity and objective standards. It is simply not the case that what counted as an objective fact for Copernicus, Kepler, or Galileo is still what counts as an objective fact today. This is not just something that needed to be hammered out in the early days of modern science. Much of the dispute about the Copenhagen interpretation of quantum mechanics is about what *ought* to count as the criteria and standards of objectivity. Objectivity is not a metaphysical or an epistemological given, it is an ongoing *achievement* – one that must be constantly rethought. This is an example of what Putnam means when he declares: "Our norms and standards of anything – including warranted assertability [and including the norms and standards of objectivity – RJB] are capable of reform. There are better and worse norms and standards" (Putnam 1990, p. 21).

Some advocates of moral realism and moral objectivity do argue as if there really are moral facts "out there" in the world independent of us. They argue as if moral objectivity and metaphysical realism are inextricably linked. But Putnam argues that this linkage is not only mistaken, it is also incoherent. Objectivity, whether in science or ethics, has *nothing* to do with metaphysical realism. Metaphysical realism in *any* realm – epistemology, science, ethics, or politics – is a "Bad." Putnam is advocating a nonmetaphysical way of thinking about objectivity in science and ethics. This is one of the reasons why he develops what he calls an "epistemological justification of democracy." "The claim, then, is this: Democracy is not just a form of social life among other workable forms of social life; it is the precondition for the full application of intelligence to the solution of problems" (Putnam 1991, p. 217). Putnam clearly accepts what he claims for Dewey.

> Nevertheless, Dewey believes (as we all do, when we are not playing the skeptic) that there are better and worse resolutions to human predicaments – to what he calls "problematical situations." He believes that of all the methods for finding better resolutions, the "scientific method" has proved

itself superior to Peirce's methods of "tenacity," "authority," and "What is Agreeable to Reason." For Dewey, the scientific method is simply the method of experimental inquiry combined with free and full discussion – which means, in the case of social problems, the maximum use of the capacities of citizens for proposing courses of action, for testing them, and for evaluating the results. And, in my view, that is all that Dewey really needs to assume. (Putnam 1991, p. 227)[9]

In a similar vein, Putnam argues that we need to give up the metaphysical picture of objectivity and "accept the position we are fated to occupy in any case, the position of beings who cannot have a view of the world that does not reflect our interests and values, but who are, for all that, committed to regarding some interests and values – as better than others" (Putnam 1990, p. 178).

> This may mean giving up a certain metaphysical picture of objectivity, but it does not mean giving up the idea that there are what Dewey called "objective resolutions of problematical situations" – objective resolutions to problems which are *situated* in a place, at a time, as opposed to an "absolute" answer to "perspective-independent" questions. And that is objectivity enough. (Putnam 1990, p. 178)

I want to go over Putnam's claims a bit more carefully, because from one perspective there is a circularity of reasoning involved in his claims about objectivity in ethical and political disputes. It is *not*, however, a vicious circularity, but something that is analogous to the hermeneutic circle. Putnam is not claiming that – as things stand *now* – there is significant moral or political objectivity. He argues that we *ought* to cultivate and institute practices – practices that he associates with discursive and deliberative democracy – that will enhance a greater objectivity and reasonable argumentation about the resolution of problematical situations. In short, Putnam is arguing for the way in which an ethical community *ought* to organize itself – and, if it does, then it will achieve the conditions required for cultivating moral objectivity. To the extent that we succeed in fostering such a democratic ethical community, then moral objectivity becomes a *real fact of the matter.* "[A]n ethical community – a community which wants to know what is right and good – should organize itself in accordance with democratic standards and ideals, not only because they are good in themselves (and they are), but because they are the prerequisites for the application of intelligence to inquiry" (Putnam 1994, p. 175). He goes on to tell us:

> It may look as if Dewey is "pulling himself up by his own bootstraps." For even if we assume that inquiry into values should be democratized, that the participants should, *qua* seekers after the right and the good, respect free speech and the other norms of discourse ethics, not instrumentalize one another, and so on, what *criteria* should they use to tell that their inquiry has succeeded? (Putnam 1994, p. 175)

But it also looks as if Putnam, too, is "pulling himself up by his bootstraps." He argues that there *ought* to be a democratic cooperative open society in which there will be a broader and deeper moral objectivity. Making such a democratic community a living reality means making the type of moral objectivity he favors a living reality. This *is* a type of "bootstrapping" insofar as it is intended to bring about a moral objectivity that does not yet fully exist. But this type of bootstrapping is not objectionable. It is consistent with the pragmatic orientation that normative considerations are relevant to discerning what ought to count as objectivity. This is why I suggest that the circularity of Putnam's argument is analogous to the hermeneutic circle.

But still another objection may be raised against Putnam. Isn't he seeking to *impose* standards of moral objectivity rather *discovering* them? If this is his intention, then isn't this goal achieved more efficiently and effectively by totalitarian regimes that enforce standards of what is right and wrong, and criteria for "objective" political and ethical judgments and decisions? But this objection also misfires; for it assumes that Putnam is not making any distinctions in the *type* of moral realism and moral objectivity he is advocating. He clearly recognizes that some forms of moral objectivity are objectionable.

> But not every defense of moral objectivity is a good thing. We live in an "open society," a society in which the freedom to think for oneself about values, goals, and mores is one that most of us have come to cherish. Arguments for "moral realism" can, and sometimes unfortunately do, sound like arguments against the open society: and while I do wish to undermine moral skepticism, I have no intention of defending either authoritarianism or moral apriorism. It is precisely for this reason that in recent years I have found myself turning to the writings of the American pragmatists. (Putnam 1994, p. 152)

In Putnam's declaration of his affinity with the American pragmatists, we can discern the basis for the difference that makes a difference here – for distinguishing objectionable forms of moral objectivity and moral realism from those he is advocating. He places the stress on how we ought to achieve this objectivity – through discussion, open debate, deliberation, and reasonable argumentation. These are the democratic practices he praises, and these are the practices that need to be cultivated and instituted. These practices are not merely Putnam's "subjective" preferences. He *argues* that these provide better norms and standards for achieving moral objectivity.

In his essay, "Pragmatism and Moral Objectivity," originally delivered at a conference dedicated to specific ethical and political issues of justice and equality in developing societies, Putnam concedes that his paper was more "abstract" than most of the others. He explains and defends this abstractness when he declares: "If it ended up being more 'abstract' than most of the others, that is not because the author got 'carried away' by a particular line of abstract thought. Rather, it is because it was my conviction . . . that positions on the 'abstract' question of moral objectivity have real world effects." And he adds, "to show that the justifications which are offered for ethical skepticism at a philosophical level will not stand up to examination, that the foundations of the idea that there is no rationality beyond purely instrumental rationality are in trouble, *may* help to combat that instrumentalization and that manipulation" (Putnam 1994, p. 151). This is a modest but extremely important claim about the role of "abstract" philosophical discussions and "real world effects." I am sympathetic with, and strongly endorse, Putnam's arguments against ethical skepticism, his defense of an enlarged conception of rationality, and a more open and liberal sense of moral objectivity. I do think he is effective in showing the entanglement of fact and value. He has elucidated a way of thinking about moral objectivity that escapes the snares of moral metaphysical realism. He is also effective in criticizing the *dichotomy* between science and ethics, and in exposing the inadequacy of all appeals to "absoluteness." But I also think that his general line of argument is "abstract." It is as if he is clearing the space for a proper deliberative democratic way of dealing with value judgments and decisions. But a good pragmatist will also want to know how this really *works* when we get down to the nitty-gritty, how we are to decide what is right and wrong, and which value judgments are true and false in specific situations. It is not good enough to be told that this will always depend on context and the background assumptions of the participants in the dispute. This is true, but unhelpful. The really hard moral and political issues concern just how we are to figure out what is to be done and how we are to judge competing claims. On the abstract level, Putnam has made a good case for a non-metaphysical way of thinking about moral objectivity. But he has not (yet) shown us how we are to determine which of our concrete value judgments are objectively true and which are false. I am not asking for clear and determinate criteria or demanding more exactness of ethical and political objectivity than the subject matter warrants. Aristotle taught us this lesson long ago. But an abstract argument for moral objectivity must at least be complemented with *some guidance* about how we decide what is right and wrong, true and false, when we are confronted with seriously competing claims. This is especially pressing in a world where extremist positions are becoming more fashionable, where there is a violent clash of absolutes, and where there is little agreement about what really counts as an "objective" solution to an ethical or political problem. If we are to be fully persuaded by Putnam, then it is these sorts of questions that must be answered. What Putnam has already shown us is extremely illuminating, but it is still only an abstract sketch – one that requires the filling in of its concrete details.

Notes

1. See James Conant's excellent introductions to Putnam (1990) and Putnam (1994) for an overview of Putnam's philosophical development.
2. See Putnam's perceptive discussion of Hume in the history of the is-ought and fact-value dichotomies (Putnam 2002, chap. 1).
3. He shows this in detail and with specific reference to the discipline of economics in *The Collapse of the Fact/Value Dichotomy*.
4. Putnam frequently does not make a *systematic* distinction between "values" and "norms," although he speaks of norms when he wants to emphasize standards of correctness and standards of what ought to be. Not all values are norms. One of his major disagreements with Habermas concerns what Putnam takes to be Habermas's rigid dichotomy between values and norms.
5. For an explanation of what Putman means by "indispensability arguments" see Putnam (1994, pp. 153–160).
6. Putnam thinks that James is more helpful in thinking about ethical decisions and Dewey is more illuminating in dealing with political decisions and values. Nevertheless, Putnam rejects a *dichotomy* between ethics and politics. Indeed, ethics requires an ethical community, and the cultivation of the *practices* required for such a community is itself a political project.
7. In his strategy of argumentation, Putnam also shows the influence of pragmatism, especially the pragmatism of Peirce. Peirce argued that, in philosophy as in the sciences, we ought to "trust rather to the multiplicity and variety of its arguments than to the conclusiveness of any one. Its reasoning should not form a chain which is no stronger than its weakest link, but a cable whose fibers may be ever so slender, provided they are sufficiently numerous and intimately connected" (Peirce 1932–1935: 5.265). For Putnam's multifaceted critique of Williams's dichotomy of

science and ethics, and Williams's concept of absoluteness, see Putnam (1990, pp. 165–178); and Putnam (1994, pp. 188–192, 217–218).

8. This is a statement that Putnam made in his concluding remarks at a conference dedicated to his pragmatism, held in 2000 at the University of Münster.

9. Putnam rejects the idea that there is a *single* "scientific method." But he also thinks that this is not what Dewey meant when he appealed to scientific method in solving ethical problems, but that he was appealing to experimentation, imaginative construction of alternative hypothetical solutions, open discussion, debate, and ongoing self-corrective communal criticism.

References

Peirce, C. S. (1931–1935). *Collected Papers*. Ed. Charles Hartshorne and Paul Weiss. Cambridge, MA: Harvard University Press.

Putnam, H. (1990). *Realism with a Human Face*. Cambridge, MA: Harvard University Press.

(1991). A Reconsideration of Deweyean Democracy. In M. Brint and W. Weavers, eds. *Pragmatism in Law and Society*. Boulder, CO: Westview Press, 217–242.

(1994). *Words and Life*. Cambridge, MA: Harvard University Press.

(1997). Interview with Hilary Putnam. *Cogito*. 314:44–53.

(2002). *The Collapse of the Fact/Value Dichotomy*. Cambridge, MA: Harvard University Press.

Sellars, W. (1956). "Empiricism and the Philosophy of Mind." In H. Feigl and M. Scriven, eds., *Minnesota Studies in the Philosophy of Science, Vol. 1*. Minneapolis: University of Minnesota Press.

Index